Looking at Greek Art

Looking at Greek Art offers a practical guide to the methods for approaching, analyzing, and contextualizing an unfamiliar piece of Greek art. It demonstrates how objects are dated and assigned to an artist or region; how to interpret the subject matter and narrative; how to reconstruct the context for which an object was made, distributed, and used; and how we can explore broader cultural perspectives by looking at questions of identity, gender, and relationships to surrounding cultures. Each section focuses on different theoretical approaches, providing an overview of the theories, key terms, and required evidence. Case studies serve to demonstrate each process and some key issues to consider when using a given approach. This book explores a variety of media, including terracotta, metalwork, and jewelry, and includes examples of art found in major museum collections in the United States and Europe.

Mark D. Stansbury-O'Donnell is a Professor of art history at the University of St. Thomas in St. Paul, Minnesota. He is the author of *Pictorial Narrative in Ancient Greek Art* (Cambridge, 1999) and *Vase Painting, Gender, and the Social Identity of Archaic Athens* (Cambridge, 2006). He has published in the *American Journal of Archaeology* and has contributed to several other books on Greek art and vase painting.

Looking at Greek Art

Mark D. Stansbury-O'Donnell

University of St. Thomas

Cambridge
University Press

CAMBRIDGE UNIVERSITY PRESS
Cambridge, New York, Melbourne, Madrid, Cape Town, Singapore,
São Paulo, Delhi, Dubai, Tokyo, Mexico City

Cambridge University Press
32 Avenue of the Americas, New York, NY 10013-2473, USA

www.cambridge.org
Information on this title: www.cambridge.org/9780521125574

First published 2011

Printed in the United States of America

A catalog record for this publication is available from the British Library.

Library of Congress Cataloging in Publication data

Stansbury-O'Donnell, Mark, 1956–
Looking at Greek art / Mark D. Stansbury-O'Donnell.
p. cm.
Includes bibliographical references and index.
ISBN 978-0-521-11038-9 (hardback) – ISBN 978-0-521-12557-4 (pbk.)
1. Art, Greek. I. Title.
N5630.S735 2010
709.38 – dc22 2010031500

ISBN 978-0-521-11038-9 Hardback
ISBN 978-0-521-12557-4 Paperback

To my teachers and students

CONTENTS

ILLUSTRATIONS

Acknowledgments

This book had its origins in my need to grapple with various theoretical approaches to Greek art, first as a student and then as a scholar and teacher. Discussions over the past few years with colleagues and students encouraged me to attempt a book that is both theoretical and practical, focusing on the questions we ask about Greek art and how we can begin to answer them. As a synthesis, this book is deeply indebted to the work of many scholars of Greek art, whose work provided models or examples for the various approaches explored here. I hope that this book will serve as a gateway to their work and be a practical guide for students.

I especially thank Elizabeth Langridge-Noti and Vanessa Rousseau for reading an earlier version of the manuscript, commenting on it, and thinking about how it could work for a class or research projects. Their suggestions improved the book considerably.

Several of my undergraduate and graduate students also served as readers of one of the drafts of the manuscript and provided their perspectives on what worked well and what did not. I thank Lauren Graff, Elizabeth Henderson, Andrew Herkert, Amy Nygaard, and especially James Wehn, who compiled their comments and provided an overview of the range of reactions.

In addition, I thank the following individuals who listened to the ideas I was developing for the book along the way and whose responses were helpful barometers for the project: Judith Barringer, Sheramy Bundrick, Kenneth Lapatin, François Lissarrague, Susan Matheson, Richard Neer, Jerry Pollitt, David Saunders, Alan Shapiro, and Ioulia Tzonou-Herbst.

I thank Beatrice Rehl at Cambridge University Press for her support and guidance of the project.

I am also grateful for a faculty grant from the University of St. Thomas that provided course releases for writing and funding for visiting museums in Greece and London to study issues of display.

For help with photos and permissions, I thank the following: Irene Bösel, Staatliche Antikensammlungen und Glyptothek, Munich; Jacklyn Burns, J. Paul Getty Museum; Kalliopi Christofi, École française d'Athènes; Tracey Cullen, American School of Classical Studies; Maureen Goldsmith, University of Pennsylvania Archaeological Museum; Dr. Joachim Heiden, Deutsches Archäologisches Institut Athen; Dr. Nikolaos Kaltsas, National Archaeological Museum, Athens; Dario Lanzuolo, Deutsches Archäologisches Institut Rom; Craig Mauzy, American School of Classical Studies, Athens; Agata Rutkowska, British Museum Images; Ann Sinfield, Chazen Museum of Art; Michael Slade, Art Resource, New York; Tricia Smith, Art Resource, New York; Carol Stein, American School of Classical Studies; Dr. Alexandra Villing, British Museum; Kathrin Weber, Badisches Landesmuseum Karlsruhe; and Kristen Wenger, British Museum Images. I especially acknowledge Michael Slade for his persistence in working with a number of museums in getting images, and Craig Mauzy for his photo and assistance in getting permission for it.

One

The Study and Presentation of Greek Art

Studying Greek Art and Historical Narratives

When one opens a textbook on Greek art, or even the history of art generally, one almost always find an illustration and discussion of the sculpture from the Siphnian Treasury at Delphi (Figure 1). We will discuss this building and its sculpture extensively throughout this book, along with a bronze mirror (Figure 2) and a ceramic drinking cup (Figure 3), but let us begin by describing the treasury. The original structure was a small building with a porch at one end and an enclosed room behind it (Figure 4). Made of marble, the elaborate architectural decoration, particularly its sculpted pediments and friezes that are now on display in the Archaeological Museum at Delphi, would belong on virtually any top-fifty list for Greek art, and probably on many top-ten lists.

The consensus of art historians is that this is an important monument of the Archaic period (c. 600–480 BCE). In part, this is because of the condition of the reliefs and pediments that crowned the building, as other examples of relatively well-preserved, sculpted architectural relief before the fifth century BCE are rare. Further, the building was one of the most luxurious treasuries at Delphi, made of imported marble with lavish ornamental moldings in addition to the reliefs. The scholarly discussion of the sculptural reliefs focuses on either their style or their subject matter, or both. Regarding style, it is significant that two clearly distinguishable sculptors worked on different sides of the building, one of whom inscribed a partially effaced signature on

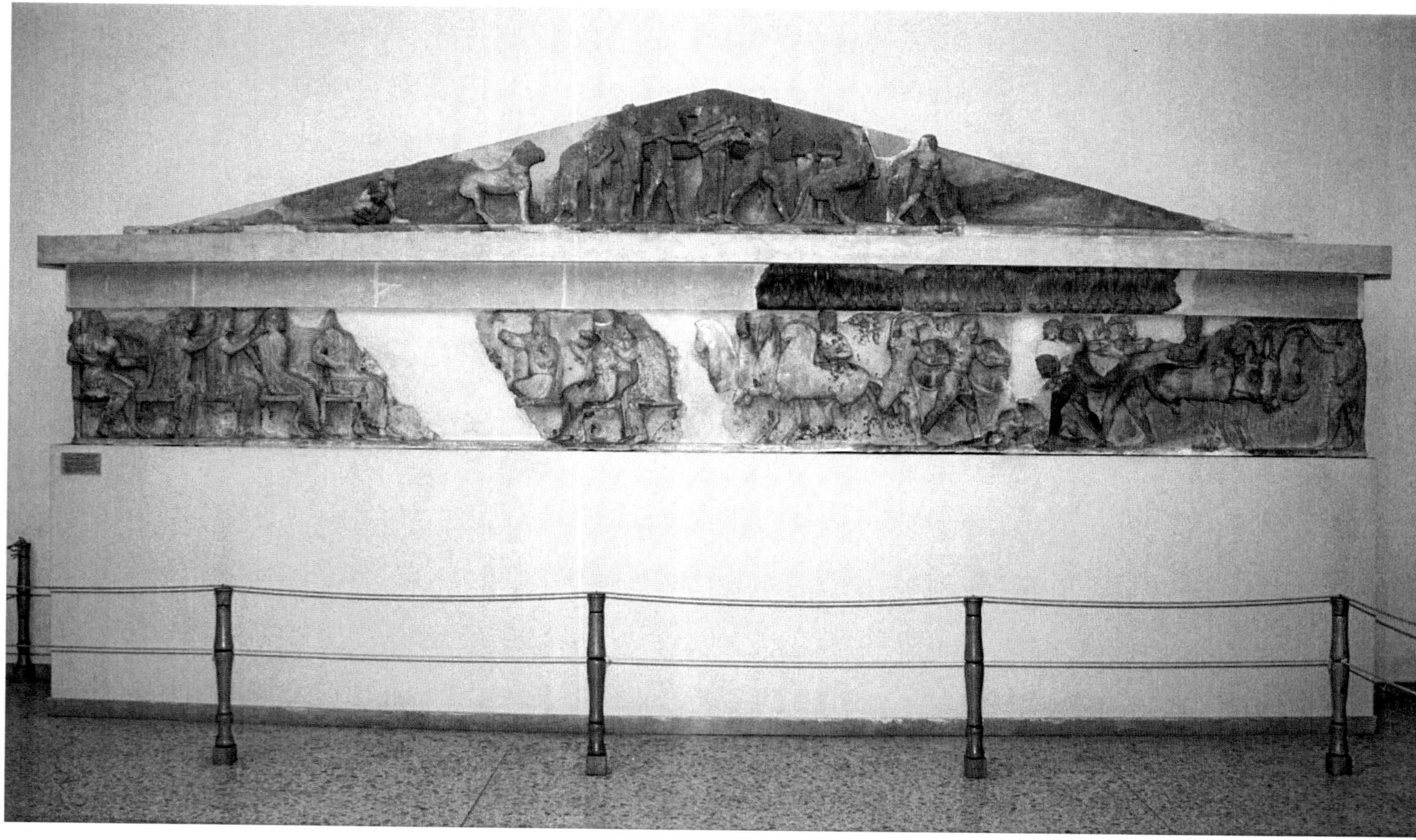

Figure 1. East frieze and pediment, Siphnian Treasury, Delphi, C. 525 BCE. *Delphi Museum. Photo: Vanni/Art Resource, New York.*

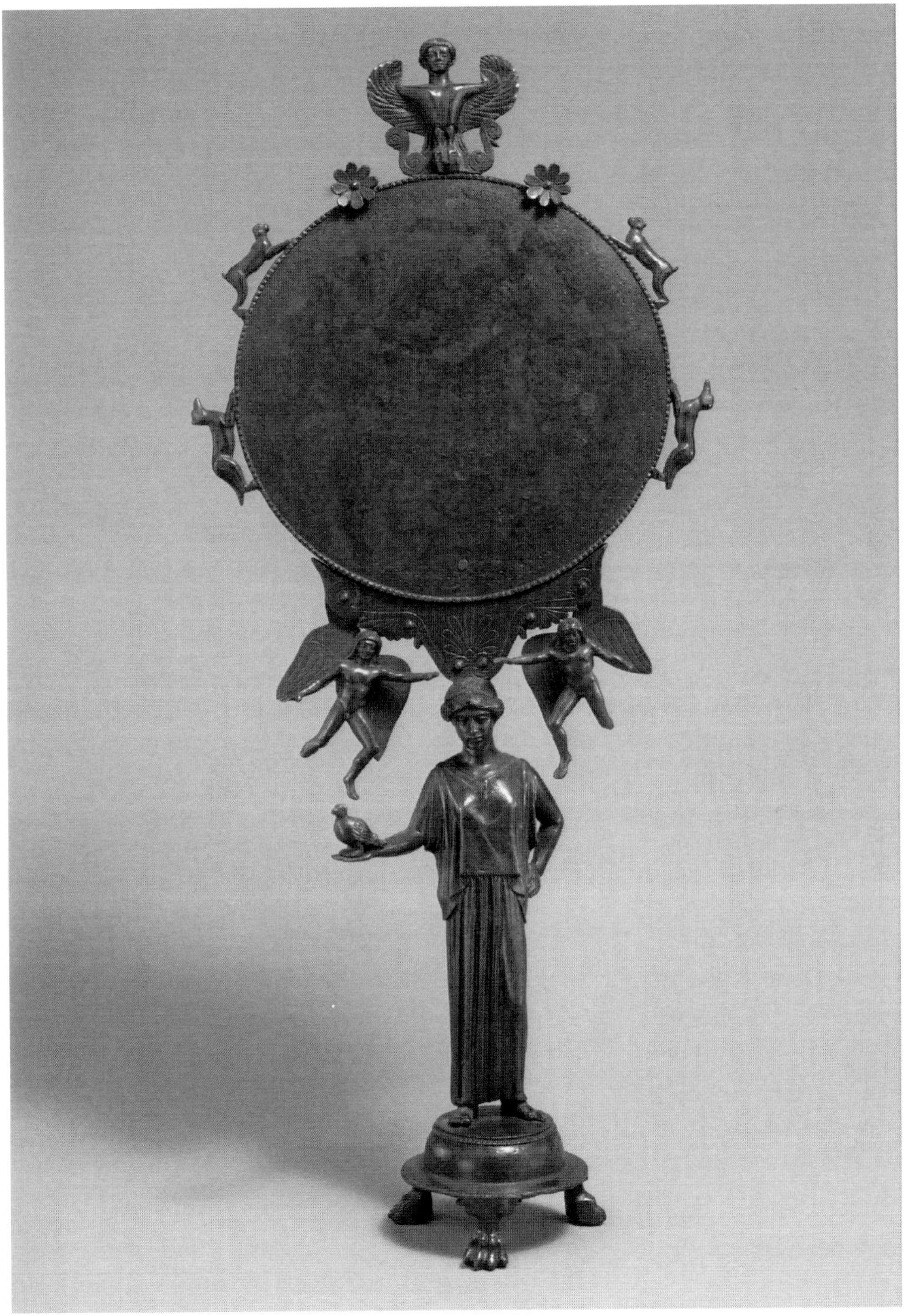

Figure 2. Bronze Argive caryatid mirror, mid-fifth century BCE. *New York, Metropolitan Museum of Art,* 1972.118.78. *Image Copyright © The Metropolitan Museum of Art/Art Resource, New York.*

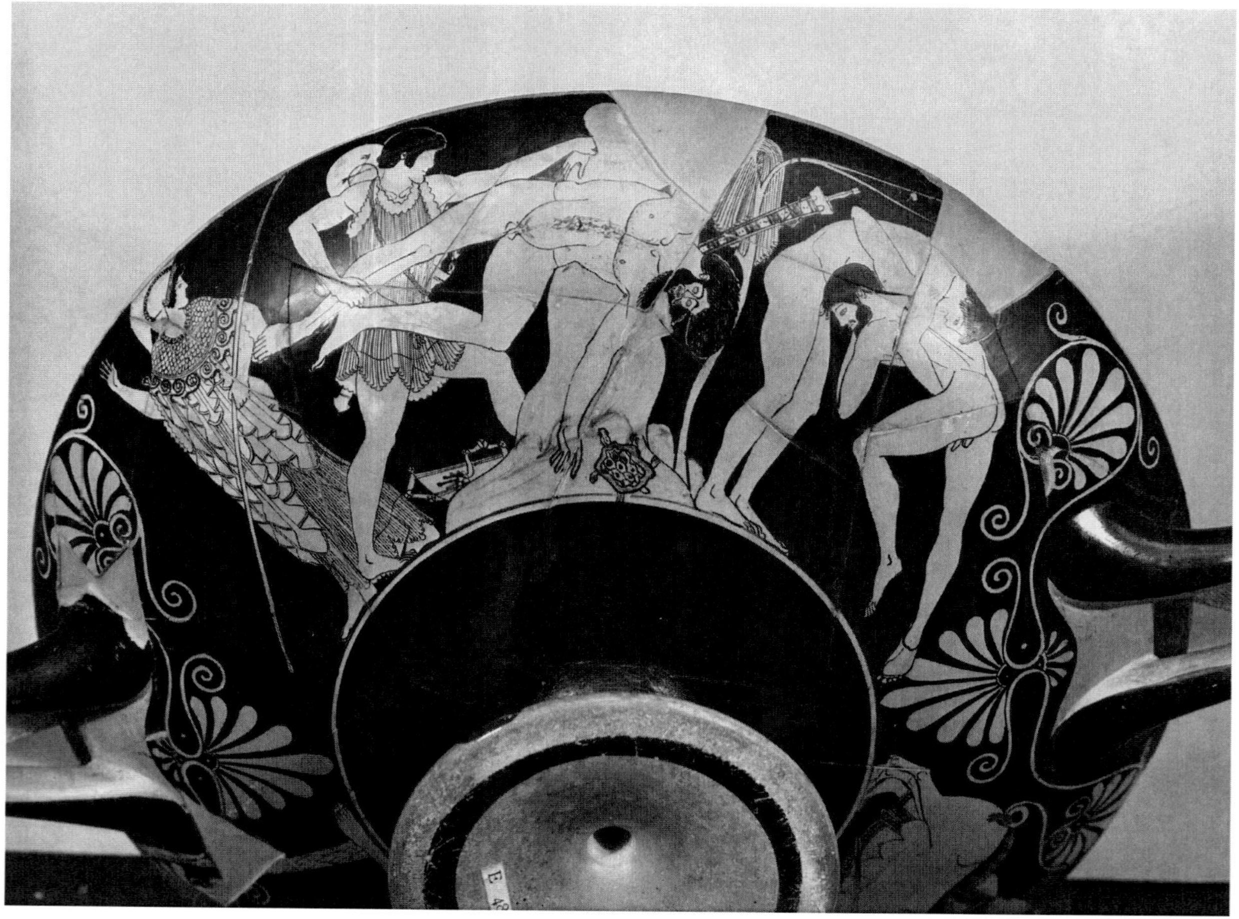

Figure 3. Attic red-figure kylix attributed to Douris, c. 490–480 BCE. *Theseus and Skiron; Theseus and Kerkyon.* London, British Museum, E48. Photo: © Trustees of the British Museum.

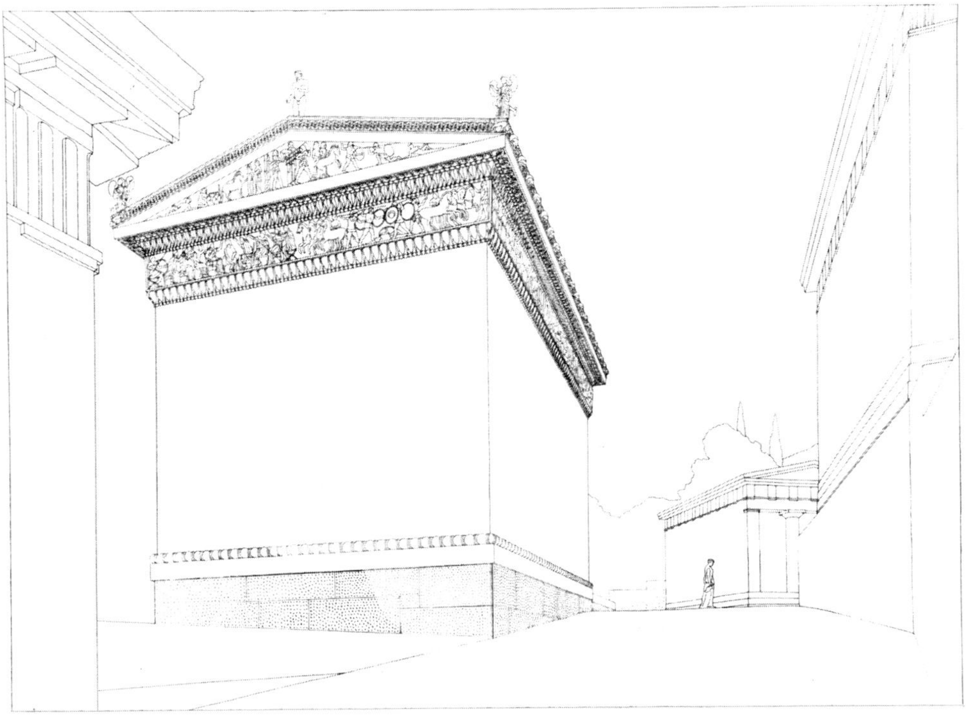

Figure 4. Reconstruction of the Siphnian Treasury and Sacred Way at Delphi. Photo: École française d'Athènes/E. Hansen.

the north side. The composition of that frieze, showing a Gigantomachy, or battle between the gods and the giants, is noted for its greater use of overlapping and the relatively complex movement of the figures compared with contemporary monuments (Figure 5). The other subjects are also noted and described, as is their broader significance and relationship to other representations of the same scenes. Finally, the work is important for the history of Greek art in that there is secondary documentation that links its construction to around the year 525 BCE, making it a key marker for the chronology of Greek art. The Siphnian Treasury is important for art historians and archaeologists, then, for a variety of reasons.

The second-century CE doctor and traveler Pausanias, who wrote a guidebook to Greece and gave a detailed description of the sights at Delphi that equals or exceeds the length of most modern guidebooks, mentions the Siphnian Treasury in his account. In contrast with modern histories, he tells us simply that "the Siphnians too made a treasury, the reason being as follows."[1] He then recounts the story of the wealth and troubles of the Siphnians, but says nothing about the building's appearance or its artistic program. It is just one of several "treasuries" that do not contain treasure and do not seem sufficiently striking on their own to merit any further description, unlike several other monuments at Delphi that he describes in detail. The historian Herodotos, writing earlier in the fifth century BCE, also mentions the story behind the construction of the Siphnian Treasury, but of the building itself he adds only that it is "equal to the richest ones there."[2]

Why are there such differences in interest and conclusions between these two ancient observers of this building in its original condition and setting, and recent scholars, who can view only its incomplete fragments in a modern museum? First, one has to recognize that neither Pausanias nor Herodotos is trying to explain the history of Greek art; their agendas are quite different from that of a modern archaeologist or art historian. For Pausanias, the Siphnian Treasury pales in comparison with other monuments at Delphi that he describes in more detail. Herodotos is writing a history of Greece, and the action of the Samians, who attacked Siphnos, is his primary focus; the Treasury is evidence of the wealth of the Siphnians.

More important, it is necessary to understand that any history, ancient or modern, is a story. In practical terms, historians must be selective in what they describe or recount if they are to achieve their main goal: understanding the causes of events and relationships among events, people, and things. Unnecessary or extraneous details would bog down the narrative and its point. In that sense, modern archaeologists and art historians share the same approach as Herodotos. However, the specific objective of a history of Greek art will make the fabric of the Siphnian Treasury itself more significant for the archaeologist and art historian than it was for Herodotos. Finally, any historian must work with the available evidence, and consider its completeness and reliability, in selecting which details to include and exclude from the account. For Pausanias, there were other sights more engaging at the time he was at Delphi, but many of these are now lost or are in much worse condition than the sculpture of the Siphnian Treasury.

For modern art historians, the importance of the Siphnian Treasury derives not only from the accidents of preservation and documentation, but also from its inherent artistic qualities. The chronology and development of artistic style have been fundamental goals of art history since its beginning; for this story line, the Siphnian Treasury is indeed a key piece of evidence. When the site at Delphi was excavated by French archaeologists beginning in 1892, there were no labels or manuals to guide them. The conclusions that current texts draw about the Treasury's style and composition are the result not just of looking at the remains, but also of the methods and theoretical approaches that have helped scholars to analyze them. Just as the

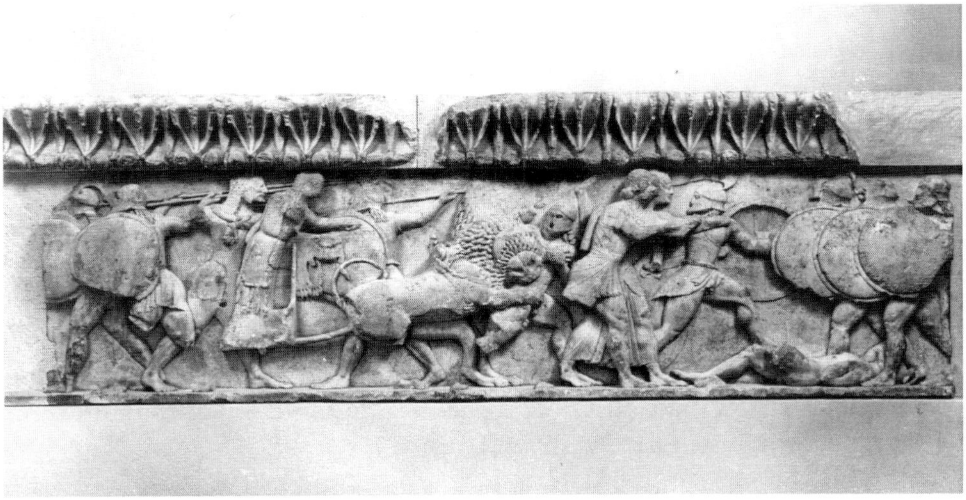

Figure 5. North frieze of the Siphnian Treasury at Delphi, c. 525 BCE. Gigantomachy. Delphi Museum. Photo: École française d'Athènes/Ph. Collet.

agenda of the modern art historian gives importance to the Siphnian Treasury, the particular theory or approach that art historians take affects their understanding and conclusions.

There are many more dimensions than style and date to consider when looking at a work of art such as this, however. What it means, why it was built, how it was used, and how it represents the identity of the people and culture who made it are all important questions for the art historian. Which of these receives attention depends, at least in part, on the issue that the art historian is exploring and on his or her need for constructing a plausible story/history of Greek art. If one were only interested in funerary art and architecture or mural painting, then one might well leave the Siphnian Treasury aside, in spite of its canonical status.

Rather than the history of Greek art, what is of interest for this book is the variety of questions that we want to ask about monuments such as the Siphnian Treasury, or any other work of Greek art, and how we can start to answer them. We could construct many different types of histories; considering some of the processes and theories that are available for such a task can help us articulate what we might want to know about an object and whether or how we can learn enough to begin to engage with its place in history.

I envision two types of readers for this book, both of whom are confronted with works of Greek art and seek to make sense of them. One is the student in a class on Greek art history or archaeology who may have to study actual objects as part of a research project or essay. The other is a visitor or traveler interested not only in the well-known works housed in places such as Athens, Paris, London, Rome, Munich, and New York, but also in any collection of Greek art in cities such as Minneapolis, Chiusi, or Nemea. When either type of reader goes to look at Greek art, each becomes an art historian in a way, looking to make sense of the artifacts and objects on display.[3]

No ancient artwork in a museum was ever meant to be in such a place, and almost everything in a museum was found without any documentation or guide to its interpretation. Although labels help, you as a viewer must define what interests you about what you see. What questions can you ask about the work of art? What more do you need to find out to understand things more deeply? How do you connect the work to others, whether in the same room or elsewhere? Understanding how methodology and theories work on a practical level can help us to consider these and other questions.

Encountering Objects and Narratives of Display

As noted earlier, both Herodotos and Pausanias could see the Siphnian Treasury intact and complete, but we can see only its base on the grounds of Delphi and some of its remains in the nearby museum. Looking at these artifacts, however, is not as simple as it might first seem. The preservation and means of display of an ancient work of art are important factors in the way we encounter an object today, and our viewing experiences are quite different from those of its original makers and users. Furthermore, no museum has enough space to display everything in its collection, so curators must select what to put into display cases. How a single object is set up and placed into groups with other objects affects how we think about it. Displaying and looking at artifacts thus involve choices and decisions; thinking about how we encounter objects today can serve as a prelude to studying them more intensively. Before laying out the specific plan of this book, then, we should consider briefly the circumstances in which we look at Greek art today, as it is the work of art itself that engages us.

For example, we might consider a small object such as that found in many museums with collections of Greek art. In looking at the object in Figure 2, without any prior knowledge, one might be surprised on reading the label that it is a mirror, as it does not seem as if it would give a clear reflection of its user. Looking at the picture printed here, it seems as if the mirror is in a good state of preservation, as indeed it is, but looking at the actual object rather than a photograph, one can see that the surface is a bit rough, somewhat like fine sandpaper in areas. A new bronze object would have had a smooth, polished, and highly reflective surface quite different from what we see today. The present mottled discoloration is the result of a chemical reaction; the original color would likely have been lighter, more metallic, and uniform. When cleaned and polished in a new state, one could imagine seeing one's reflection and the glint of light off the surface, making the original experience quite different from the one we have today. Two centuries ago, such a work might have been "restored" to its "original" appearance. Today we try to conserve rather than restore works, but this does have the effect of making the work less as it was for its original owner.

Not only is the appearance of the mirror different than it was originally, but the viewing experience is different as well. One would have held an object such as this as one holds a modern mirror, or one could have looked at one's reflection from a close distance while the mirror stood on a flat surface. Today, when the object is protected in a display case by glass or Plexiglas, one certainly can not hold it and move it around, and in most displays, it would be unlikely that you could get directly in front of it at the proper distance for usage, even if it were still shiny and reflective. Thus, one cannot experience the work as a user but only as a detached viewer, losing the intimate, personal dimension of the original work. This is unavoidable, because letting viewers touch objects such as this would quickly damage these objects.

This detached viewing of a work increases substantially when we see the work reproduced in publications. Most Greek art is three-dimensional, but the limits of publication typically result in only one view, such as that in Figure 2, being printed for the discussion of an object. The back side, though, is revealing: the joins and rivets of the mirror are apparent, as is the rougher and greener quality of the surface of the disk (Figure 6). Because the back would not have been polished over and over again, as was the reflecting front, its surface was probably less protected from the elements when it went from being a household object to a buried artifact. Even adding a back view, however, does not fully convey the three-dimensional quality of the mirror. From an oblique rather than a perpendicular angle, one can see that the figure stands in a slightly twisted and asymmetrical stance, as a real person would stand, and that the arm holding the bird projects toward the front. You realize in actually looking at the object that reaching out to grasp it would not have been a casual act; you would have to reach under that arm to wrap your hand around the bottom part of the figure.

Seeing the object, then, is important. Although the limitations that we have considered might seem to be huge disadvantages for the modern viewer, there are aspects of the museum that in fact make it easier to see an object.

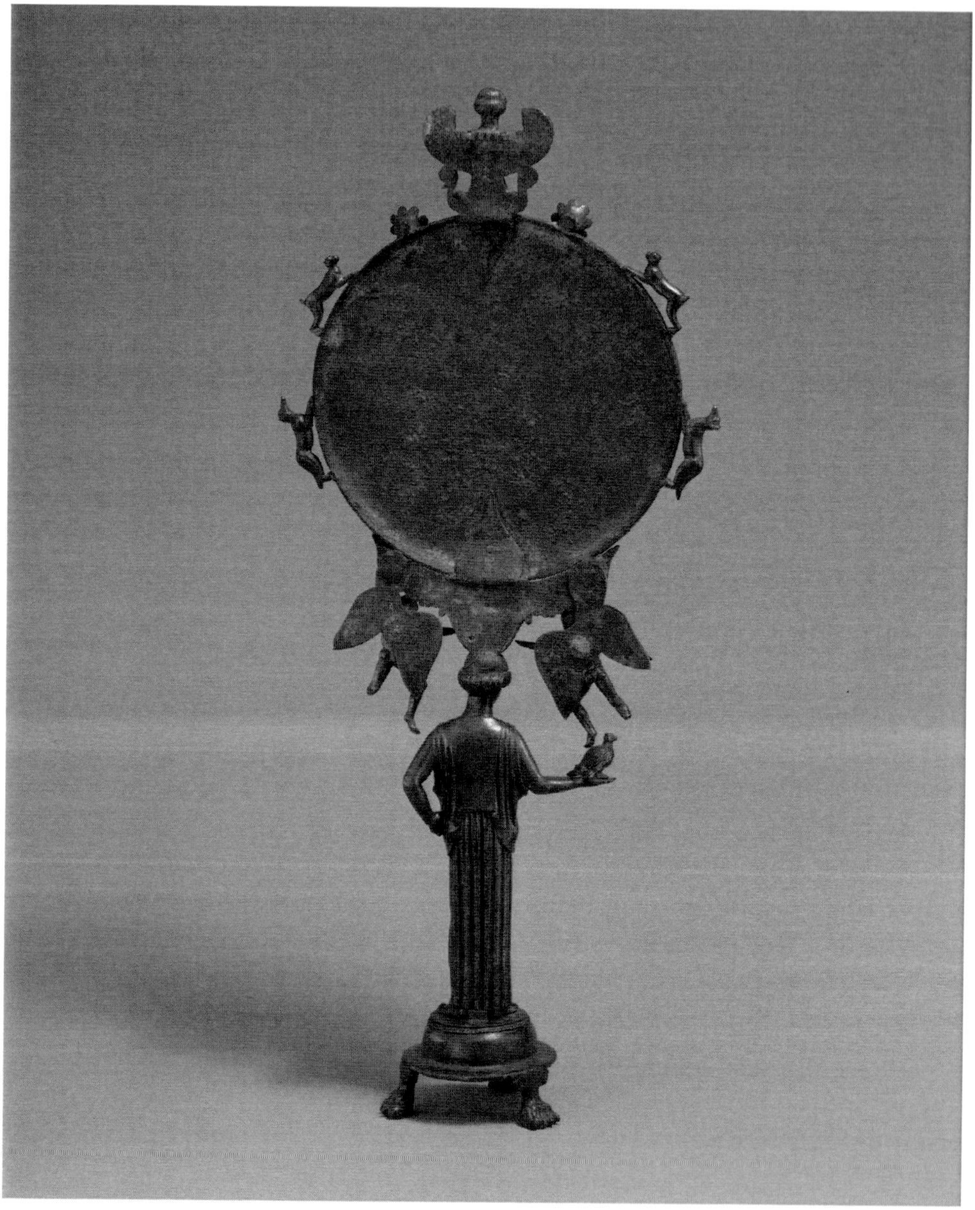

Figure 6. Bronze Argive caryatid mirror, back, mid-fifth century BCE. *New York, Metropolitan Museum of Art,* 1972.118.78. *Image Copyright © The Metropolitan Museum of Art/Art Resource, New York.*

The modern museum usually provides better viewing conditions in terms of climate and lighting, and objects are often displayed so one can see them distinctly and from multiple angles. The care given to their presentation and handling means that they will likely be the same when you see them

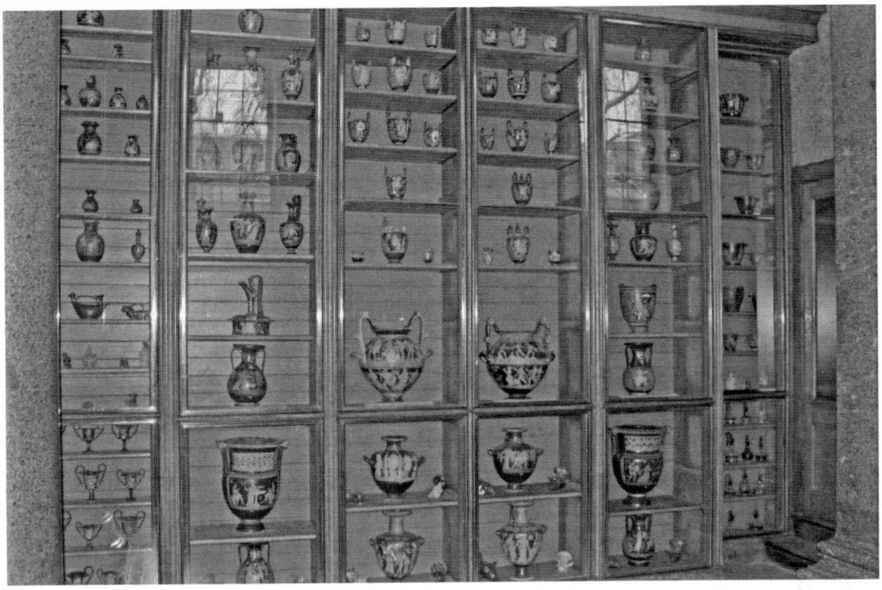

Figure 7. View of vases in Room 1, British Museum. Photo: author, used with permission.

for a second time. If one had seen such a mirror in a house in its original context, it might well have been damaged accidentally while being used a week later, or sold and melted down for its material value a month or a year later, dedicated in a large pile of votive offerings, or buried in a grave along with its owner. In a real way, the original context was often not conducive to the preservation of ancient art.

In a museum one can also look at other objects at the same time; the ability to compare and note similarities and differences is crucial for seeing what is typical and what is unique about a work of art. Display space is limited, though, and museums cannot show everything that they have or just randomly set objects on shelves. Like a history textbook, a gallery must have some kind of order to guide its visitors. Many works that are in the same display case never belonged together in the ancient world, and come into direct contact with each other only thousands of years later in a vitrine. As in a textbook, the way in which the object is presented conceptually is as important as its physical display when considering one's encounter with and reaction to a work.

Let us first consider an older style of display. Room 1 of the British Museum formerly housed the library of King George III; today it displays objects in a manner similar to that found in museums and galleries during the eighteenth and nineteenth centuries.[4] On one wall, there are dozens of vases stored in glassed cabinets running from floor to ceiling (Figure 7). The cabinets were

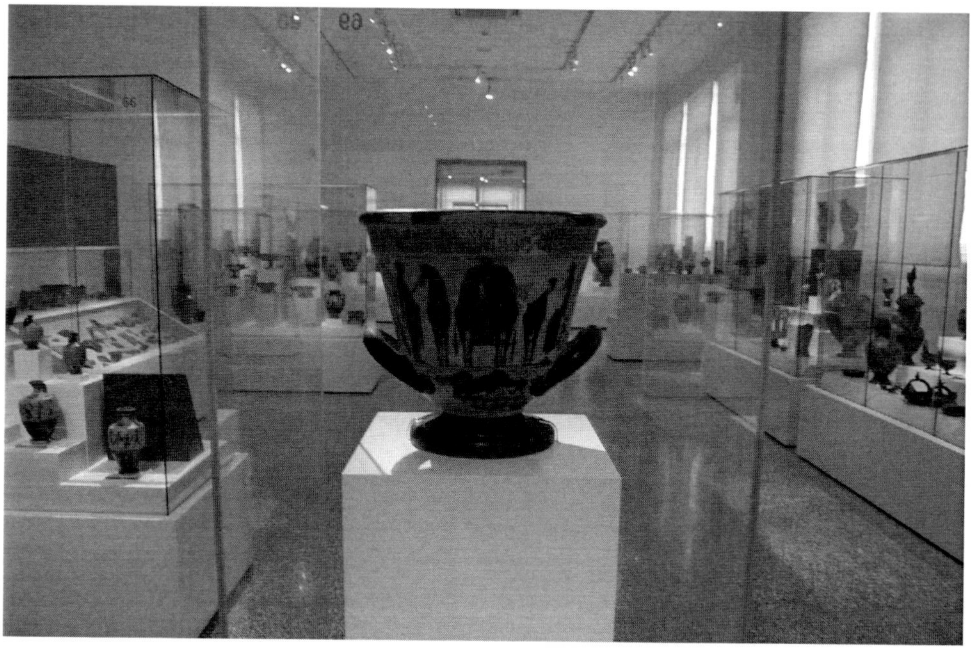

Figure 8. View of gallery in the National Archaeological Museum, Athens. Photo: author, used with permission.

made for books rather than vases, but the presentation of hundreds of objects closely packed together and similarly sorted by shape and vase type is like that of other early museums, and quite different from a spare, modernist aesthetic of presentation. As in the early museums, most of the objects are without labels except for the inventory number stuck on some, and those on the top shelves are very hard to see. The display does reflect some of the initial efforts of art historical scholarship going back to the Enlightenment: the classification of thousands of artifacts.[5] The lack of labeling implies some expectation of prior expertise for the observer to appreciate what he or she sees. Further, although these are clearly three-dimensional objects, their reverse sides are mostly inaccessible to the museum visitor.

A more typical modern display can be seen on the second floor of the National Archaeological Museum in Athens (Figure 8). Here the objects are placed on neutrally painted bases; the glass enclosures are thinner and less noticeable (in some museums these are replaced by lighter Plexiglas). What is interesting about this gallery view is that one object, a black-figure krater, has been placed on its own pedestal in the center of the room. This sets it apart and draws attention to it, leaving the side cases with their multiple occupants in the background. This particular vase is attributed to

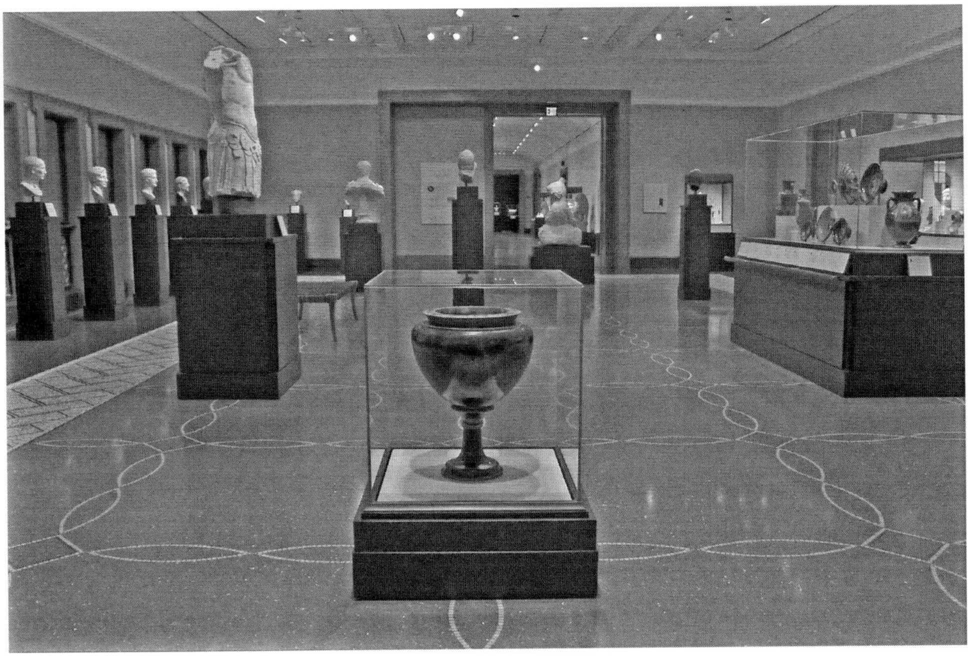

Figure 9. View of gallery in the Getty Villa, Malibu. Photo: The J. Paul Getty Museum. Villa Collection. Malibu, California.

the manner of Exekias, a vase painter and potter whose work usually appears in any survey of archaic Greek vase painting. The krater is a relatively big vase, and its figures are defined with precise and fine detailing. Being large in scale, the figures are visible from a distance and are more monumental than those of the other vase paintings in the room.

Placing the vase by itself on the central axis of the room gives it a prominence that would be appropriate for a masterpiece. Placing it at eye level allows the museum visitor to appreciate the painted figures fully, but doing so presents the object in a way quite different from the way it would have been seen in the sixth century. When it was originally used, it would have sat on the floor and been used for mixing wine and water for a drinking party. This is the way another type of mixing bowl called a *dinos* is displayed in the Getty Villa (Figure 9). Here one looks down at the vase, close to the way it would have been seen originally. In this case, the main painted decoration is on the top part of the vase, so this is actually conducive for the modern museum viewer. However, putting the Exekian vase in Athens on the floor, although this is more like the original context, would mean that a museum visitor there would have to kneel on the floor to see the figural decoration fully. A curator must make a choice: whether to emphasize the object as a functional piece of pottery or as a painting for the modern viewer to see. Either choice affects one's impression of the work and each choice has its limitations.

As this last example points out, the concept or theme behind the selection and organization of the objects also affects one's impression of the work. Like textbooks, museums and exhibitions create art-historical narratives. The narrative theme will guide the selection of works and their arrangement, but a museum, unlike a book, is limited by the availability of objects to construct this narrative.

Perhaps the most common scheme of organizing an exhibit is by period and chronology. Works that share common stylistic features are placed together in a common period or region, and the exhibit leads the viewer from the oldest material to the most recent. Doing this allows the viewer to see changes in style or technique over time and to understand the impact that innovations might have had on artistic culture as a whole. By mixing painting and sculpture in the same gallery, one could also see the similarities and differences across media at the same point in time. However, this combines things in ways that would not have happened in antiquity and obscures other themes that could be explored.

Other organizational strategies are possible and are found with increasing frequency in museums, either in galleries of their own or as subsections within the broader period/chronology scheme. For example, works in the same medium, such as painted vases, bronzes, or glass, are shown together. Works from the same geographic area or site, such as objects from the Greek cities in southern Italy and Sicily, can be grouped together.

With art that has narrative or representational images, subject matter can be a theme. For example, a display case might feature the exploits of Herakles, the episodes of the Trojan War, or representations of women. In these cases, the need to address a theme, such as representing all twelve deeds of Herakles, may mean mixing objects of different media, periods, regions, and artistic quality that never would have appeared together in antiquity. Alternatively, one could focus on archaeological context by displaying objects that were found together, such as those from the same tomb or shrine. Even here, though, the viewer does not see them as they were found, typically all jumbled together and covered with dirt. Not only have the objects been cleaned and conserved, they are spaced apart in a more orderly fashion to allow a viewer to see all the objects clearly and study them. This can be seen in the objects from the so-called Tomb of the Rich Lady from the Agora in Athens (Figure 10). The photo mounted in the case shows all the objects

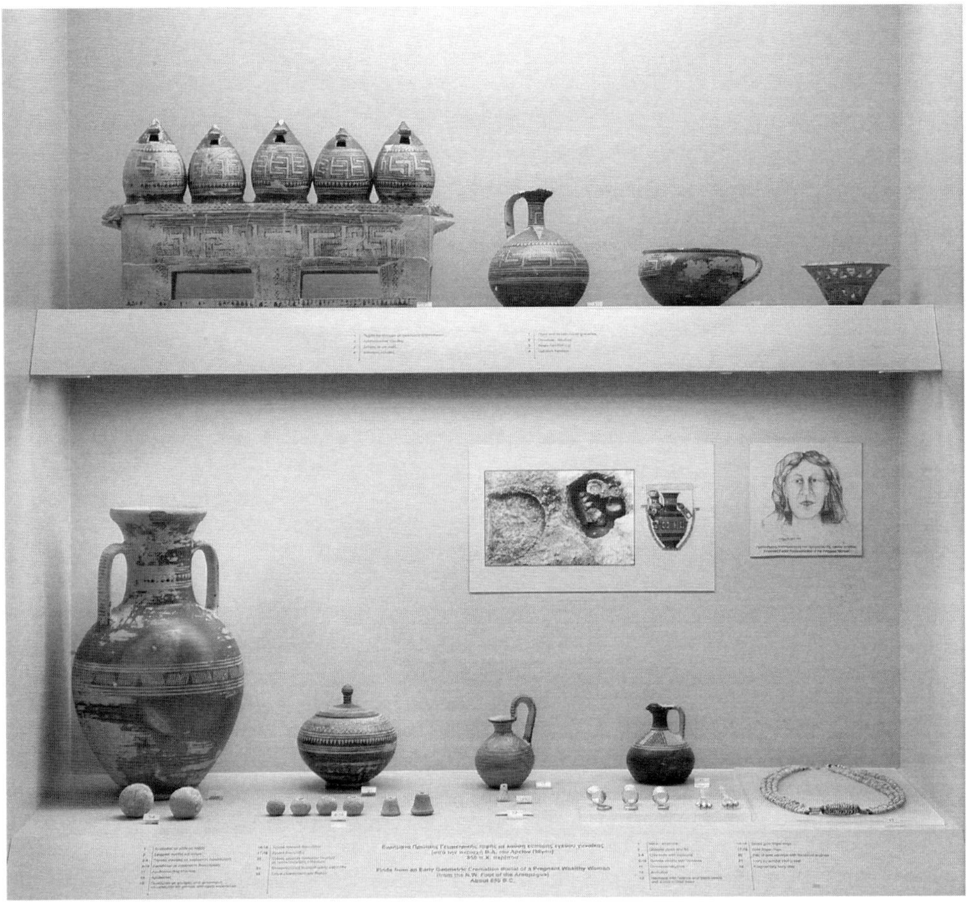

Figure 10. View of the material from the Tomb of the Rich Lady, ninth century BCE. *Agora Museum, Athens. Photo: Craig Mauzy, American School of Classical Studies in Athens.*

piled into a pit dug into the ground, quite a different order from that in the museum. Of course, once the objects were placed into the tomb by the family, they were not meant to be seen at all, so giving them proper space in a museum for a contemporary viewer seems reasonable.

Finally, one also must consider that the objects on display have frequently been found broken and damaged. Many have been pieced together and missing fragments have been filled in, usually with neutral coloration to distinguish the original fabric from the new, as can be seen in a small cup in the British Museum (Figure 11). Many fragments are too small or few for such treatment and remain in storage.

Looking at an object, then, is influenced by the interpretive strategy or strategies a museum chooses in designing its exhibition. Museum displays are like stages, on which the objects act out the scripts that art historians

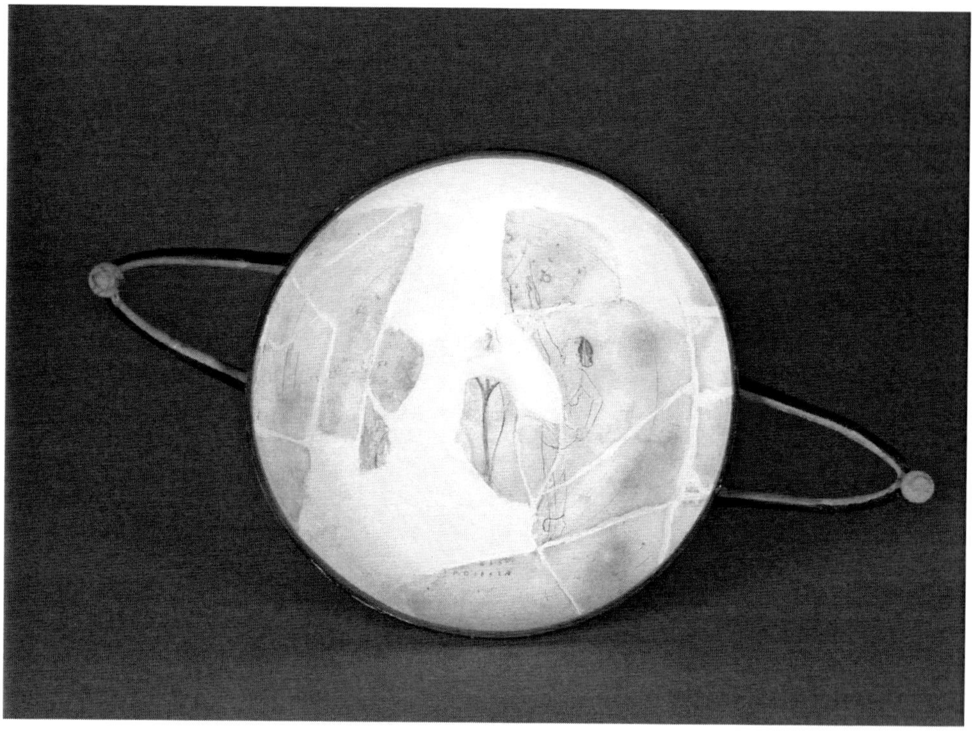

Figure 11. Attic white-ground cup attributed to the Sotades Painter, c. 460 BCE. London, British Museum D6. Photo: © Trustees of the British Museum.

have developed to explain the history of art.[6] As with a text, article, or book, this narrative is a choice that focuses on some themes but not on others. Given the need for economy in label copy, this focus is a necessity, but there are further constraints. Unlike written accounts of Greek art history, which can choose illustrations from virtually any collection, a museum exhibition is limited by the objects that are available for display. This too limits the themes that can be explored, and leaves questions for viewers to explore on their own.

Questions and Approaches

We can turn to one more object to consider the types of questions and the associated methodologies and theoretical approaches that we explore in this book. We consider these under four broad categories: style, meaning, context, and identity. Metaphorically, we could think of each of these areas as the leg or support of a table. Each has a particular focus and set of concerns, processes, and evidence. Individually, each helps us to study and analyze an artwork; together, they provide support for a tabletop, on which we could set the object for study.

Figure 3 is a painted ceramic vessel with figures on both the outside and inside of the bowl and is the third work that we will be discussing throughout this book. There are handles on either side; there once was a foot on the bottom of the cup, but this is now lost. As virtually nothing is found with a manual or identity papers, we must begin with a close visual examination of the work.

Basically, we would like to classify the work: What is it, where was it made, when was it made, and who made it? Just by looking at the object, we could make some guesses about the materials, shape, and other physical properties, but it would be only by comparison with other objects that we could develop more detailed answers. For example, many works such as this are found in Italy, but study has shown that this object was produced in Athens and then exported. By classifying thousands of objects using methods such as stylistic analysis and formal analysis, and correlating this with internal and external evidence, it has been possible for archaeologists and art historians to develop knowledge of regions, schools, and individual artists and connect these chronologically and geographically. Thus, as we shall see in the discussion of **style** in Chapter Two, we can attribute this drinking cup to an Athenian painter named Douris, who was active in the first decades of the fifth century BCE. Deciding this, we can then place it within the history of Greek art.

A second set of questions can be grouped together under **meaning**, which will be the focus of Chapter Three. Who are the figures that decorate the cup, and what story is being represented? What would the story have meant to the ancient viewer? What principles, ideologies, or morals does it represent, and why might they have been important to the artist, the viewer, or the society? How is the representation similar to or different from the literary versions of the story, and is there even a relationship between literary and pictorial narratives? Is this version of the story common, or is it unusual in some way? Answering these questions requires the use of other methodologies, although once again close visual observation and comparison are necessary. Iconographic analysis, semiotics and structural analysis, poststructuralism, information theory, hermeneutics, and reception are all methodologies and theories that have been developed to structure our observations and fill in the gaps of our knowledge so we can consider and interpret the meaning of Greek art.

Still another set of questions considers the work of art as an artifact that interacts with people and settings. A drinking cup, for example, is a practical, functional type of object; in Chapter Four we will consider broadly the **context** of art as a field of inquiry. How was this cup made, how was the workshop organized, and how much was the artist paid for it? How did it get distributed to its eventual owner, and how did this fit within the trade and economics of the ancient world? What was its value to its owner? Did its use affect familial, social, or political relationships? How was it adapted or configured to fulfill its functional purpose? Again, there have been a number of approaches that try to answer such questions, including economic and political analyses associated with Marxist theory, ritual theory and analysis, object biography, and agency. When there is sufficient evidence, these can provide a way to understand how a work of art fit into the activities of a culture.

One final set of questions has to do with who and what people are; in Chapter Five we will consider these perspectives under the heading of **identity**. For example, with the Douris cup, how would the experience of a young man drinking from the cup contribute to his social, gender, sexual, and ethnic position within his culture? If we consider that much of ancient art was seen not in solitude, but within a group setting and social activities, we can ask how using an object and looking at its subject matter both shaped and expressed the self-identity of the viewer. How would the experience of an older man drinking from this cup differ from that of a younger man? How would an Etruscan owner identify with the decoration of an Athenian work of art? Approaches such as psychoanalysis, and area studies such as feminism and gender analysis, sexuality, ethnicity, and status all offer perspectives about the experience of a work of art for the ancient viewer.

The use of different theoretical approaches in the study of Greek art has expanded considerably in the past couple of decades. As we will see in each chapter, the rationale and details for each approach will be found in lengthier scholarly discussions. What we want to do in this book is to develop an overview that provides links to more detailed, scholarly discussions. To take a practical approach to theory, we will focus on the following:

- The basic purpose or goal of a theory or methodology and its fundamental questions;
- The process or sequence of steps that should be followed in using a specific approach, or the framework to be used;
- Some key terms and concepts for each approach;
- The type of evidence that is needed to undertake a particular approach.

In addition to this sketch of the methods, we will also use a series of case studies that demonstrate, albeit all too briefly, how an approach might be carried out. To provide some continuity across the next four chapters, we will be looking at the three works featured in this introduction – the Siphnian Treasury (Figure 1), the caryatid mirror (Figure 2), and the Douris cup (Figure 3) – in each of the following chapters. Doing so will demonstrate how our understanding is extended by alternative approaches, and how we might begin to integrate the range of questions and answers into a more comprehensive understanding of a work of art. For reference, these have been listed in the index as Delphi, Siphnian Treasury (Figure 1); mirror, caryatid (Figure 2); and cup by Douris (Figure 3).

In all cases, this book is meant to be a starting point for questions, research, and analysis. In looking at an object in a museum or in researching a work for a paper, one will want to identify what questions are of interest and what approaches would be fruitful for answering them. Doing so will depend on delving more into the theory and approach, and for that purpose each chapter has some suggested reading at the end. These works are intended to be starting points for learning a method and understanding both its madness and insights. The lists are not exhaustive, and they focus on literature in English, given the readership of this book, but students should be prepared to pursue the wide range of scholarship in other languages found in the literature.

Further Reading

There are two books that I have found to be particularly useful in developing the historiography of methodology and theory and in taking a practical bent toward their application. Eagleton 1996 considers literary theory rather than art history, but his synthesis is particularly engaging for a student of art history. D'Alleva 2005 takes a broader approach to the historiography and application of theory in art history generally. Both should be consulted in developing the use of a methodology for a project. Hitchcock 2008 is also very useful from a classics perspective for the intellectual background of many of the theories introduced in this book.

For general histories of Greek art, see Robertson 1981, Biers 1996, Boardman 1996 and 1997, Spivey 1997, Osborne 1998, Fullerton 2000, Whitley 2001, and Pedley 2007.

For some surveys of different archaeological and art historical approaches, see Morris 1994 and Alcock and Osborne 2007.

For museums and issues of display, see Preziosi 1992 and 1993 and Hooper-Greenhill 1992 and 2000.

Two

Description and Visual Analysis

An object in a museum display case has a label that generally describes its period, region, artist (if attributed), medium, date, object type, and subject matter (if any). Sometimes information such as the findspot is listed when it is known, but this is often not the same place as the one where the object was made. Vases found in Etruscan tombs were initially thought to be Etruscan, for instance, but the use of Greek inscriptions led early archaeologists to realize that many of the vases in Etruscan tombs were from Greece, and that there were many regional and chronological variations among Greek vases. To situate a work within the history of Greek art, it is first necessary to classify the wide range of objects and to synchronize their chronologies and geography.

Because objects do not come with certificates that record their creation or history, one must begin with the study and description of the work itself. In this chapter we explore stylistic and formal analysis as approaches that describe the visual characteristics of a work and its artistic effect. These methods also compare one object with others, whether found together with it in the same archaeological context or found in other locations. Such comparison allows the classification of a work relative to others, defining categories of similar and dissimilar works as well as a chronological sequence. Understanding typology and sequence then allows us to consider broader questions about the development of artistic forms and ideas and the qualities of specific periods or artists.

Stylistic and Formal Analysis

Before we can analyze a work of art, we must first describe it. We can do this objectively by measuring the dimensions of the work and identifying the materials used to make it, the techniques employed in its fabrication, and the type of object. Complete objectivity, however, is difficult to maintain. Even some straightforward quality, such as the object type, requires prior familiarity with a culture's objects. In the case of fragments, we often must guess what type of object it was when whole; even some intact objects are puzzles as to what they are and what they did. Objectivity becomes even more difficult when we move to describe verbally the specific visual qualities of a work of art. Precisely what color something is, the variation of the tones or saturation of the color as it is applied over a surface, and the quality of its preservation require making choices among a range of descriptive adjectives and nouns that may elucidate what we see, or may fall short of the subtleties.

With this in mind, it is all the more important to be systematic. Visual analysis, in the broadest sense, begins by describing the properties of the work of art, its *forms*, in as much detail as possible. These forms of a work are its more purely visual features – such as line, shape, texture, and color – and their arrangement or composition, in contrast to the subject matter or content. From the close observation of these forms, one can use a sequence of steps and vocabulary for several different purposes. The goal of **formal analysis** is to understand the visual or aesthetic effect of a work and the way in which it creates an impression on the viewer. The goal of **stylistic analysis** is to associate or differentiate a work of art with or from others, creating stylistic categories on the basis of a specific set of visual qualities and object properties.

An underlying premise in both types of analysis is that in making a work, the artist fashions and manipulates materials to create the finished work. In doing so, artists rely on techniques and training that will create a certain consistency in how they fashion the forms that we see, such as a human figure. The assumption of stylistic analysis is that these repeated renderings are habits that transfer from one work to another, just as a person's handwriting is relatively consistent from one page of writing to another. Like handwriting analysis, stylistic analysis presumes that we can associate some works with one another as belonging to the same time, place, group, and/or individual on the basis of the visual qualities of the forms. Furthermore, we can differentiate works from one another in varying degrees, according to artist, region, or period.

Meyer Schapiro, in a fundamental discussion about the theory of style and form, articulated the general components of visual analysis:

> Although there is no established system of analysis and writers will stress one or another aspect according to their viewpoint or problem, in general the description of a style refers to three aspects of art: form elements or motives, form relationships, and qualities (including an all-over quality which we may call the "expression").[1]

These three aspects constitute a sequence of analysis, moving from the detail to the collective effect. The basic level consists of the *form elements* or *motifs* (a more common French term used in lieu of *motives*): the specific details of form that contribute to the collective visual effect. These include elements such as line, shape, color, texture and surface quality, lightness or darkness, mass, volume, space, and dimension. Even when focusing on the construction of an anatomical feature, such as an eye, one should focus on the use of shaped lines or ridges, color, and texture that make up what we actually see and then interpret as an eye.

Form relationships are the overall interactions or combinations of the form elements. For example, what is the relative size and scale of the work, and what are its general proportions? What is the composition or arrangement of the parts, and what kinds of rhythmic patterns are created by the placement of the elements, the use of light and dark, mass and space, and the like? Are the forms open, extending into space, or closed and circumscribed? What are the lines of movement (horizontal, vertical, diagonal) and how do they create the order and balance of the work?

Finally, with the *form qualities* one becomes more evaluative than descriptive, looking at the distinctive visual expression created by the work. For figural imagery, one can ask whether the figures are *naturalistic* (appearing to the eye as they would in nature) or *abstract* (more schematic and reduced). Are they *realistic* (looking like real people, warts and all) or *idealized* (following a particular standard of beauty or proportions, which may vary by time and place)? A work can be both naturalistic and realistic, but it could also be naturalistic and idealized, or somewhere between the two. Deciding where on the spectrum of these concepts a figure is situated helps to understand the form quality. More broadly, what is the general effect of the work? Is it balanced or directional? Is it dynamic or more self-contained in relation to its surroundings? Is it, for instance, dramatic, elegant, or delicate? One way to approach the form qualities is to consider what would change if a motif or relationship were different; how would the expression of the work be different if the colors or scale were changed, or the rhythmic order altered?

This division of the process into three levels is useful, as it builds from the observation of small, specific details into the analysis of their collective pattern of deployment and visual effect. To these forms, we may also add materials or media and techniques as important contributors to the visual qualities of a work of art. Certainly the medium has an impact on what it allows an artist to do, but frequently one will find a similar style used in both marble and bronze, despite the very different properties of the two materials.

As Schapiro noted, the process will vary in its details depending on the purpose of the analysis, and many times in scholarly work the details are described or treated summarily. A good example of the process in its intricacies can be found in the work of Sir John Beazley, who published an article in 1922 on a series of vases that he attributed to an unknown painter to whom he gave the name the Berlin Painter, after a vase in the Antikensammlung in Berlin. Beazley had already been working on creating lists of vases that he felt belonged to individual artists, and in this article Beazley was careful to explain his methodological approach in extensive detail as a foundation for his goal of stylistic attribution.

One of the works Beazley attributed to the Berlin Painter is a vase, called an amphora, now in the Metropolitan Museum of Art (Figure 12). We can begin by describing some of the form elements/motifs of the vase itself. It is 41.5 cm high, about two times as high as it is wide. From a narrow and curved foot, the contour swells in a curve until the midpoint, where it flattens, then narrows with a sharper curve in the upper third to create the narrow neck, and flares out again to the rounded rim. The handles are also rounded, and are looped and set vertically at the shoulder of the vessel. The surface is a mostly dark, burnished black slip that reflects the light and surrounds the central figure. The silhouette of the figure is an orange-red color that is the bare surface of the clay, on which thick black and thinner brown lines describe its anatomical details. One could say much more about the vase – a more complex or detailed description and analysis would demand a much lengthier treatment, as is typical of exhibition and museum catalogues and recent volumes of the *Corpus Vasorum Antiquorum* – but this is sufficient for our purposes to illuminate some aspects of the form elements/motifs.

Next, we can analyze the form relationships of the elements/motifs. Overall, we can say that the proportions of the vase are vertical. The lines of the handles and the S-like curve of the profile further contribute to the verticality of the work, but give it a rhythmic undulation, like a sine wave, that is capped at both ends by the horizontals of the rim and base. The verticality is enhanced by the placement of the orange-red standing figure on the vertical axis of the vase, symmetrical between the handles. We can see some of the same undulating lines of the vase in the contour of the figure and the drapery hanging from his body, creating repetition and a rhythmic pattern in the vase.

In describing the form qualities of the vase, we might say that the vase emphasizes flowing line and balance and is rather restrained in its decoration. This allows the warm color of the figure to project from the dark background and creates a certain statuesque or monumental quality for the figure and vase, giving it a large scale and isolation that draw the attention of the viewer. Beyond its verticality, there is also a tenuous sense of balance in the vase. The base is only about one-third of the diameter of the wide belly of the vase, creating a more dynamic balance even while sitting on the ground. One way to consider an effect such as this would be to imagine a different type of relationship of elements: What would happen if the base were twice as wide, with the contour from the belly to the foot much straighter? This would give the vase a squatter appearance that would seem less prone to tipping, changing some of the form quality and effect. What if the background were red and the figure were black? What if the handles were located at the sides and turned horizontally? Considering these alterations allows one to see the form qualities and articulate them more concretely.

So far, we have been considering the formal effects of the vase, but we can also use this approach to point to the distinctive form motifs, relationships, and qualities that would allow us to attribute the style of this vase to a specific region, period, group, or artist. Details of human figures are particularly appropriate for this, as they give us many more diagnostic elements to consider.

We can begin by noting that the artist has defined the contour of the figure with a thick band of slip about 2 mm wide; this is raised slightly above the level of the black slip painted on the remainder of the vase. To define the interior details of the figure, the painter used a combination of black, raised lines, usually called thick lines, to describe major components of the body, and used a diluted, brown-red, washlike line to define the smaller details. For example, the chin, eyes, ears, and nose are defined by thick lines, whereas two brown lines define the tensed sternomastoid muscles of the neck. The contours of the clothing are outlined in thick black lines, whereas

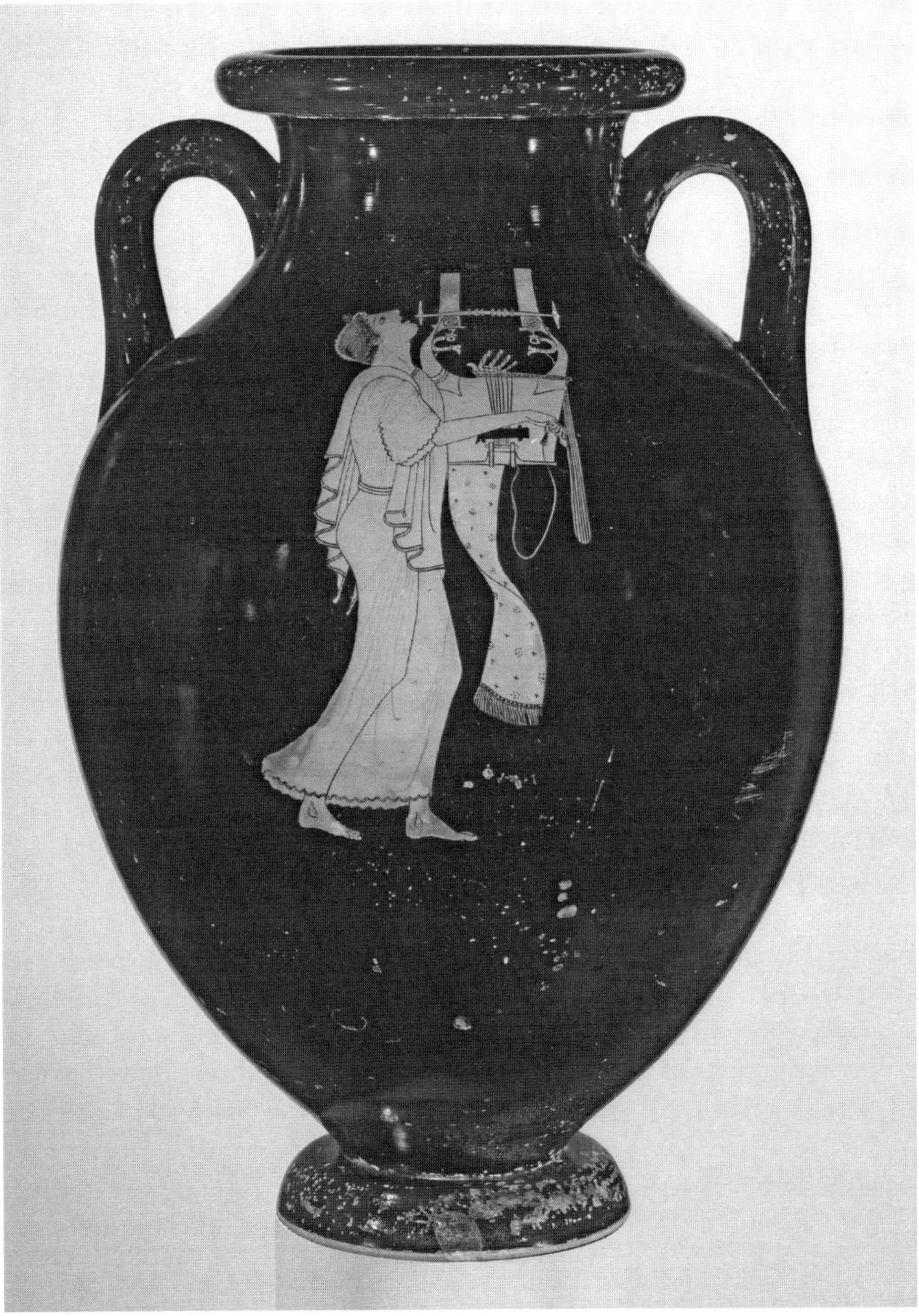

Figure 12. Attic red-figure amphora attributed to the Berlin Painter, c. 490 BCE. Kitharode. New York, Metropolitan Museum of Art, 56.171.38. Image Copyright © The Metropolitan Museum of Art/Art Resource, New York.

the interior folds of the fabric are in brown lines. The edges of the mantle are indicated by a double black line and the folds are set in an undulating pattern like a zigzag, but with rounded rather than angular valleys. The eye is almond-shaped and the pupil is a solid black disk located toward the front end; the eyebrow above is an even line following the curve of the eyelid. The chin is heavy and rounded and is defined in part by a black line dividing it from the neck. Farther down we can see that the painter emphasized the forward contour of the near leg with a thick line, over which brown lines are drawn in alternating hooks. The ankles are rendered by two black lines, one in a hook shape.

Each of these features can be called a form element or motif, the rendering of a figural feature in a very specific way using the materials of the medium. Overall, they form a system of renderings, as Beazley termed it, to represent the human figure. Beazley's system of renderings belongs to the level of form relationships as we have defined it. To this, we can add that the figure is shown with a slight movement, and there is some extension of the figure vertically and horizontally. Generally, though, we can say that the forms are basically closed, rather than open and extending into the pictorial space vigorously. There is relatively little emphasis on foreshortening or the illusion of three-dimensional space created by the figure.

At the level of form qualities, we can say that the figure is generally naturalistic, but that there are some abstract elements. The eye is still somewhat frontal on a profile head, there is some simplification of complex forms such as the ear and hand, and the drapery falls too regularly in a zigzag pattern to be truly lifelike. The figure is also more idealized than realistic in its quality, as it is somewhat longer in proportion than the average person and its appearance is more graceful and composed. Still, as a figure performing at a public venue, there would be an extraordinary level of dress and behavior, so the idealization does conform to the expectations of the time. The lack of extensive subsidiary ornament on the vase is distinctive and concentrates attention on the figure, giving it what might be described as a statuesque quality, especially with its restricted movement.

Natural forms, of course, are not made up of thick and thin lines, but of undulations of three-dimensional surfaces that a painter translates into two-dimensional shorthand. In doing so, an artist will rely on a convention or system that describes the feature. As with handwriting, these conventions will vary from one artist or group to another, so the particular details of motifs, along with their combination and pattern of deployment, allow us the possibility of classifying works as belonging to a distinct group with

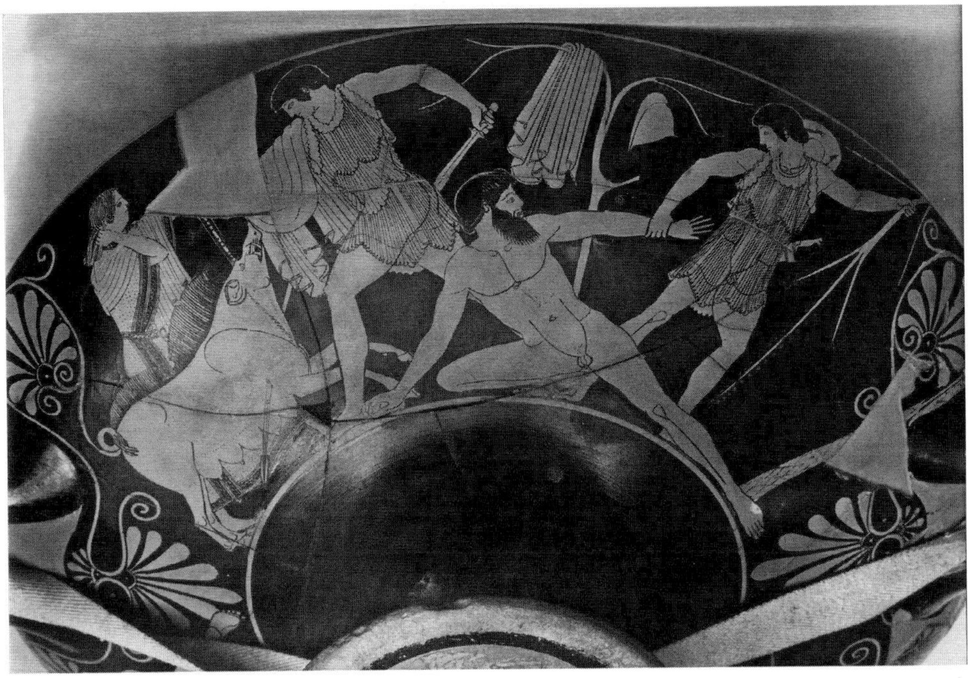

Figure 13. Detail of Attic red-figure kylix attributed to Douris, c. 490–480 BCE (other side of Figure 3). Theseus and sow; Theseus and Sinis. London, British Museum, E48. Photo: © Trustees of the British Museum.

similar features, such as the works of a specific artist. One of the key elements for this purpose is comparison with other works, which show how distinctive or common this pattern of elements/motifs, relationships, and qualities is.

Turning to the cup in the British Museum introduced in Chapter One (Figure 3), we can see a different approach toward the decoration. Rather than a single figure, the exterior of the cup is filled as a frieze with a series of overlapping figures, and the surface around the handles is decorated with palmettes and tendrils. The overall effect is to emphasize the horizontal quality of the cup itself, which as a shape provides a very different kind of surface for the artist and creates a more open form than the amphora. Overall, there is a busier effect, one that forces a viewer to sort out the relationship of the various figures within the picture.

In looking at the figures themselves, we can see some similarities to the *kitharode*, or kithara player, on the amphora in Figure 12. The eye of the striding figure with the sword on the other side of the cup is almond-shaped and defined by thick lines, but the pupil is an open circle compared with the dot of the kitharode's eye (Figure 13). The eyebrow on the cup is a more arched line that flares in thickness in the middle. The artist uses both thick and thin lines throughout, but there is a stronger use of thick black lines to describe the details of the drapery. Indeed, the short garment of the young man creates a strong visual impression of closely spaced, vertical black lines. In spite of this, the details of the underlying body are also indicated by black lines, so there is a more active intersecting of lines that make the details somewhat less clear. The folds of the drapery are also set into zigzag-like folds, but the angles are sharper and less rounded.

Overall, the forms on the cup are more complex visually. The artist uses several diagonal lines in the picture, such as the limbs, which create a different and more active formal effect than the statuesque quality of the kitharode. There is a strong interest in foreshortening and multiple viewpoints, so we see frontal, profile, and three-quarter views that make a deeper space around the figures. Indeed, one can see the bottom of the foot of one figure at the far right of Figure 3 and the tops of two other feet, one on each side of the cup and all on the opponents of Theseus. We should not assume, however, that this is simply an effort to be more naturalistic, as the twisted feet and frontal face require a somewhat unnatural twist of the body that shows the strength of the hero. It is an artistic tour de force as well, one that fits in with some of the same visual tricks of other artists developed during this time.

In comparing the amphora and the cup, we can note a number of similarities. The techniques and materials are the same, and we can attribute both to the same region, in this case Athens, based on a wider pool of comparanda. The similarities of the renderings of anatomical features would suggest that they are closely related in time as well as place, but there are enough differences in motifs, relationships, and qualities to suggest that these are not by the same artist. Indeed, Beazley attributed the amphora to the Berlin Painter, an artist whose name we do not know, whereas the cup is inscribed with the name of Douris, a name that appears on a number of other vases, especially cups. We can find numerous other examples of both artists' works based on stylistic comparisons; from this we can see that they did favor certain shapes of vases and composition types, as well as some specific motifs and system of renderings.

Developing a description and analysis of a work can allow us to begin to understand the artistic qualities of a work and to associate or differentiate works. One should keep in mind, though, that there are limitations in the effectiveness of words describing visual forms, as well as elements of judgment and subjectivity that enter into description and analysis.

For example, a couple of paragraphs ago I noted that the artist had a strong interest in foreshortening and multiple viewpoints. How objective, though, is the word "strong"? When compared with the Berlin Painter amphora, there is certainly more use of foreshortening in the cup, but "strong" implies an intentionality that is a subjective judgment. This may be justified on the basis of comparison with other works and detecting a broader pattern in the use of forms.

So, too, in noting that something is similar or different, there is a question of degree. Not all the eyes of the figures on the Douris cup are precisely the same; how much variation do we allow before we decide whether a different artist is at work, even on the same vase? Given the complexity of the drawing, it would seem unlikely that two artists painted the same cup, but it is important to remember that stylistic analysis and attribution are a question of probability rather than absolute certainty. Some vases, for example, have a decidedly simpler rendering of the figures on one side than on the other; is this side "B" the work of the same artist as side "A," but with less time and effort, or might it be the work of an assistant? Deciding these questions on the basis of style and form requires experience and judgment, and the number of attributions that say "close to the style of Douris" or "in the manner of the Berlin Painter" in Beazley's lists points out that stylistic analysis needs to be prudent.

The effort to describe the individual object and its forms and to associate or differentiate them from others is of critical importance, however, if we are to undertake the next stages of analysis by reconstructing the sequence of art and begin to consider the qualities and characteristics of artistic groups, regions, and periods, as we consider in the next section.

Region, Chronology, and Medium

One of the results of stylistic comparisons is being able to associate or differentiate two works and, ultimately, to be able to situate an individual work within a particular time, place, and artistic group or individual. In other words, some points we would like to know are: Where was it made, when was it made, and who made it?

As we have seen in the Berlin Painter amphora and the cup by Douris, similarities in technique, medium, and renderings suggest that these works are by different artists who worked at about the same time and place. Although vases such as these were originally thought to be Etruscan because they were found in Italy, further study and classification determined that they were produced in Athens. A comparison of Athenian pottery with those of other production centers, such as Corinth or Boeotia, shows differences that allow one to attribute an unknown work based on the qualities of the style and medium (compare Figures 21 and 48). On the other hand, in some periods, pottery from Euboeia and Greek cities in southern Italy closely imitates the techniques and materials of Athenian pottery, making attribution at times challenging and dependent on much closer observation of the fabric and renderings.

Not only can art move from its region of origin, but artists can also move from one place to another, bringing their individual styles with them to a new location. Thus, sculpture from one area could be closely related to that of another if the sculptor were to move to a new project, applying established tools and techniques to local stone or materials. Stylistic analysis can, therefore, show how a new way of rendering forms can spread, creating an interregional or international style that can coexist with or supplant a local style and potentially stimulate changes in other media.

Determining **chronology** is also complicated. Excavation can help to determine the *relative chronology* of works – that is, the sequence in which they were produced or used. However, works found together in a deposit might not have been made at the same time. Some could be significantly older, such as an old object that is deposited in a tomb along with work contemporary to the burial. Determining a fixed date or *absolute chronology* for a work is very hard to do, as there are very few works or contexts that have precise dates associated with them. Given the scarcity of works with fixed dates, those that have them become the touch point for stylistic comparisons and for determining approximate dates based on the degree of similarity or difference from the anchored works.

A case in point for considering the relationship of style across time, region, and media is an amphora attributed to the Andokides Painter (Figure 14). Looking at the work, one can see that the similarity in medium to the Berlin amphora and Douris cup would suggest that the work was from the same place. A look at the system of renderings, however, shows that the figures are drawn in a more abstract convention, with profile heads, hips, and legs but frontal eyes and chests (compare with Figure 12). The figures are very angular in their poses, and there is a much greater emphasis on decorative pattern that is less connected to the movement of the body than in the amphora and cup. Based on this comparison and other information about relative chronology, we would argue that the Andokides Painter amphora is older than the Berlin Painter amphora or the Douris cup. Indeed, based on

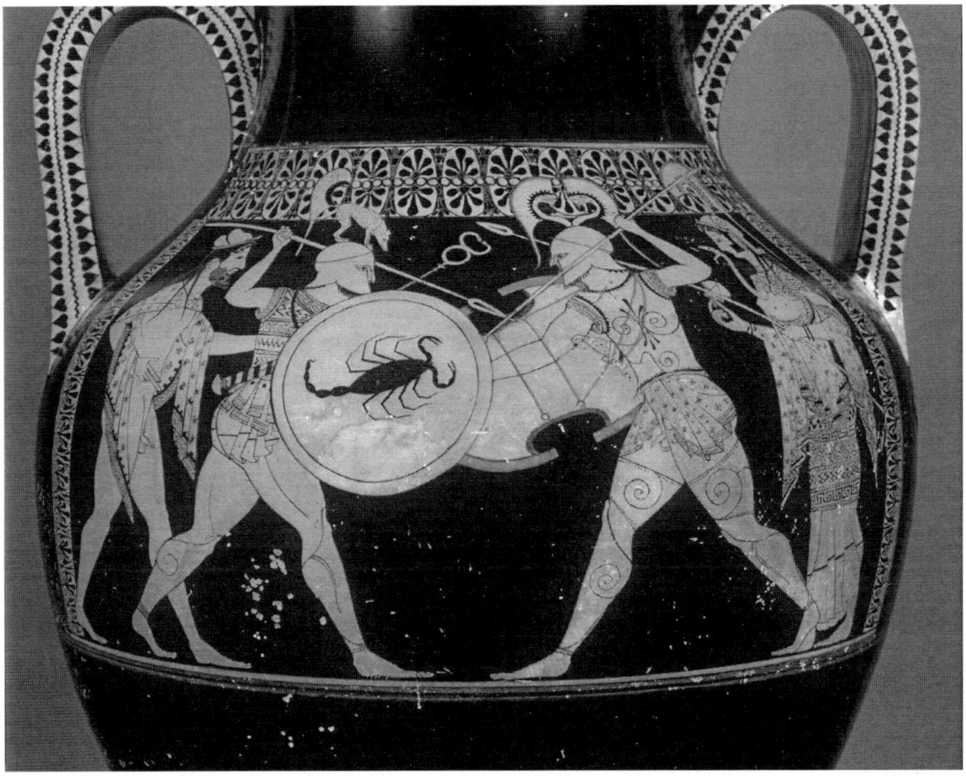

Figure 14. Attic red-figure amphora attributed to the Andokides Painter, c. 530–520 BCE. Warriors fighting. Paris, Musée du Louvre, G1. Photo: Réunion des Museés Nationaux/Art Resource, New York.

stylistic comparison with other red-figure and black-figure works, scholars would agree that this vase is in a group with the earliest red-figure vase paintings, produced at a time when black-figure painting was the dominant technique (compare, for example, Figure 28). Many vases associated with this painter also use black-figure painting on the other side of the vase from the red-figure painting. This makes the date of a vase such as this particularly important, as it can be tied to the introduction of a new technique that became common and dominant in later decades, and thus is an important example of a significant historical development for both medium and style.

We can compare the Andokides Painter amphora to a black-figure hydria, or water pitcher, produced in Italy, perhaps by a Greek or Greek-trained workshop (Figure 15). The type is called Caeretan, but the number of vases and painters attributed to this fabric are small when compared with Attic or Corinthian painting and show less stylistic range, suggesting that this type

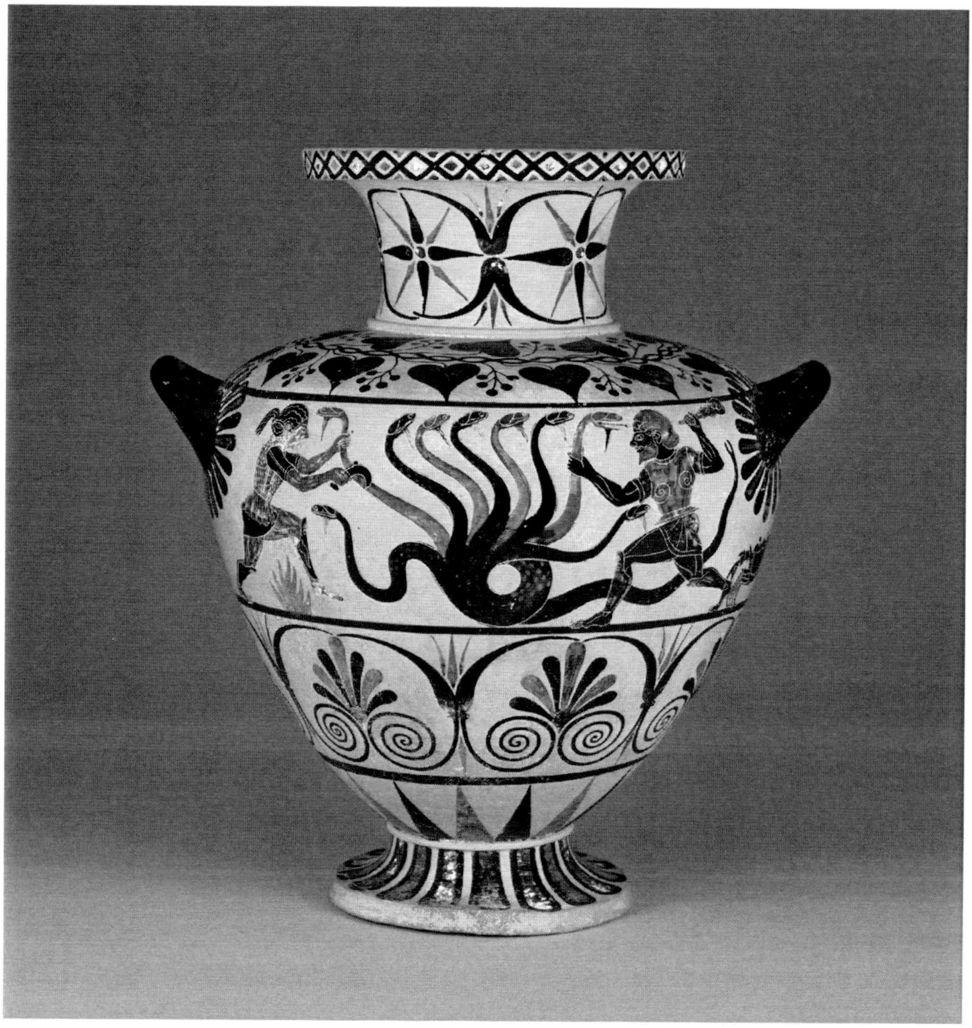

Figure 15. Caeretan hydria attributed to the Eagle Painter, c. 530 BCE. *Herakles and Hydra. Malibu, Getty Villa, 83.AE.346. Photo: The J. Paul Getty Museum. Villa Collection. Malibu, California.*

of painted vase was not produced over an extended period of time. If we look at some of the key diagnostic features, such as the pose, anatomical proportions, and renderings of specific features such as the eyes, there are some similarities to the Andokides Painter amphora, and both vases are usually dated to the same period. The Caeretan vase, though, looks distinctly different from Attic black-figure work, making use of a three-color palette of a cream background and alternating use of black and brown-red in both figures and decoration. This patterning, as well as rounded forms and more

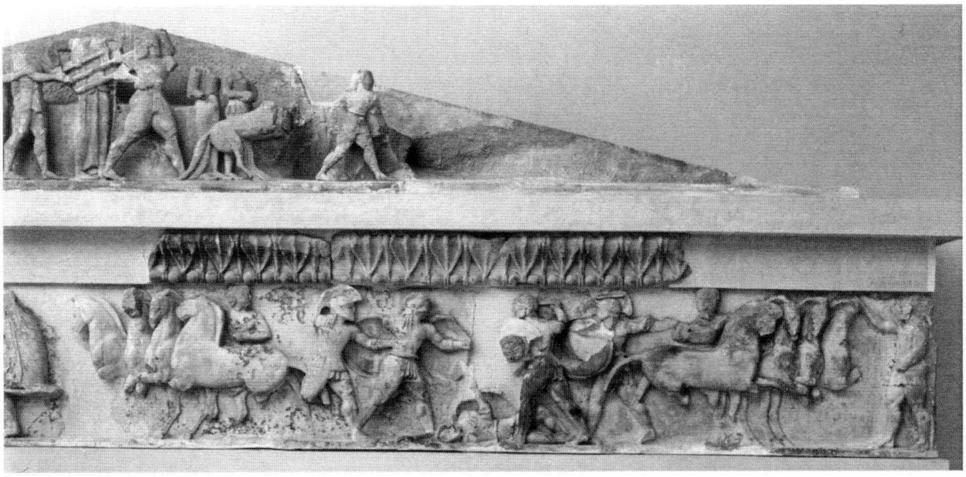

Figure 16. Detail of east frieze from the Siphnian Treasury at Delphi, c. 525 BCE. Memnon and Achilles. Delphi Museum. Photo: École française d'Athènes/P. Amandry.

extended silhouettes, creates a more dynamic movement and different formal effect than that of the Andokides Painter amphora.

Because this vase comes from the geographic margins of the Greek artistic world, we need to balance similarities and differences when comparing works produced in different regions. Attic pottery was available through trade in this region of Caere, so comparing similarities is worthwhile, but we also need to account for a different aesthetic produced by locally based artists.

Neither vase, however, can be tied to an absolute date on its own. Assigning a date to a work such as the Andokides Painter amphora requires looking at a datable work with a similar style. The east frieze from the Siphnian Treasury (Figure 1) has a very similar scene of warriors fighting. If we compare the warriors from the Andokides Painter amphora with a detail of that frieze (Figure 16), we can see that the conventions for pose, body proportions, drapery, and composition are very similar to one another, similarities that would have likely been more apparent when the frieze was intact and painted. As studies by V. Brinkmann have shown, the background was painted dark blue and details of the figures were in reds and green. The color contrast is similar to the dark background with lighter figures in red-figure vase painting, and the painted details of costume and armor on the reliefs might have made the decorative effects of the works closer than they appear to be now. Stylistically, we can say that there is a great deal of similarity between the works, even though they were produced in different regions (Athens, versus marble from Siphnos and Paros worked at Delphi) and media (vase painting versus relief sculpture).

The comparison becomes still more intriguing when we look at a different section of the Treasury reliefs, this time from the west frieze (Figure 17). Although these are less well preserved, there are some significant differences between the south and west friezes on one hand and the north and east friezes on the other (see Figures 5 and 16). The west figures are not rounded at their edges, but are cut sharply from the background, as if by a cookie cutter. The decorative patterns, such as the hair of the horses' manes and tails, are more regular and repetitive. Those poses are rigidly unlike the experiments with three-quarter and profile views on the north and east friezes. Indeed, if one were to compare the two friezes without knowing that they were from the same building, one might say, based on stylistic analysis, that the south frieze was somewhat older than the north and east friezes.

Being part of an architectural project and built into the fabric of the structure, the friezes would almost certainly have been done at the same time as the construction of the building. Given the stylistic differences between the two sets of friezes, we would then have to attribute them to different artists and, indeed, the traces of an inscription on the north frieze tell us that "[missing name] made these subjects and those at the back," or east end of the building. The implication is that another sculptor made the south and west friezes, and stylistic comparison would confirm this.

The importance of this for stylistic analysis and chronology is that Herodotos tells us that the building was the result of a tithe offering by the Siphnians to Delphi from the revenue of their gold and silver mines. Herodotos also tells us that Samians attacked the island in 525 BCE seeking the wealth of the Siphnians, and that the mines were closed in the aftermath of the attack. Therefore, the date of the attack must be a *terminus ante quem*, or point before which the tithe would have been given. Using this external chronological marker, the date of the Treasury is usually given as c. 525, allowing for a range of a few years before that date, and possibly a little after 525, as work might have continued once the material and money were already in Delphi. As one of the rare, absolute chronological points for sixth-century art, the Siphnian Treasury becomes a base for stylistic comparison with works in other places and media, such as the Andokides Painter's amphora. Given the latter's stylistic similarity to the west frieze, it is usually assigned a date range of 530 to 520 BCE, or nearly contemporary with the frieze.

The vast majority of scholars agrees with this dating of the Siphnian Treasury and with the relative and approximate chronology built by extension from it. While reasonable, this makes some assumptions. First, stylistic

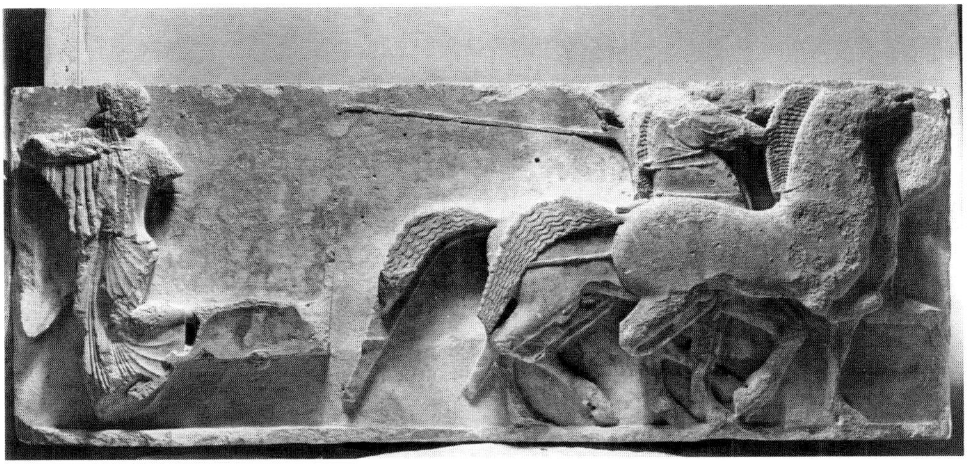

Figure 17. Detail of west frieze from the Siphnian Treasury at Delphi, c. 525 BCE. *Delphi Museum. Photo: École française d'Athènes/G. de Miré.*

comparison across media assumes that figures and motifs that are very similar in their details and patterns must be close in date to one another. Second, stylistic comparison within a medium sequences works found in different contexts based on their stylistic qualities, assuming that changes in style are relatively evenly distributed within a particular locale. Thus, the progression of rendering the human figure from very abstract in the eighth century to very naturalistic in the fifth century provides a continuum on which we can place a work through association and approximate date based on distance from a fixed point such as the Siphnian Treasury.

There has been criticism of both this process of stylistic attribution as well as the sequence derived from the Siphnian Treasury by E. Francis and M. Vickers. They have argued two points: (1) we are not sure that the building is the Siphnian Treasury, as there is no identifying inscription on the building, and (2) that the mines of the Siphnians continued to operate into the fifth century and that the caryatids featured on its porch were only invented after 479, according to Vitruvius, making the date of the building in the 470s, rather than 530–525. If true, this would vastly alter the entire chronology of early Greek art and make the Siphnian Treasury just before the Temple of Zeus at Olympia (see Figure 52), a hallmark of the Early Classical period for which we have some external evidence for dating. If the Andokides Painter amphora is also of the same date as the treasury, then the chronology for Athenian vase painting is also in question.

Mineralogical analysis has determined that the treasury walls were made with marble from Siphnos, and that marble from Paros was used in the friezes. The expensive importation of Siphnian marble to Delphi would be plausible for its treasury, making it appropriate to identify these friezes as part of the Siphnian Treasury. Herodotos as a direct source on the building, rather than the indirect evidence of Vitruvius, has been defended as stronger evidence. On balance, the date of 525 is the most logical assessment of the various pieces of evidence that we have. Nonetheless, the controversy over the proposed redating does remind us that dating and attribution are methodological issues, and we should always be aware of the strength and quantity of the evidence that we have in making a judgment.

To return to the two artists of the frieze itself, if the friezes had been found apart and unassociated with the same building, based on style we might suggest that the west frieze was older than the east frieze, following normal conventions. Because they come from the same time, however, do we attribute their differences to the age of the artists (one older and working in the style of that artist's youth, and one younger in a new style); to a different regional background for the sculptors (marble from Siphnos, Naxos, and Paros was used in the building, and perhaps the sculptors came from different regions as well, whether from these islands or the mainland); or, perhaps, to a combination of both scenarios? Should we assume that these artists are relatively constant in their style, or do they change over the course of their careers? The stylistic changes seen in comparing the Parthenon metopes to the later Parthenon frieze would suggest a development and refinement of individual styles that resulted in more consistency as the sculptors worked together over the course of a little less than a decade. Attributing differences in style to differences in artist, region, or date requires balance and judgment, realizing that the answer will vary according to the particular circumstances.

History and Development of Style

In looking at the history of Greek art, one finds a narrative that has been constructed concerning its stylistic development. Human figures begin to appear with regularity as subjects in the eighth century BCE; these are very abstracted and geometric in their form, hence the name Geometric, derived from the stylized patterns used in this period (see Figure 35). Gradually, artists begin to draw the human figure with more details and action, in part because of new techniques and materials. Furthermore, in the Orientalizing period of the seventh century we see new experiments in form and style (see Figure 48). In the Archaic period, from the end of the seventh century into the beginning of the fifth century, there is an increasing refinement and detailing of the style and an increasing naturalism of the figures. The Siphnian Treasury would stand near the midpoint of the Archaic period and its developments, whereas the Berlin Painter amphora (Figure 12) and Douris cup (Figure 13) would come at its end.

In the succeeding Classical period, we see the development of naturalism in the representation of the figure and more three-dimensional effects of volume and space in two-dimensional painting. The early phase is often called the Severe Style because of its relative simplicity of form and detail, but this gives way to the apex of idealism and naturalism seen in the Parthenon (see Figure 29) and the Doryphoros of Polykleitos (see Figure 25). After this brief period in the third quarter of the fifth century, the late Classical period introduces more refinement, illusionism, sensuality, and emotion in art (see Figure 82). The Hellenistic period sees greater drama and theatricism in its early stages, as well as a revival of some of the earlier styles of art (see Figure 22). There is also the development of a stronger realism in some of the arts (see Figure 39), as well as the development of portraiture.

This model is generally one of progressive, evolutionary development from simple beginnings to an apex of idealized naturalism, followed by an increasing individualism and diversity. This storyline, which I have vastly oversimplified, is built on detailed stylistic and formal analysis, but it finds confirmation in the accounts about the development of Greek art in ancient sources.[2] When examining a new work, we would try to fit it into this model of stylistic development.

In looking at the female figure that forms the handle of a bronze mirror from the previous chapter (Figure 2), we could say that the two Erotes floating above her head have the same type of vigorous movement as Herakles on the Caeretan hydria, but the handling of their anatomy and proportions is much more lifelike. The drapery of the female figure has abandoned the rigid zigzag folds seen in the work of the Berlin Painter and Douris, and although they fall in roughly even and regular folds, there are small asymmetries that suggest that the drapery is responding to the slight movement of the body underneath in a more naturalistic fashion. Of particular note is the figure's stance, with the right knee bent and projecting forward, pulling the drapery along the contour of the leg, while the left leg is hidden behind the curtain of the cloth. This weight shift, or *contrapposto*, is a more complicated type of standing pose than that of the kitharode in Figure 12 and is more lifelike. The left hand is on the hip, pushing at the upper drapery and creating a diagonal crease that is a response to the pressure on the costume. The pose is quiet and the features are broadly defined and seem contemplative.

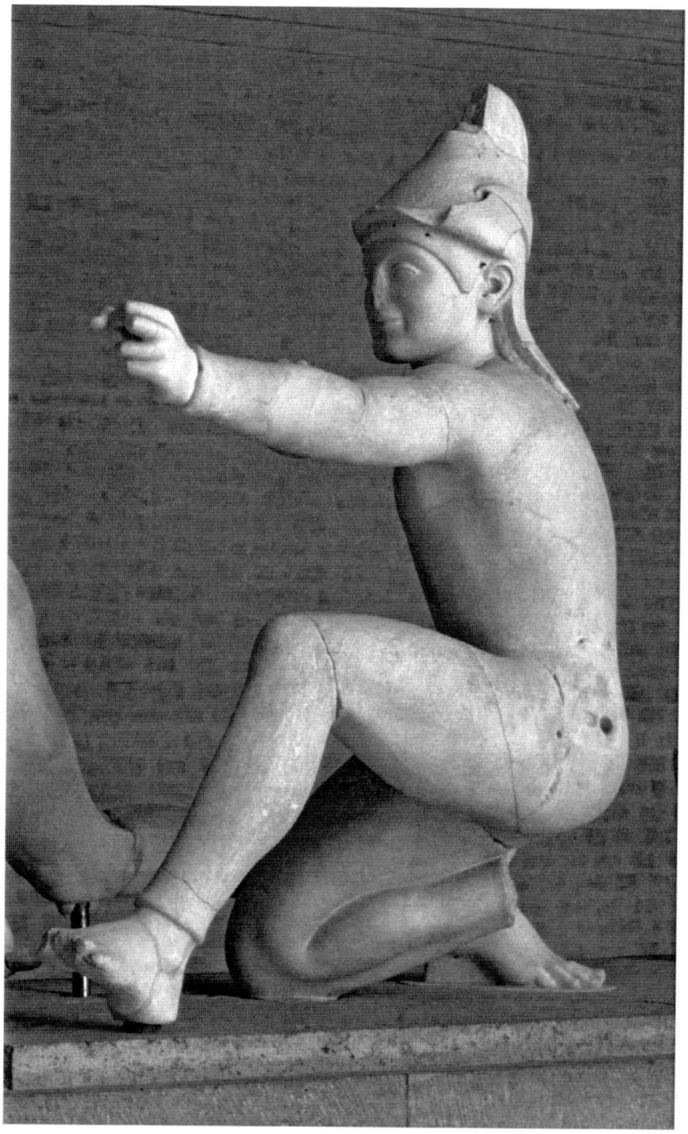

Figure 18. Archer from the west pediment of the Temple of Aphaia at Aigina (West 11), after 480 BCE? Munich, Glyptothek, Aeg W 11. Photo: Renate Kühling. Staatliche Antikensammlungen und Glyptothek München.

Rather than an interest in complex foreshortenings, this figure has a more convincing representation of a body in an active standing pose. There is also the suggestion of an inner contemplation or self-awareness expressed through the facial expressions and gaze. As J. J. Pollitt has explained, the artist here has an understanding of the coordination of the body's parts to carry out a movement – what the Greeks called *rhythmos*. There is also an

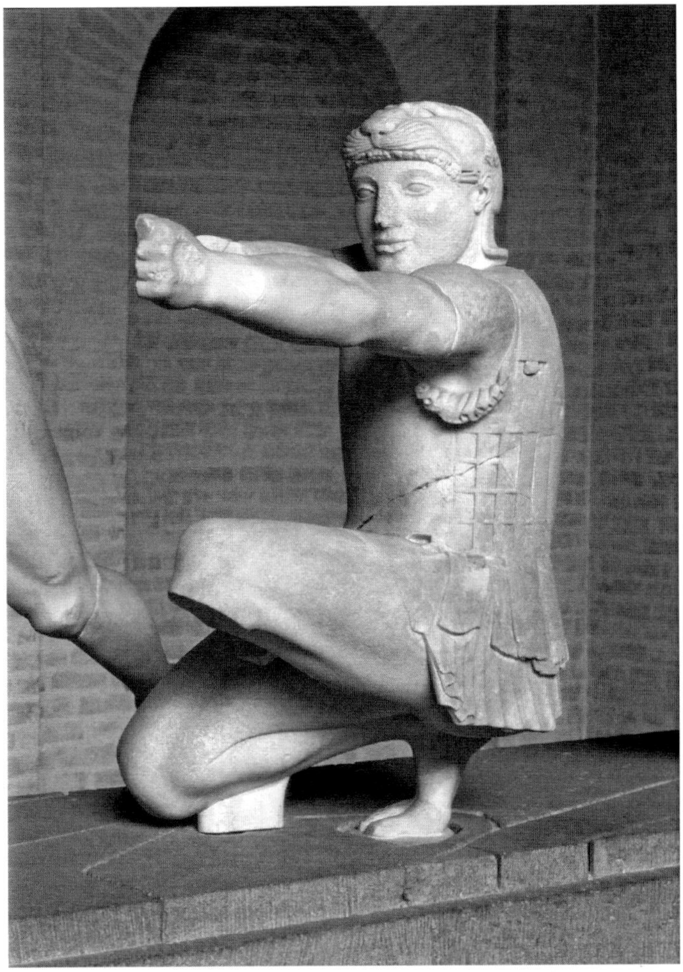

Figure 19. Archer (Herakles) from east pediment of the Temple of Aphaia at Aigina (East 5), after 480 BCE? Munich, Glyptothek, Aeg O 5. Photo: Renate Kühling. Staatliche Antikensammlungen und Glyptothek München.

ability to convey an emotional state, or *pathos*, through the use of gaze, facial expression, and gesture.[3] Altogether, we get a suggestion of the character, or *ethos*, of the figure, a quality that is seen as the key to the flowering of Greek mimetic art. Based on stylistic analysis, this mirror would be dated a generation after Douris and the Berlin Painter, toward the middle of the fifth century BCE, somewhat in anticipation of the style of the Parthenon.

This mimetic style, imitating the appearance of natural figures and forms, is linked to the development of the Severe Style that flourished in the Early Classical period, c. 480–450 BCE. The style finds its most monumental expression in the figures of the pediments and metopes of the Temple of Zeus at Olympia, which, on the basis of external historical references, are dated to between 470 and 457 (see Figure 52). Copies made in marble and plaster of a bronze statue group known as the Tyrannicides, or Tyrant Slayers, also belong to this style (see Figure 50); the original bronze sculpture was dedicated in the Athenian Agora in 477–476, thus giving us some absolute chronological markers for the style. In looking back at the Berlin Painter's amphora (Figure 12), we can see that it has some restraint and simplification of drapery when compared with earlier Archaic works, such as Figure 14, as well as some understanding of rhythmos and pathos in the demeanor of the singer. Does the Severe Style, then, develop gradually from a series of smaller innovations or experiments, or does it have a defined starting point? Should we follow a model of progressive and incremental development for artistic style, or one that mixes graduated change with more episodic changes or, to borrow a term from evolutionary theory, punctuated equilibrium? In other words, do significant changes in style result from specific innovations and works, followed by a period of synthesis and refinement but less dramatic changes?

To see the contrast between these two models of stylistic development and their impact on the history of style, we can look at the figures from the east and west pediments of the Temple of Aphaia at Aigina, one of the traditional examples of art history surveys (Figures 18 and 19). Using the similar figures of two crouching archers placed at the side of the gable in a limited space, we can see that there are some significant stylistic differences. The archer from the west pediment (Figure 18) still bears the smile associated with the Archaic period, his eyes bulge, and although there is an indication of some of the muscle groups, their detail is obscured by the close-fitting costume that he is wearing. The anatomical details would have been even more obscured by the original paint, featuring a strongly colored diamond-check pattern that would have drawn the viewer's attention away from anatomical details.[4] In contrast, the east archer (Figure 19), who is identified as Herakles by the lionskin on his head, has less of an Archaic smile, his eyes are more set back in their sockets, the muscles and tendons are more articulated, and the drapery has more weight and movement that responds subtly to the body's motions. The use of paint was also more restrained in its use of color and pattern than it was in the west pediment, allowing more focus on the figure's movement. If one were to sequence these works, based on style, most scholars would place, and have placed, the west archer about a decade or so before the east archer.

Typically, pedimental sculptures would have been done at the same time as part of the building's construction program, so this stylistic difference is puzzling. Additional sculptures were found at Aigina that belonged to an ensemble set on the ground, and the theory has been that the original pediments were replaced successively by two new pediments, each done in the style current at the time of its manufacture. The west pediment has been usually dated to 500–490, and the east pediment to just before or after the Persian destruction of Athens in 480, at the cusp of the new Severe Style, although dates as early as 500 and late as 470 have been offered for the whole ensemble. The sculptures were dug up in the early nineteenth century, unfortunately not through a controlled excavation; therefore, the scenario has been based primarily on the analysis of the sculptures themselves.

In 2008, Andrew Stewart reconsidered the range of datable works associated with the development of the Severe Style in sculpture. His conclusion about the sculptures from Aigina, based on more recent excavations of the temple's foundation and of the pottery found in the construction fill, however, was that the temple likely was built after 480, not around 500 as hypothesized in the previous scenario. If this is the case, then a reasonable hypothesis is that the two pediment groups would have both been carved at the same time during the 470s, firmly within the Classical period. The work on the east pediment, which was carved by a different group of sculptors from those who worked on the west pediment, not unlike the situation in the Siphnian Treasury, was more influenced by the new Severe Style, whereas the sculptors of the west pediment were more conservative in their approach. Both groups would have been aware of the new style, as it was on display in Athens by 477–476 in the Tyrannicides of Kritios and Nesiotes (see stone copy in Figure 50). Because none of the Severe Style sculpture in his survey can be placed before 480 on the basis of archaeological context, Stewart proposes that the Severe Style might have been inaugurated by Kritios and Nesiotes with their publicly commissioned Tyrannicides, one of the early works of Athenian reconstruction following the destruction of the city by the Persians in 480.

The importance of this hypothesis, from a methodological point of view, is that Stewart proposes a different model for the development of a style, one that looks to specific artists and a specific circumstance and production for the genesis of a new style. This innovation created reactions among contemporary sculptors of varying degrees of resistance or acceptance, but the dominance of the style in the succeeding decades stemmed from this beginning point. The earlier model, working from the same observations of stylistic differences, explained them as the result of progressive developments toward naturalism, so each pediment was up to date at the time it was done, and not "retro," as would be the case if they had been done at the same time.

Rather than a steady linear model, we should probably consider the history of style as more likely to follow a mixed model. There will be episodes of strong change and particularly influential and significant works, but there will also be periods of more gradual alteration.

Stylistic Plurality

If we consider the Tyrannicides and both pediments at Aigina as being nearly contemporary, we must conclude that style is not necessarily uniform in a specific time and place, and may rather be plural at any one time, not only across widely separated regions such as Delphi, Athens, and Caere in the 520s, but even within the same city or building site or work of art. We can see this even at a miniature scale in a gem made of glass and showing Diomedes carrying the Palladion, or cult statue of Athena, from her temple in Troy (Figure 20). Looking at the crouching figure of Diomedes, there is an effective three-quarter view of the torso, with the midline of the chest and abdomen articulated and the muscles on either side foreshortened or lengthened to accommodate the perspective. The eye is in profile and matches the profile view of the face, and the figure appears to be hiding behind the statue and its shield, as if facing an unseen opponent.

The shield of the Palladion is set as a foreshortened oval, but the statue itself is completely frontal and symmetrical, with no indication of movement or weight-shift as in the caryatid figure of the mirror in Figure 2. Rather, this is a figure that resembles the kore figures of the Archaic period (see, for example, Figure 53). The style of the Palladion at first glance appears archaic, but the foreshortening of the shield shows the conventions of classical perspective, so we must label this figure as neo-archaic, or an archaic revival. The reason for choosing to represent one figure in an older style is likely because of its status as a cult statue. The oldest examples of cult statues were venerated because of their antique and "primitive" style, which gave them age and authenticity. When reproducing cult statues, an artist would make it in a less naturalistic and more archaic style while rendering the other, living figure in a more lifelike way.

The gem is dated to the last quarter of the fifth century BCE based on stylistic criteria. The Diomedes figure has many of the traits of the classical

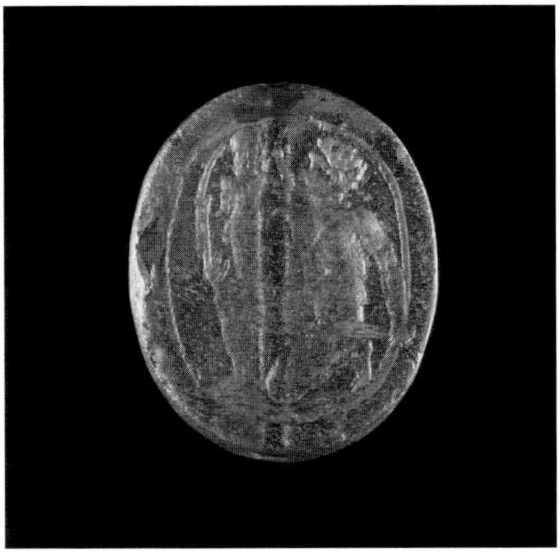

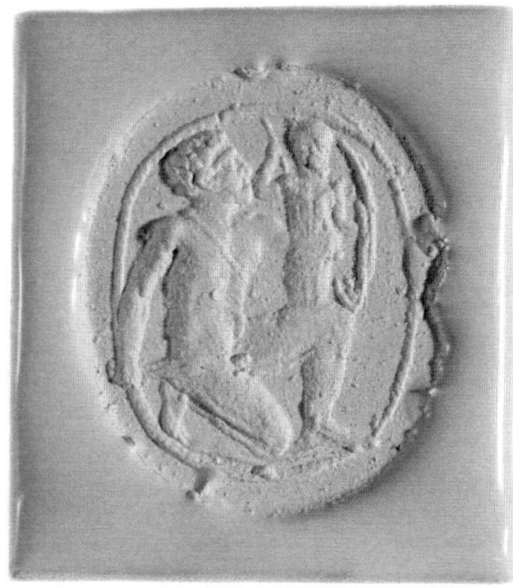

Figure 20. Glass gem and impression. Diomedes stealing the Palladion, c. 425–400 BCE. Malibu, Getty Villa, 81.AN.76.53. Photo: The J. Paul Getty Museum. Villa Collection. Malibu, California.

style: naturalism in the rendering of the anatomy, idealism in the proportions and actions of the figure, and a relative restraint in detail and composition (compare Figure 25). This classical ideal is not universal, as we can see on a nearly contemporary cup from Boeotia (Figure 21). This Cabiran kantharos,

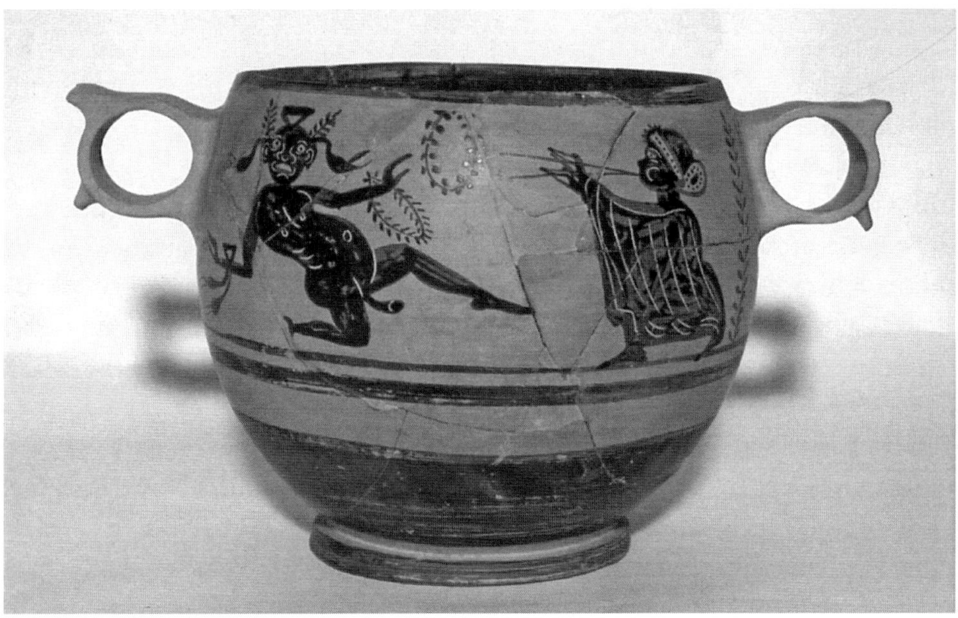

Figure 21. Cabiran kantharos attributed to the Mystai Painter, late fifth century BCE. Athens, National Archaeological Museum, 425. Photo: National Archaeological Museum, Athens. © Hellenic Ministry of Culture/Archaeological Receipts Fund.

named after the sanctuary in Cabiros with which the cups and other vases are associated, shows a woman playing the double flute on the right while a nude male bedecked with garlands and ribbons appears to be dancing. His figure is hardly the classical ideal, as it features a large potbelly and phallus. His head has exaggerated features, and whether this and the enlarged belly and phallus are part of a costume or are a caricature, his vigorous and unsustainable pose shows a boisterousness and lack of poise often associated with satyrs. The flutist is less caricatured, but even so she is much squatter and rounder in proportions and has more animation than a composed musician providing accompaniment would have.

The figures are made in black-figure, a technique that continued to be used at a small scale in the fifth century, even after the developments of red-figure painting in the late sixth century. Many black-figure vases can be associated with cults and rituals such as those at Cabiros, as well as in Athens on Panathenaic prize amphorae made every four years for the Panathenaic games. Although we are not sure about the nature of the Cabiran rituals and what role a cup like this would have played in them, the style is distinctly recognizable when encountered in a museum and forms a strong contrast to the more idealized and naturalistic red-figure vases that usually dominate displays of Classical art. They suggest that a specific style can have a particular expressive purpose.

The range of styles that develops within Greek art is even wider if we look at a later example of the theft of the Palladion, this time from the monumental marble sculptures found in the grotto at Sperlonga (Figure 22).[5] The two fragments belonged to a group of Diomedes and the Palladion with Odysseus. There has been a great deal of controversy over the interpretation of the action, but for the purpose of stylistic analysis, one can focus on the sharp contrast between the rendering of the head of Diomedes and the statue. The former is carved in what has been labeled as the Hellenistic baroque style, featuring deeply undercut forms, strong facial expressions, the use of dramatic poses, and tensed and bulging muscles. The contrast between the bulging tendons in the hand of Diomedes and the smooth surface of the Palladion are effective in portraying the drama of the statue's theft from Troy in the middle of the night. The face of Diomedes shows some strong emotion or pathos through the turn of head, the direction of the gaze, the movement of the locks of hair, the creases of the face, and the set of the mouth. The turn of his head seems to engage with something unseen off to his left, whether an unseen foe or perhaps the figure of Odysseus

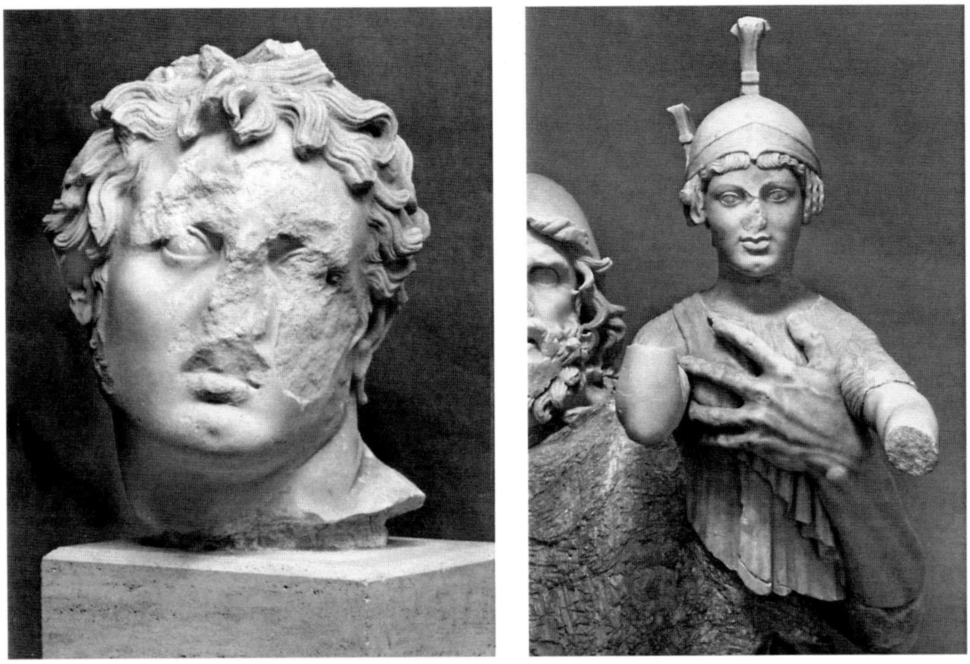

Figure 22. Palladion group from Sperlonga grotto sculptures, second-first century BCE. *Diomedes (left) and the Palladion (right). Sperlonga Museum. Photos: Deutsches Archäologisches Institut – Rom/ Fellbermeyer, Neg. D-DAI-Rom* 1965.0087 *and D-DAI-Rom* 1965.0104.

who, according to many accounts, drew his sword on Diomedes to take the Palladion for himself.

The sculpture conveys a sense of drama that was supported by the placement of the group in a cavelike grotto that had pools of water in the center; the sculpture was placed on a walkway to one side, and three additional monumental sculpture groups were set in other sections of the cave. One of these, showing the ship of Odysseus attacked by Scylla, is inscribed: "Athanodoros son of Hagesandros, Hagesandros son of Paionios, and Polydoros son of Polydoros, the Rhodians, made [it]." These same three sculptors are mentioned by Pliny as the creators of the Laocoön sculpture in the Vatican Museum today, and the stylistic similarities would corroborate that testimony.

The link of a signed, surviving work to artists known from literary sources is rare. The Sperlonga sculptures are also linked stylistically to the Hellenistic baroque style of the Pergamon altar, and this has created a number of different reconstructions of the origin of the Sperlonga sculptures and the artists. Because the actual Sperlonga sculptures were created specifically for their setting, they must have been made in the later part of the first century BCE, as the grotto is linked to the emperor Tiberius and to the family of Augustus. The Pergamon altar, however, is generally dated at least one hundred years earlier, to sometime in the second century BCE, and is associated by some with a stylistic school connnected with the island of Rhodes, home of the Sperlonga artists. This creates of a problem of chronology, in that the Hellenistic baroque style has often been seen as flourishing in the late third into the second century; its works were frequently copied afterward, when the school and style itself were no longer current. Thus the following questions arise:

- Are the Sperlonga sculptures first-century copies of second-century originals made by Athanodoros, Hagesandros, and Polydoros?
- Are they second-century originals made in Rhodes by these artists and then brought to Italy for the grotto?
- Are they first-century originals by these artists, made for the grotto?
- Are they free adaptations (rather than copies) by these artists of earlier Hellenistic works?
- Are the named artists merely the copyists of original works by unknown masters?
- Are these Roman or Greek works?

Although some Greek originals were copied in the Roman period, scholarship has recognized that Roman artists and patrons were not beholden to ideas of stylistic purity and were at times more attuned to content than to questions of style and attribution in purchasing works.[6] Further, the modern distinction between copy and original makes too sharp a dichotomy, as Greek artists had been exploring some of the same ideals and forms for centuries. After all, the male nude is hardly an original idea, and there are only so many novel ways of representing it. "Formulaic" might be a better way of thinking about the relationship of style and content and composition, with variables that allow some range of individualization, if desired, for a specific work. Indeed, ancient artists and patrons did not always prize originality in the way that modern artists and viewers do, and frequently comment on cost, scale, materials, and the quality of execution as important.[7]

Choosing which of the previous questions is the correct one to answer depends in large part on how one judges stylistic quality and history, as well as innovation versus familiarity within a work. It will probably be some time before a consensus is reached about the Sperlonga works, but the notion that these were first-century sculptors from Rhodes working in Italy for Roman clients, creating a commissioned set of sculptures that used familiar stories and identifiable figures based on well-known symbols and compositions, thus making the works both Greek and Roman, is plausible and can find support from nonstylistic analysis.

B. Ridgway, in reference to these issues, put the variability of style in the Hellenistic period very succinctly:

> I believe that any form of chronology based on style is dangerous, since aesthetic expression seems to have been conditioned by content. And I am convinced that the last decades of what we call the Late Hellenistic period . . . saw masters from all parts of the Greek-speaking world . . . producing works in a variety of styles to serve the purposes of new clients.[8]

Indeed, this is a reminder that formal analysis, which seeks to explain the visual and aesthetic effect of a work of art, can sometimes arrive at a different understanding from stylistic analysis, even though both are built on detailed observation of the form elements and relationships.

Medium and Quality

Methodologically, description can be applied meticulously to any type of object. The terracotta statue of a woman in Figure 23 was one of thirteen found in a tomb excavated at Myrina in 1883. The figure's features are naturalistic, but the proportions appear elongated because of the scale of the head relative to the overall height. The figure stands in a contrapposto pose and wears two garments, a chiton that falls to the ground and covers all but the front of one foot, and a mantle that wraps over her arms and shoulders and pulls up over her head. The arms are set out slightly from the body, creating a more active stance, and the body twists about 90 degrees from the foot to the turn of the head. The twisting of the body creates pulls in the fabric covering it; these ridges and furrows not only help to convey the form of the body underneath the drapery, but also are important in suggesting the vigor of the stance, particularly in the strong diagonals that radiate from the figure's right elbow. The resulting tension of the outer garment is used to show the texture of the undergarment, particularly in the way it pulls across the deeper vertical channels of the chiton and creates the illusion of bridges that cross over the valleys, a drapery-through-drapery effect.[9]

This textured effect and the three-dimensionally twisting stance appear in other media of sculpture, such as marble and bronze. If we compare the Myrina figure to the roughly similar marble statue of a woman named Kleopatra, found in the courtyard of her house in Delos (Figure 24), we

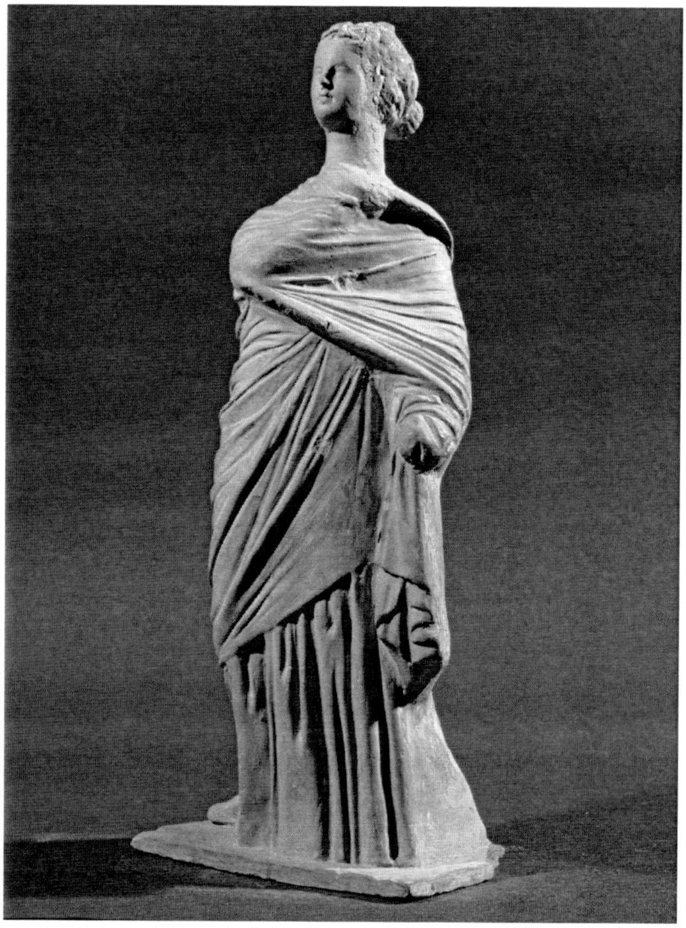

Figure 23. Terracotta figure from Tomb A at Myrina, third century BCE. *Paris, Musée du Louvre, Myr234. Photo: Eric Lessing/Art Resource, New York.*

can see the same stylistic ideas. The change of material and scale allows deeper channels to be carved in the undergarment and more complicated subdivisions of the folds and creases of the fabric than we see in the smaller terracotta work. The effects are both more detailed and subtle and more dramatic, with a stronger contrast between the lighted surfaces and the dark shadows of the recessed areas.

In describing the differences in visual effect, however, there is also an issue about the status and quality of the work. Large works in marble or bronze are routinely called "statues" and belong in the category of sculpture, whereas small works in terracotta are "figurines" or "statuettes" and are not usually included in the history of "sculpture." Rather, they belong to the "minor arts" or the "decorative arts," along with pottery, textiles, metalwork, jewelry, and

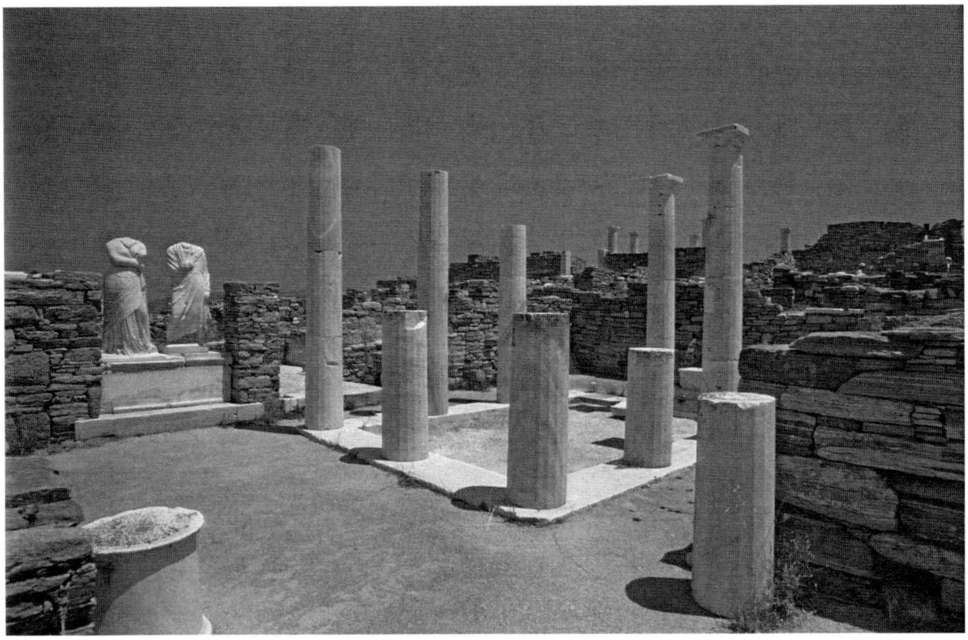

Figure 24. Statues of Kleopatra and Dioskourides from the House of Kleopatra, Delos, c. 138/137 BCE. In situ. Photo: Vanni/Art Resource, New York.

the like. In creating a history of art on the basis of formal analysis, there has been a tendency to restrict art to the "fine arts" – that is, painting, sculpture, and architecture. In part, this is a result of the fact that terracotta statues were produced in great quantities and were made with molds, making them less "original" and unique as works, whereas marble statues are more individual and were not mass-produced. The supposition is that the minor arts imitate developments in the fine arts, so we would look for the origin of a stylistic trait such as the textured drapery in a medium such as bronze or marble, and follow its migration into terracottas. Curiously, however, the dating of the effect of textured drapery depends on excavated deposits in the Athenian Agora of terracotta figures that can be dated to the late third century BCE, whereas the Delos statue is from the second century.

This is not to say that monumental sculpture does not influence terracotta figures, or that an over-life-size figure does not have the potential for making a more dramatic aesthetic effect on the viewer – but that is frequently the presumption. It is impossible to describe in minute detail every work of art, so some selectivity will always be at work. Further, it is important to keep in mind that description entails a choice of words that may be somewhat subjective on the part of the writer, for describing visual effects through language is not natural or apparent. Being aware of the problem can help us to understand where subjectivity becomes difficult and to approach the issue of stylistic analysis aware of its strengths and limitations.

The Artist and Biography

We can end this chapter by thinking about the artist. As we have seen, one goal of stylistic analysis is to attribute works, whether to anonymous artists with pseudonyms given by scholars, such as the Berlin Painter, or to artists whose names appear on the works themselves, such as Douris. The inscriptions on vases show that a division by type of labor was sometimes practiced in this medium. Some vases, such as a cup in London, are inscribed by two figures. One inscription is *Python epoiesen*, or "Python made [this]." The other is *Epiktetos egraphse[n]*, or "Epiktetos drew/painted [this]." The majority of scholars interpret these inscriptions to mean that Python was the potter, whereas Epiktetos painted the cup and its figures, thus dividing the labor. From inscriptions on other vases, we know that Python worked with other painters, such as Douris (see Figure 3), and that Epiktetos worked with other potters, such as Hischylos, so there was some fluidity in these arrangements. Other vases bear only the inscription of either the potter or painter, leaving open the question as to whether the same person did both parts of the work, whereas some vessels have inscriptions of an artist as both potter and painter, such as Exekias, and some artists sign as both potters and painters on different vessels.[10]

Although we have hundreds of such signatures or names on vases, we have virtually no information about these individuals and their lives. We can use stylistic analysis to attribute other uninscribed vases to them; by comparing styles of different artists, we can see that some are closely related to each other but differ in their date, so they may be different members of a workshop, perhaps teachers and pupils. Thus, we speculate that the Berlin Painter is related to the Pan Painter and the Achilles Painter, who worked into the next two generations of the Classical period. Tracing these relationships moves us into the realm of understanding the relationship between art and the individuals who produce it.

The goal of an artistic biography is to combine stylistic and formal evidence about an artist's work with literary evidence about the career to understand the relationship between an artist's career and works. This would include determining the sources or influences on the artist's work, including teachers or schools, as well as the legacy and importance of the artist's production and any artistic descendants and pupils. Further, one would like to understand the artistic principles or theoretical foundation for the works to see how the idea is realized in the forms that we see in the artwork. One would also want to explore the connection between changes in the artist's work and the artist's biographical events.

Information about the artist's life comes from literary evidence – occasionally inscriptions, but more frequently literary sources such as Pliny's *Natural History* or Pausanias's *Guide to Greece*. This evidence is variable in its source material, consistency, and reliability, but does provide some information on a number of elite artists, especially painters and sculptors of the Classical period. Unfortunately, none of the mentioned works of the named painters survives. Of the sculptors, we have perhaps a few originals from the hand of the artist, but we do have works that, sources say, were supervised by well-known sculptors. There are also copies of some works that provide a secondhand glimpse of some of the work. By studying and comparing copies of a specific work, we can look for some stylistic similarities and try to connect them to what we know of the artist's career.

Stylistically, the Doryphoros (Figure 25) could be regarded as representative of the High Classical style, along with the architecture and sculpture of the Parthenon (see Figure 29). The figure is a highly naturalistic rendering of the male figure, with well-defined musculature and limbs that convincingly represent the movement and forms of the body. The figure has a smooth face with a neutrally set mouth, displaying little in the way of emotion. The figure is proportioned like that of a well-conditioned athlete, but is relatively contained in its form, so we get the sense of readiness to act rather than strong action. This is heightened by the weight-shift or contrapposto, with one foot lifted up on its toes, as if being picked up to start moving or being planted as if stopping.

This last point about the motion of the figure makes sense based on direct observation, but its significance is also magnified by the details about the career of Polykleitos. According to Galen, Polykleitos wrote a treatise called the *Canon* that articulated the principles of his art. In particular, we learn from Galen and other sources that the proportions of the figure were commensurate with each other and with an ideal perfection defined by the ratios of one part of the body to another, such as the length of the finger compared with the palm and wrist. This has been understood to indicate that Polykleitos developed a system of numbers that prescribed the ideal proportions of the human figure, derived from the observation of nearly ideal examples of the human figure. One of two quotes preserved from the

Canon states that "perfection . . . arises *para mikron* [little by little] through many numbers"; a table describing ratios and proportions is thought to have accompanied the treatise.

Polykleitos emerges, then, not just as an artist making works, but also as a theorist who defined the principles of art that guided its conception and actual design. As Jeremy Tanner has proposed, this was a new position for the artist in the fifth century BCE, moving beyond the practical details of design and production to a more intellectual expression of the rationale behind an idealized and naturalistic sculpture.[11]

The sources state that Polykleitos executed a sculpture, also titled the *Canon*, which was a demonstration of his principles. A Roman rhetorician, Quintilian, states that the Doryphoros was the appropriate model for outstanding painters and sculptors, a position that Cicero states was the case for the fourth-century sculptor Lysippos, who used the Doryphoros as his model. On this basis, most scholars would link the Doryphoros with the written and sculpted *Canon* as a demonstration of Polykleitan principles of sculpture.

The intellectual basis of Polykleitos's work and its reliance on numbers and proportions as the expression of artistic ideals has led to discussions of Polykleitos's connection to Pythagorean philosophy, which flourished in the same period. The emphasis in Pythagoras on number as well as the mean, or balance, fit nicely with what we know of the Polykleitan *Canon*. This has led to the idea that the balancing between the Pythagorean opposites that were the underlying order of the universe, such as light–dark, motion–rest, and so on can also be found in the Doryphoros. The figure is neither youthful nor old, but at a median point of perfection; he is not too muscled or too thin, his figure is balanced in the arrangement across left–right and up–down, and finally he seems to be caught between a state of rest and of motion, balanced on one leg but lifting the other foot.

If one could show that Polykleitos was a follower of Pythagoras, and if some part of his treatise talked about motion and rest and the arrangement of the limbs, one would be able to link idea and form and comprehend the way in which the thought of an artist is manifested in the work. The literary testimony, from sources who lived four to six centuries after Polykleitos, articulate the influence and status that both his work and theory had in the ancient world, giving him historical importance.

In the absence of abundant and detailed literary evidence and original works, we must remember the tentative quality of such a conclusion of artistic biography. Comparing original works directly and indentifying patterns in

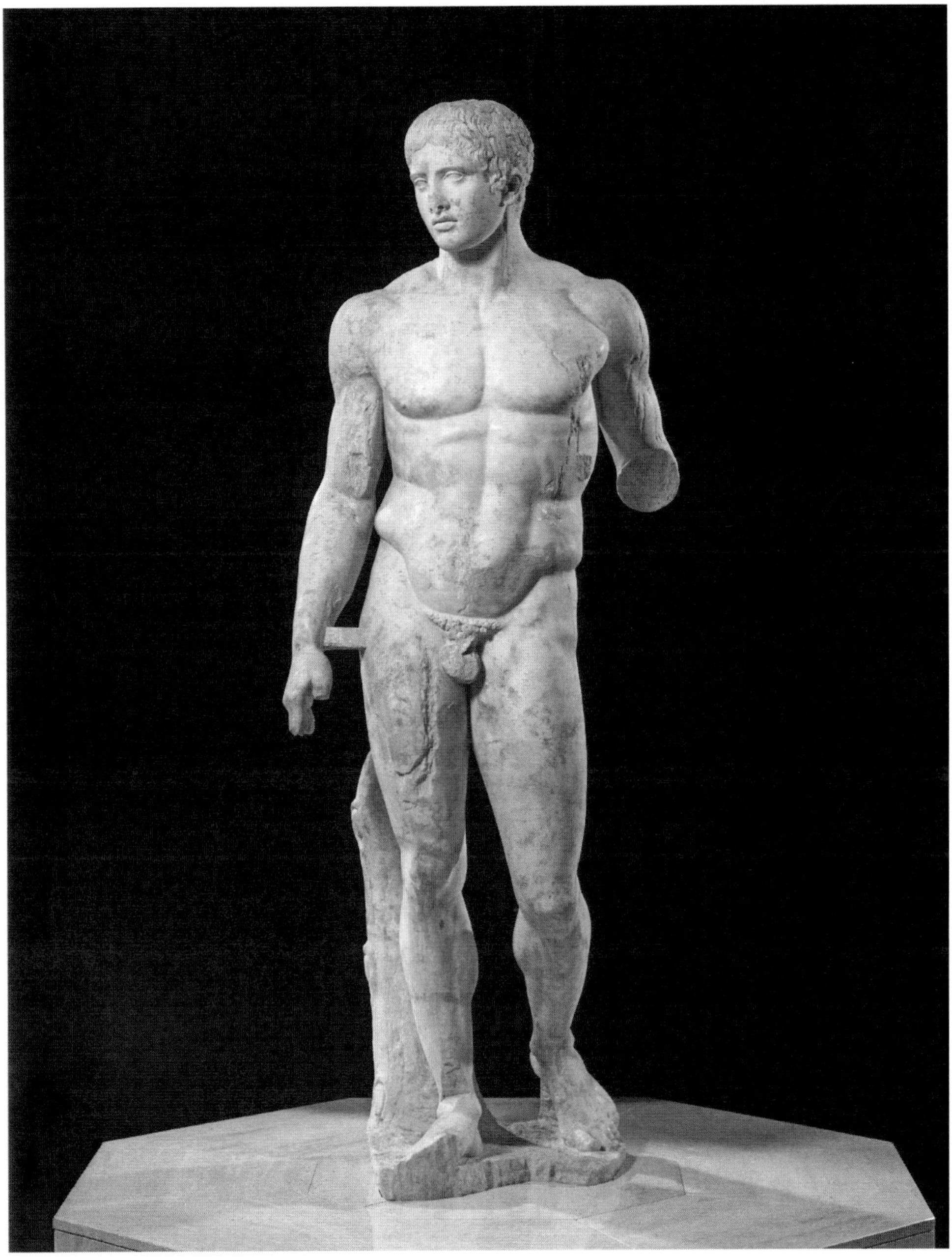

Figure 25. The Doryphoros of Polykleitos. Hellenistic copy of bronze original. Minneapolis Institute of Arts, The John R. Van Derlip Fund and gift of funds from Bruce B. Dayton, an anonymous donor, Mr. and Mrs. Kenneth Dayton, Mr. and Mrs. W. John Driscoll, Mr. and Mrs. Alfred Harrison, Mr. and Mrs. John Andrus, Mr. and Mrs. Judson Dayton, Mr. and Mrs. Stephen Keating, Mr. and Mrs. Pierce McNally, Mr. and Mrs. Donald Dayton, Mr. and Mrs. Wayne MacFarlane, and many other generous friends of the Institute, 86.1. Photo: Museum.

the relationships among works or between artists can compensate to some degree for the lack of external evidence. In either case, whether we have external or internal evidence, a biographical approach offers an opportunity to consider the link between an artist and a body of works.

Conclusion

The beginning of this chapter discussed the process of visual description and analysis, and the end has stressed some of the conclusions that have been drawn based on formal and stylistic analysis. Even though there has been some criticism recently of Beazley and attribution generally, one still needs to begin asking questions and thinking about Greek art by looking intensely at the works, whether monumental or modest. To make sense of the hundreds of thousands of works that survive, one must also make the effort to sort and classify them to see the historical patterns and circumstances that are behind their production and use. Such historical synthesis is always a work in progress, and new examples, information, or approaches may require adjustments in our hypotheses, as we have seen – but this too is part of the process of inquiry.

In looking at a work in a museum, then, one might begin by noting what is its most noticeable visual feature. Is it the shape, the color, the size, or some internal detail of the work? What visually draws the eye to that feature? What are some other distinctive details of the work? Does it seem balanced? Is it self-contained, or does it project itself visually into the space around it? Does it get lost in its surroundings, or does it draw attention away from other things in the room? What about it is different from works around it? What is similar? Is there a figural subject, and does it dominate the visual impression? Is this work pleasing, or not so pleasing?

These questions are rather general, but answering them requires thinking about what one sees, beginning with the form elements and building from there. This also serves as a foundation for looking at the work of art from other vantage points, such as content, meaning, and context, which will be addressed in the next chapters.

Further Reading

General, Stylistic and Formal Analysis

On the theory of formal and stylistic analysis, see Schapiro 1953 and Gombrich 1968. Many textbooks have lists and definitions of forms; a good overview is in D'Alleva 2006. A fundamental and minute demonstration of the process is in Beazley 1922.

For some recent discussions of stylistic analysis and description, see Neer 2002 on vase painting and Donohue 2005 on sculpture. On the history of vase painting scholarship, see Sparkes 1996.

On color in Greek sculpture, see Brinkmann and Wünsche 2007, Brinkmann 2008, and Panzanelli 2008.

On aesthetics and ancient terminology, see Pollitt 1974, and the translation of literary sources in Pollitt 1990.

On challenges to Beazley and attribution, see Vickers 1985a, 126–8.

Resources on Media

On style and its history in Greek sculpture, see the series of books on Greek sculpture by Ridgway (1970, 1977, 1981, 1990, 1997, 2000, 2002) and the handbooks by Boardman (1985, 1991a, 1995) and Smith 1991. On sculptural media, see Spivey 1996, Mattusch 1996, Grossman 2003, Palagia 2006. For terracottas, see Higgins 1967. For jewelry, see Williams and Ogden 1994.

On painting generally see Pollitt, forthcoming.

On vase painting generally, see Rasmussen and Spivey 1991, Clark, Elston and Hart 2002, and Moignard 2006. For histories of vase painting generally, see Cook 1997, Boardman 2001. On Attic vase painting, see the lists of Beazley (1956, 1963, 1971, 1989), the handbooks by J. Boardman (1974, 1975, 1989), as well as Beazley 1986, Robertson 1992 and Lissarrague 2001. On non-Attic painting, see the handbooks by Boardman 1998 and Trendall 1989 and their bibliographies. For Corinthian pottery, see Amyx 1988. For Caeretan pottery, see Hemelrijk 1984. For Cabiran pottery, see Mitchell 2009, 248–79, although this is mostly on content. On the medium, see Noble 1988, Schreiber 1999, Cohen 2006. For approaches to vase painting, see Rasmussen and Spivey 1991 and Yatromanolakis 2010. The range of approaches can also be seen in the compilation of papers from two conferences: Oakley, Coulson, and Palagia 1997; Oakley and Palagia 2009.

On architecture and its history generally, see Lawrence 1996 and Barletta 2001. On materials and techniques, see Coulton 1977 and Korres 1995 and 2000.

Chronology

On chronology generally, see Biers 1992. On the dating controversy of the Siphnian Treasury and other monuments, see Francis and Vickers 1983,

Vickers 1985b, among other articles. Countering their arguments, see Cook 1989 and Neer 2002, 186–205.

History and Definition of Style

On the history of style, see Boardman, Ridgway, and Robertson, above. On rhythmos, pathos, and ethos, see Pollitt 1985. On the beginnings of the classical style, see Stewart 2008a and 2008b. For a discussion of naturalism, realism, idealism, and mimesis see Stieber 2004, esp. 4-8.

Stylistic Plurality, Copies

On Hellenistic sculpture, see De Grummond and Ridgway 2000, and also the extensive discussion of archaizing and classicizing works in Ridgway's books. On the relationship of Greek art, Roman art, and Roman patrons, see Marvin 1989 and 2008 and Kousser 2008.

Artistic Biography

On artistic biography generally, see Tanner 2006. For literary sources, see Pollitt 1990. For examples of artistic biography, see Stewart 1977 and Palagia and Pollitt 1996. On the sources for Polykleitos, see Pollitt 1990, 75–79 and 222–3; see Borbein 1996 and Moon 1995 for historiography and recent assessment. For examples of retrospective exhibits of artists, see Bothmer 1985; Euphronios 1991; Moreno 1995; Pasquier and Martinez 2007.

THREE

MEANING

In this age of print and digital reproduction, we often take an abundance of images for granted and do not always think of art as a common format for conveying meaning or messages. Still, images were a part of the visual landscape of the Greeks; objects that now sit in museums were once a part of the fabric of visual communication. Images filled the pottery and furnishings of Greek homes, the textiles and jewelry that individuals wore, the grave markers and goods of the cemeteries, the interiors and exteriors of their public buildings and monuments, and the votive offerings dedicated in sanctuaries. Most of the time these images were likely to have been seen, but not actively contemplated and interpreted unless some action, such as preparing for a festival, wedding, or funeral, brought the object and its imagery to the foreground. Thinking about what these images meant to their viewers, and what they mean to us today, is not straightforward. It is similar to learning a foreign language, with some strange words as well as familiar-sounding words, some of which may be false cognates and end up meaning quite different things than we expect.

When we see a picture of an athlete on the Olympic podium today, we mentally conjure the spectacle of the Olympics and the athletic competitions, and may well have watched the original events "live" in a processed and recorded form. We can think about the particular achievements of the athletic feat, and can think about the personal, national, and international levels of meaning in the ceremony. Excerpts from such ceremonies seen in another context, such as a gold medal or an athletic apparel logo, carry their own meaning that we can easily decode as members of the culture that produced the object and its associated events. This example of visual language is one that we do not always think about in detail. So, too, the words we speak are not always well considered or thoughtful, yet they have meaning, and we can stop and think about what they mean at a deeper level if we need to do so. Trying to understand what ancient images "mean," however, is complicated by the fact that we do not have that cultural infrastructure or visual language firsthand, and must recover it through systematic study.

The traditional method for exploring the meaning of images is iconography, which developed alongside stylistic analysis as an early art historical approach. More recently, there has been interest in using methods developed from other disciplines, such as semiotics, structural analysis, hermeneutics, and poststructuralism. There can often be overlap in the processes, particularly at the descriptive level, as well as in the conclusions of these different methods, but it is important to keep in mind some of the underlying assumptions that each approach takes and the types of evidence it uses.

Iconography and Narrative

Erwin Panofsky set out the fundamentals of iconography in an essay titled "Iconography and Iconology: An Introduction to the Study of Renaissance Art," and this still serves as a basic guide to the process (see the summary in Table 1). The word itself derives from the Greek word for image or portrait, *eikon*, so iconography is the study of images.[1]

Table 1. Iconographic analysis (from Panofsky 1955)

Stage	Object of Interpretation	Act of Interpretation	Equipment for Interpretation	Corrective Principle
1	Primary or natural subject matter	Preiconographical description	Practical experience	History of style
2	Secondary or conventional subject matter	Iconographical analysis	Knowledge of literary sources	History of types
3	Intrinsic meaning or content	Iconological interpretation	Synthetic intuition	History of cultural symptoms or "symbols"

The first stage of iconography, *preiconographical description*, is related to stylistic analysis in that it calls for a detailed description of the significant forms or motifs found in the image. Because mimetic art generally looks like what it represents, this is fairly straightforward, but a knowledge of the style of the period helps to correct oddities based on the conventions of drawing or carving of the time.

One can apply preiconographical description to the mirror introduced in Chapter One (Figure 2). The handle is in the shape of a standing, clothed woman who pulls at her garment with her left hand while holding out her right hand, on which is a bird, perhaps a dove. To either side of her head are nude, winged male youths who hold out their nearer hands toward the head of the woman. At the top of the mirror disk is a bird with a female head and lion claws, and on either side we have a dog chasing a hare toward the top of the mirror. One can go into more detail, and many iconographical studies concentrate on just a few details at this stage, but this is sufficient to identify the major motifs of the work.

In the second stage of *iconographical analysis*, one attempts to identify the figures or stories and the basic meaning of the symbols. For example, the woman-headed bird (natural subject matter) can be identified more specifically as a siren (conventional subject matter or identity), one of the creatures described in the *Odyssey* whose song lured sailors to their shore, only to have them crash and die. Although the *Odyssey* says little about their appearance, we find representations of the story showing such hybridized figures as on this mirror. Thus, based on a use of literary sources and artistic conventions, we can deduce the identity of the figure; it would probably have been common knowledge for the ancient owner or maker of the mirror.

Drawing on literary and artistic sources as well, we can identify the nude, winged youths as *erotes* (plural of Eros), minor gods of love who frequently crown brides or accompany Aphrodite. The identity of the woman is more difficult to determine. We can call her a caryatid, or structural support in the form of a female figure. She could be the goddess Aphrodite, but she might also be a mortal woman who makes an offering of the dove, depending on whether one decides that the dove is an attribute identifying a specific figure, or is an offering identified with that same goddess. The dog and hare are associated with the hunt, with the hunter left out.

Finally, one tries to synthesize the intrinsic meaning of a work in the third stage of *iconological interpretation*. Here one thinks about the overall work and draws together the elements into a program. The woman in the handle is dressed in formal attire, wearing elaborate garments and jewelry, such as the diadem on her head, that might be worn on important public occasions such as a religious festival or wedding. The pulling of the garment is a gesture frequently seen with *kore* statues, large stone sculptures of maidens found in sanctuaries (see Figure 53). This gesture could be seen as indicating solemn processional movement and making an offering to the gods. The figure then, whether Aphrodite or mortal, is intended as an ideal of a beautiful, pious woman carrying out her civic religious role – an occasion, especially before she is married, that attracts the attention of the city to her and her family. If one thinks that the mirror is an object associated strongly with women in its function, then the figure serves as a model of appearance.

The siren, whose song is beautiful, could evoke the song that such mortal maidens sang in their procession. The seventh-century BCE Spartan poet Alkman wrote a poem for *parthenoi*, or young maidens such as our caryatid figure, who sing about their performance and that of their leader, Hagesichora:

> She [Hagesichora] has sung her song today not more sweetly than the sirens (they are gods). But how we sang, we ten girls instead of the Eleven!
>
> One is trilling like a swan by Xanthos river, one with splendid tawny hair.[2]

The chorus of parthenoi modestly disclaims its own performance compared with that of its leader, who sings like the sirens. In the rest of the poem we hear about the beautiful appearance of the women, with their "luxury of purple dye . . . the carven bracelet-snake, the wimple sheer in gold." The siren and maiden on the mirror reflect the ideal performance and beauty of the chorus leader, as well as the parthenoi themselves. However, the siren also lures men with the beauty of her songs, and one can think of the woman using this mirror as also attracting the attention of men through her performance as well as her beauty. The hunt motif of dog and hare can also symbolize this hope for luring the missing hunter into pursuing her. Her triumph is to become a bride, and the association of the erotes with both Aphrodite and bridal imagery makes their adornment of her head a wish for success in realizing the transition from maiden to wife and mother.

This combination of motifs – the idealized woman holding an offering, siren, hunt, and erotes – is found on a number of mirrors. Several of the motifs appear in other contexts, such as wedding scenes, which would confirm our intuition about the iconological meaning of the program here, but we will have more to consider about this in Chapter Five.

A much more complicated program can be found on a Hellenistic relief signed by the sculptor Archelaos of Priene and probably coming from

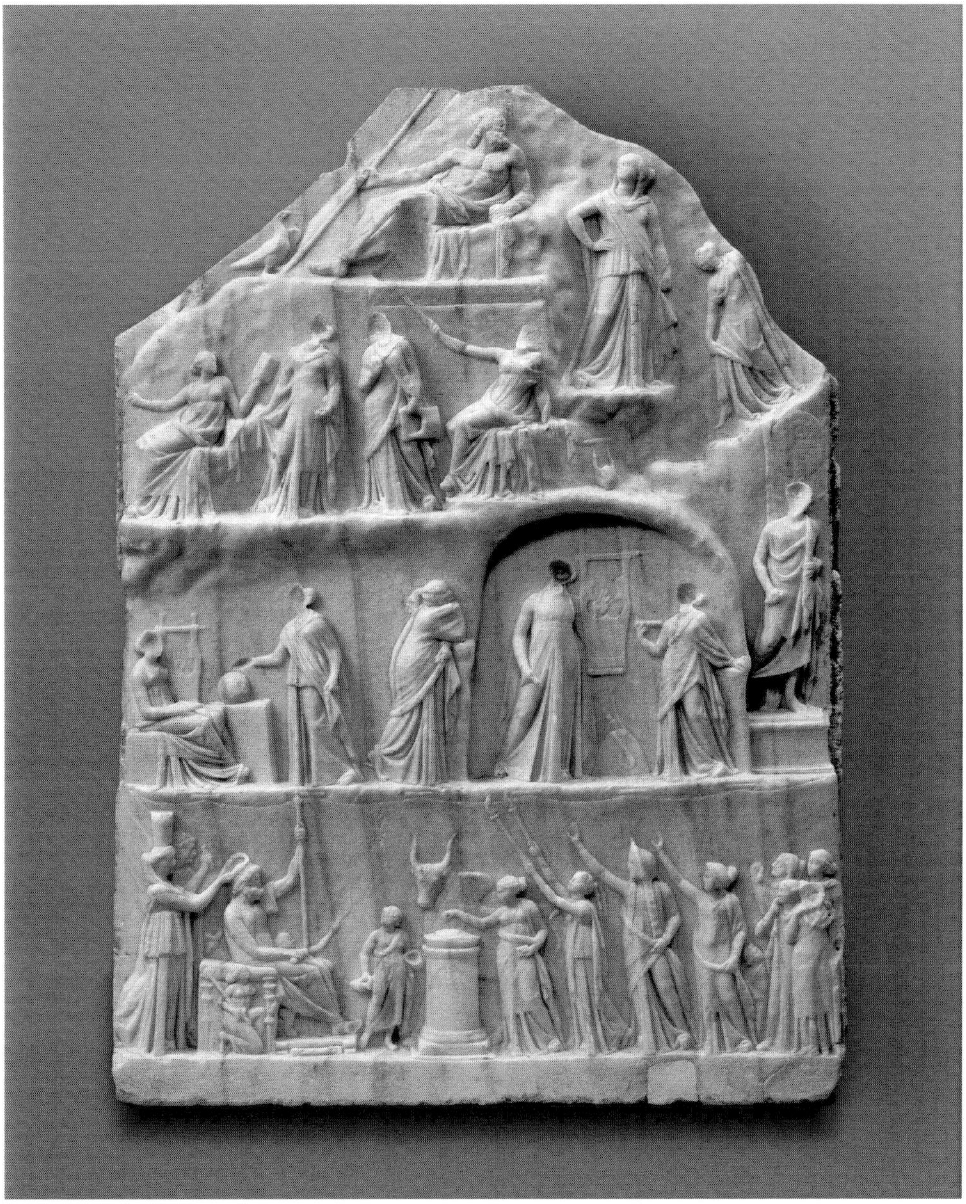

Figure 26. Relief signed by Archelaos of Priene, second or first century BCE. *Apotheosis of Homer. London, British Museum 1819.0812. Photo: © Trustees of the British Museum.*

Alexandria, although it was found in Italy (Figure 26). The stylistic dates assigned to the work range from the late third century to the first century BCE, but its iconographic program is less problematic. The relief, 1.18 m high, is divided into three registers by ground lines. At the top center is Zeus, identified by his scepter, and to our right is a female figure who is Mnemosyne, the personification of Memory. Below them and at a smaller scale are five female figures, who with the four female figures in the next register are the nine Muses, the children of Zeus and Mnemosyne. On the right side of the middle register is Apollo, patron god of poets, who plays a large stringed instrument called the kithara while wearing the long garment associated with its performers. In front of him is a stone, the omphalos, sacred to his sanctuary at Delphi. At the far right is a poet singing while standing on a pedestal, in front of a tripod that is sacred to Apollo and also represents the prize for a victory. Efforts to identify the poet on the pedestal are not supported by any internal or external evidence, and must remain unknown.

The identification of the figures in the upper register is based on numbers (nine for muses) and attributes (mask and other objects of some of the muses, kithara of Apollo, scepter and pose of Zeus). Inscriptions are essential for the bottom register, in that most of these figures are personifications of ideas. For example, at the left sits Homer with a scroll and scepter; he is now a god like Zeus but oversees the earthly realm. To either side of his throne are small children, personifications of the *Iliad* and the *Odyssey*, his progeny. Behind him are Chronos (Time) and Oikoumene (the Inhabited World) who crown him; clearly his fame is widespread throughout history and the world. These figures, however, seem to be more personalized than idealized and resemble some of the Ptolemaic kings and queens, based on comparisons with their portraits on coins and in other media. A sacrifice is being made before Homer; to the left of the altar is Myth and on the other side, from left to right, are History, Poetry, Tragedy, and Comedy. Behind them is the figure of Human Nature, who stands before a close group of four figures. These four are moral virtues: *Arete* (Excellence), *Mneme* (Mindfulness), *Pistis* (Trustworthiness), and *Sophia* (Wisdom).

The previous paragraphs combine both preiconographic description and iconographical analysis, which is typical in practice and is greatly aided by inscriptions and attributes that make identification of the figures more direct. The iconological interpretation of the piece has been concisely stated by J. J. Pollitt:

> Inspiration springs from Zeus . . . and Memory and is passed from heaven to earth by the Muses. Its foremost recipient was Homer, who is both a patron god and symbolic ancestor of the victorious poet for whom the relief was made. Homer's epics will last for all time and are universal, hence he is crowned by *Chronos* and *Oikoumene*; they celebrate both myth and history; they are the fountainhead of the literary genres that came after epic . . . and have bestowed, like all worthy poetry, essential moral virtues upon human nature.[3]

The relief seems particularly appropriate for Alexandria, home of the famous library, and would have been appropriate as a victory monument for a poetic contest. Even though we do not know the identity of the poet, the work shows how intricate and detailed an iconographic program can get. Were it not for the inscriptions, determining who the figures in the bottom register represent would be difficult indeed.

Narrative pictures present some other issues of interpretation. Most pictures that show stories are single panels, so they cannot show a sequence of actions in the same way that literature or modern media, such as film or comic books, can. We can see the challenges of interpreting narrative pictures by returning to the east frieze and pediment of the Siphnian Treasury (Figure 1).

The main group of the pediment shows four figures. Starting with pre-iconographic description, in the center is a tall figure that has lost its head and wears a long, clinging garment. In front and on either side are two male figures; the figure on our right has hoisted the cauldron end of a tripod on his shoulder and is carrying it away from the male on the left, who holds the feet to prevent its removal. A female figure behind him holds his arm in support.

Moving to iconographic analysis, we can turn to literary sources to explain the scene. In one of the many stories about Herakles, he had killed Iphitos, the son of Eurtyos, whose daughter Herakles had sought in marriage. Facing punishment for this crime, he sought to be purified and went to Delphi to seek advice. The Pythia, priestess of Apollo who pronounced the god's oracles, refused to respond to him, at which point Herakles started to loot the temple of its treasure and seized the tripod of Apollo, from which the Pythia issued her prophecies. Apollo came to retrieve the tripod from Herakles, at which point Zeus intervened to stop the fighting. This story is preserved in several literary sources, such as the works of Apollodoros (c. 180–120 BCE), Diodorus Siculus (active mid-first century BCE), and Pausanias (flourished mid-second century CE), with variations in many of the details. All these sources are later than the treasury pediment, but there are fifth-century references in Pindar to a fight between Herakles and Apollo, and a series of representations of a struggle over a tripod beginning in the late eighth century. Given the unique elements of the action, it is likely that this is the subject of the central section of the pediment, with Zeus in the middle, Apollo on the left, and Herakles on the right. The woman to the left would likely be Apollo's sister Artemis; she is not mentioned in the sources that we have, but she is found on other representations of the story and frequently balances Athena, who supports Herakles on the other side of the composition.

In making an iconological interpretation of the pediment, we should recall that the treasury lined the Sacred Way to the sanctuary of Apollo at Delphi, which is also the locale for the story. Zeus's intervention recognizes the importance of the Pythia, and also confirms that humans – even heroes such as Herakles – are subject to the will of the gods. Herakles is guilty not only of murder, but also of hubris by appropriating what belongs to the gods. Facing visitors to Delphi on their way to the temple, the scene reminds them of the role of the gods. This connection to Delphi may also help to explain the subject matter of the scenes in the sides of the pediment, which include a variety of male and female figures, horses, and a chariot. These appear to be unrelated to the center action, and suggestions for their identification include the First Sacred War at Delphi in the early sixth century, but iconographic uncertainty remains. We will return to the potential political context for analyzing the meaning of the sculptures in a different direction in the next chapter.

Turning to the frieze, the gods and goddesses are divided into two facing groups and are apparently debating with each other over the fate of their respective protégés, the Greeks and the Trojans. On the right half of the frieze, two pairs of fighters struggle over the body of a fallen warrior while charioteers and teams look on. A key iconographic detail in terms of the action is the scale held by the god in the center; this figure also sits on a more elaborate throne than the others and would surely be Zeus. We find a link between Zeus and the scales in *Iliad* 22, when Hektor and Achilles face each other and the portions of death placed by Zeus in the scale tilt toward Hektor, signaling his impending defeat; this weighing of the souls is called the *psychostasia*. The scene on the right does not match the one-on-one combat described in the *Iliad*, but it does resemble the paired fight of Hektor and Aeneas against Menelaos and Patroklos over the death of the fallen Trojan ally, Sarpedon. In *Iliad* 16 Zeus is dismayed by the fate of his son, but Hera argues that he should not intervene unless he wants to allow other gods to rescue sons fated for death. Thus, some early interpreters of the frieze proposed that the east frieze shows the struggle over the body of Sarpedon on the Trojan plain, and the counsel of the gods on Olympos on the other side.[4] The theme of the power of the gods over the affairs of men thus finds expression iconologically on both pediment and frieze.

Reexamination of the frieze in the 1980s, using infrared light, revealed traces of painted inscriptions, showing that the warriors were Aeneas and

Memnon on the left and Achilles and an unnamed warrior on the right, and that the body was that of Antilochos, not Sarpedon.[5] This is a story found in another lost epic, the *Ethiopis*, which picks up where the *Iliad* leaves off and describes the fight of the Greeks against the Amazons and the forces of Memnon at Troy, and the eventual death of Achilles. This epic survives only in a summary form, but whether it also included a psychostasia such as the *Iliad* is uncertain. This reidentification of the frieze, though, points out some of the limitations of iconography as an approach, in that it assumes that there is a single, correct identification to an iconographic problem, and draws heavily on literary sources to do so. Given the fragmentary nature of both surviving Greek art and literature, however, one will often find in scholarship cases of competing iconographic analyses and, in the case of very rare artistic subjects or very scarce literary sources, puzzles that can defy certainty in interpretation.

The comparison of literary sources and visual representations in the case of narrative pictures leads to the question of whether a single picture can present a narrative. This issue is debated, but there is ample testimony that a Greek viewer would "read" a more complicated set of actions from some pictures, even if they were a snapshot of a single time and place. Such momentary pictures have been labeled as *monoscenic* narrative, but the action can evoke moments before or afterward in the mind of the viewer. Greek artists would also frequently include more in a picture than could have existed at a single moment of action, allowing for a more complex interpretation of the picture. We can see an example of this strategy, called *synoptic* or *simultaneous* narrative for the quality of including elements from multiple moments of time or place into one picture, in a picture of the fall of Troy, or *Ilioupersis* (Figure 27).

On this amphora by Group E, we see an altar in the center on which lies an old man, recognized by his sparse white hair. A warrior with shield is attacking him; rather than wielding a sword, the warrior is flinging a young boy by the ankle, using him as a club. To either side are women who gesture outward in appeal, while the woman on the right grabs at her hair with her right hand. We know from both literary sources and funeral representations that she is pulling the hair from her head in a gesture of mourning, so she is probably a daughter of the old man, anticipating his death. In the background a nude youth runs away to the viewer's left, while a nude adult male escapes to the right past a man in a mantle who watches the action calmly. Moving from description to iconographical analysis, one can identify the scene as Neoptolemos, the son of Achilles, killing Priam on the altar of the king's palace.

Although there are no labels, there are no other stories that fit this combination of circumstances. There were two epic poems that described the fall of Troy, the *Little Iliad* and *Troy Lost* (*Ilioupersis*), and both mention that the youthful Neoptolemos, arriving at Troy after the death of his father Achilles, killed Priam. The two poems differ, however, on the fate of Astyanax, the grandson of Priam and son of Hektor. According to the *Little Iliad* of Lesches of Mitylene, Neoptolemos killed Priam by dragging him from the household altar and killing him at the door to the palace, and he killed Astyanax by flinging him from a tower at a different moment. In the *Ilioupersis* of Arctinus of Miletos, it is said that Neoptolemos killed Priam at the altar of Zeus Herceius, but Odysseus murdered Astyanax later. Neither literary account fits the picture, but the use of a young boy as a club is found on many other visual representations of the fall of Troy. It is possible that this reflects another literary tradition that does not survive, or that artists have combined the two accounts so they can suggest the death of both the current king and his potential successor, thus making the collapse of Troy complete.

This conflation shows some of the difficulties in using literary sources for interpreting pictures. Given the strong oral tradition of the ancient Greeks that is lost to us today, we must rely on literary sources, however fragmentary, for knowledge of the underlying stories. Further, we tend to think of pictures as illustrations of texts, descriptions rather than acts of narration in their own right. A Greek picture, however, is not a snapshot of a complicated action, but a pastiche of people and actions that evoke a broader range of moments from a complicated story.[6] For example, in the *Ilioupersis* picture the grieving woman would be unrealistic in a real story and more properly belongs to a later moment after the killing has stopped; she should be running for safety, as are the two running male figures. The mantled spectator has no real place in the action. His civilian dress would imply that he is a Trojan, but he acts more like a civic observer or an elder witnessing a sacrifice. The death of Priam is in a real sense a sacrifice, but the mantled figure can also stand for the viewers of the present who look at the actions of their mythic history. Iconologically, we understand the importance of the Trojan saga for the Greeks as an example of their virtue and valor. Furthermore, the Trojan War represents the triumph of justice, punishment for the abduction of Helen in violation of the laws of guest friendship that were sacred to Zeus.

Both the Siphnian Treasury and the Group E amphora use a single scene to represent their stories, as is true of most Greek narrative art. However, artists could also represent a story or series of scenes using multiple pictures in which various figures are repeated. For example, the Theseus cup that

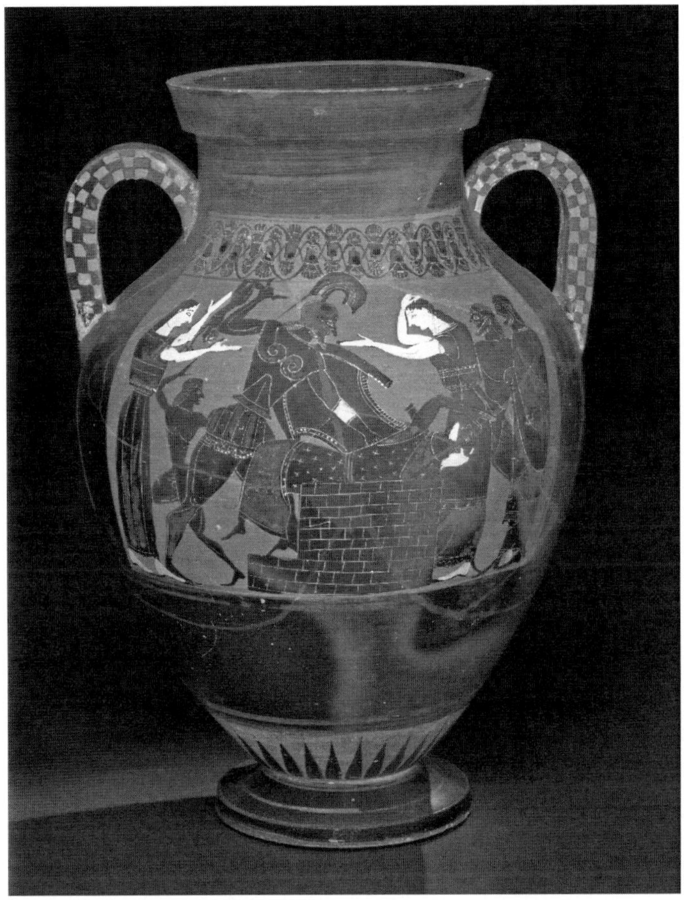

Figure 27. Attic black-figure amphora attributed to Group E, c. 550 BCE. Neoptolemos attacking Priam (Ilioupersis). London, British Museum, B205. Photo: © Trustees of the British Museum.

we examined in the first chapter (Figure 3) has two scenes of the exploits of Theseus on each side of the exterior. At the top of the cup we see Theseus throwing Skiron off a rocky outcropping that overlooked the sea (symbolized by the turtle at the base of the rock). The washbasin on the ground belongs to Skiron, who, according to Bacchylides's poem, offered to wash the feet of passersby and then robbed them and hurled them to their death. To the right Theseus is repeated, but now he is wrestling a bearded man, who would be Kerkyon, owner of a wrestling school. Continuing clockwise to the other side of the cup, Theseus attacks a murderous sow; the woman behind it personifies the meadow of Cremmyon (Figure 13). Finally, Theseus pulls at another man's hand while reaching for a pine tree. The tree is that of Sinis, who asked for help from passersby in bending the tree. Once they had grabbed hold, he let go and flung them, using the bent tree as a catapult. As Bacchylides' poem indicates, all these events took place on the road from Theseus's home in Troizen to Athens, where the hero intended to claim his rights as the son of the king Aegeus. The exterior of the cup, then, becomes a heroic adventure proving Theseus's status as he rids the world of scourges that plague mere mortals.

Playing with the form of the cup, the painter Douris placed a post-arrival scene on the interior of the cup – Theseus's battle with the Minotaur, in which he saved the youths and maidens of Athens from their sacrifice. The Minotaur scene is the signature scene of Theseus, but the exploits on the road to Athens elevate him in status as a hero of many deeds, comparable to Herakles. These cycles of deeds became popular at the end of the sixth century BCE and continued into the fifth century, and probably reflect the elevation of Theseus to an emblematic hero of Athens. Not coincidentally, this is also the period in which the constitution of Athens instituted democracy as its form of government, following the overthrow of the Peisistratid tyranny.

This type of multiple-scene narrative, in which the hero is repeated, is usually called *cyclical* (when the scenes are divided by frames) or *continuous* (no frame division, as here). The Siphnian Treasury frieze could also be considered as multiscenic, although it does not involve the repetition of figures and the two actions could be simultaneous. In that case we could call it a *panoramic* narrative, the gods on Mount Olympos to one side and the warriors on the plain of Troy on the other. If one considers the council of the gods as occurring at a different moment in time, before the battle took place, then *progressive* would be an appropriate designation. The point in using these terms is to help sort out the organization of the narrative, but it does not necessarily indicate a single "correct" order of reading. Indeed, because a drinker can only see one side of a cup, he or she can start with the scenes on only one side of the cup, whereas a companion in the same room would start with the other side and "read" in a different direction.

This variability in the order of reading brings us to other examples of scenes that present problems in formulating a definitive iconological interpretation of a work. One necessity for an iconographic analysis is textual sources that can identify the figures and their actions or attributes. When such sources do not exist, it can raise issues even when the action seems straightforward, as with the scene of Achilles and Ajax playing a game on an amphora signed by Exekias (Figure 28). The two warriors are hunched over a block and moving pieces on it. Both are identified by inscriptions, Achilles

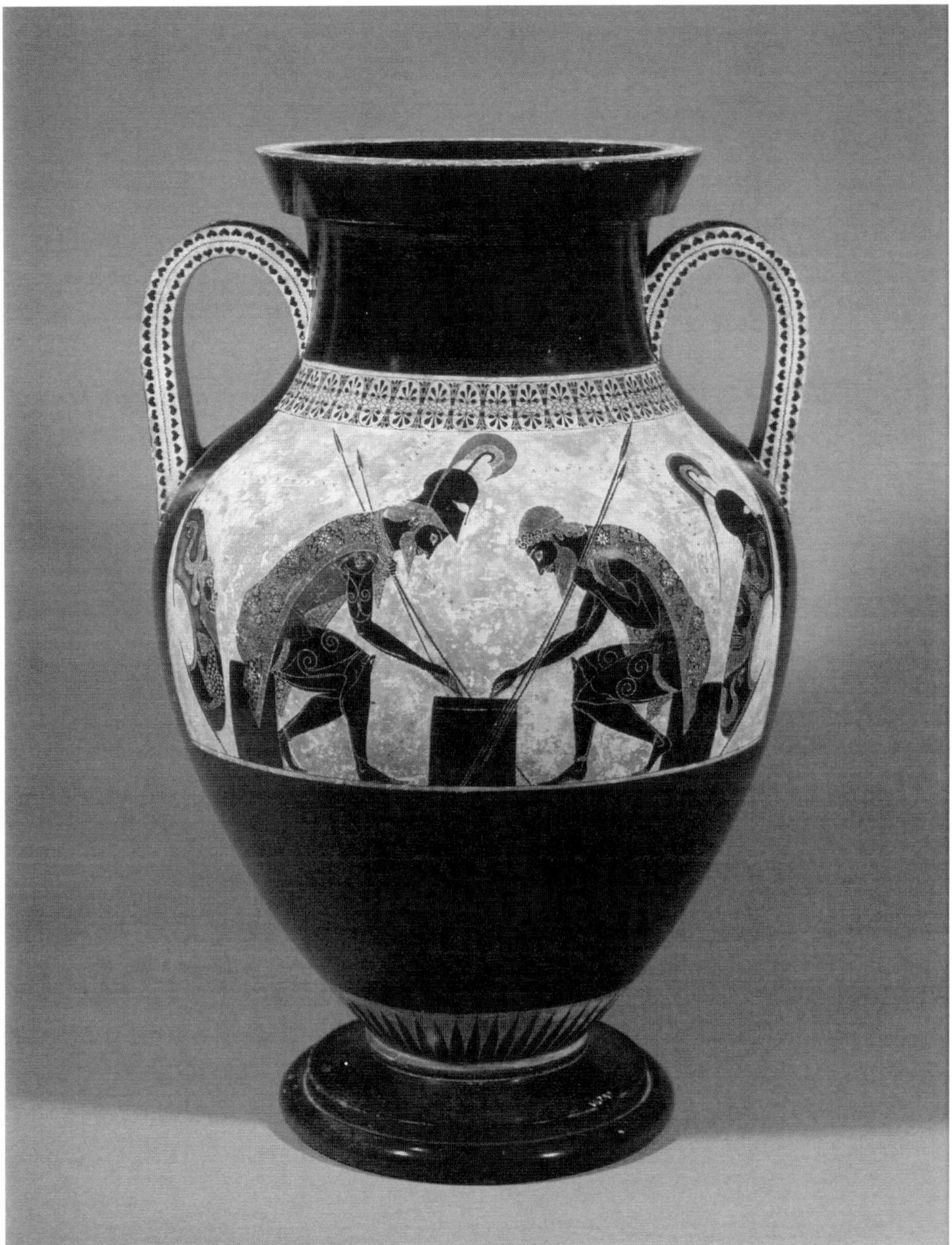

Figure 28. Attic black-figure amphora signed by Exekias, c. 540 BCE. Achilles and Ajax playing a game. Vatican Museums, Museo Gregoriano Etrusco 344. Photo: Scala/Art Resource, New York.

on the left and Ajax on the right. Speech words, apparently the numbers that they have rolled, come out of their mouths: respectively, *tessera* (four) and *tris* (three, written backward so the first letter is closest to Ajax's mouth, just as with Achilles). Although both hold spears, their shields are set to the side, as is Ajax's helmet, and they are clearly not concerned with battle at the moment. There is no literary source that mentions such a scene; explanations have noted that Palamedes invented games for the Greek warriors while they were stuck at Aulis, waiting to sail to Troy, and speculate that one of the lost epic poems might have been the inspiration for the scene.

The assumption behind this theory is that artists follow poets in finding narratives to represent. They become illustrators, who may alter the source to make a more vivid scene, but are not independent storytellers in their own right. Without a surviving literary source, one speculates as to a lost poem. In fact, though, mythological stories were not canonical and poets felt free to draw on the vast tradition of tales and to alter or add to them to fit their own purposes. In the case of Achilles and Ajax playing a game, it is entirely possible that it is an artistic invention, perhaps like the use of Astyanax as a club in the death of Priam that we saw earlier. As Susan Woodford suggested,

> Could not Exekias (or whoever originated the theme in the plastic arts) have simply been doodling mentally with ideas about the tedious length of the siege of Troy, the boredom of the heroes and the clever inventions of Palamedes to arrive at an image of Ajax and Achilles playing a game? No epic is needed, nor even an informal poem or story.[7]

Indeed, the Vatican amphora stands as the earliest surviving Attic example of a long series of representations of this theme, many of them from workshops related to Exekias. Woodford lists 129 examples of the theme, which flourished into the first half of the fifth century BCE. Even though many of these lack labels and could be generic warriors rather than specific heroes, it is clear that the scene caught the fancy of both painters and purchasers for more than a half-century. If the scene is an artistic invention, we must approach the image afresh, with some of the attendant ambiguity that must surround any innovative subject put before the public. The certainty that iconography seeks and its reliance on literary sources for evidence have limitations in such cases.

We can also see the limitations of iconography by looking at one of the most famous sculptural works from ancient Greece, the Parthenon frieze. Much of the early scholarship described this as a Panathenaic procession, which took place as part of an annual festival (*Panathenaia*) during which the

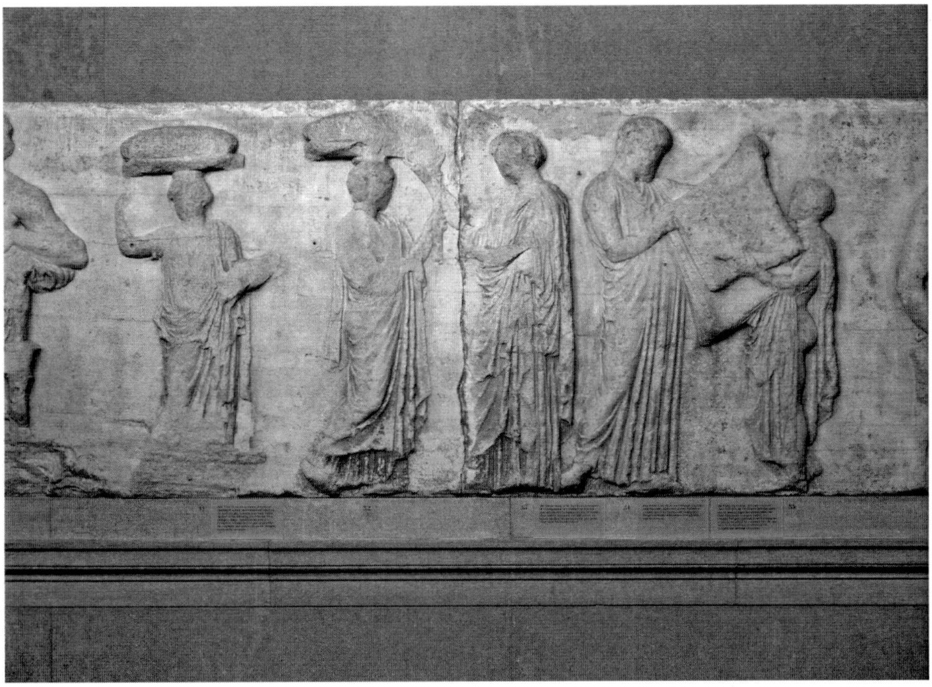

Figure 29. East frieze of the Parthenon, 442–438 BCE. Central peplos scene. London, British Museum. Photo: © Trustees of the British Museum.

citizens of Athens would bring an offering of a new garment for the cult statue of Athena. The sources that describe the procession are fragmentary and later than the frieze itself, and the inconsistencies between those sources and the frieze have long been noted and debated. A full analysis of the frieze would fill, and easily has filled, a book.[8] For our purposes in thinking about how we seek to interpret subject matter and meaning, we can look at the main scene that once stood over the doorway into the main chamber of the temple (Figure 29).

There are five figures arranged in two groups. To the left is an older woman and two girls who carry stools with cloth on them; they look as if they belong to a religious procession such as the Panathenaia. To the right is a bearded priest who holds a heavy, folded cloth with a young figure whose garment gaps open and shows the buttocks. Here we run into a problem at the very first stage of preiconographic description: is this a boy or a girl? The figure is too badly damaged to be certain; still, some scholars have argued on the basis of minute observation that it is a boy and others that it is a girl.[9] If it is a girl, the display of flesh would be very odd and inappropriate for the Panathenaia; if it is a boy, it contradicts our sources that indicate that the activity associated with giving the new and taking away the old garment is assigned to young maidens. Such gender change is not without precedent; the water carriers on the Parthenon frieze are male, but in the Panathenaia they were female foreign residents, or *metics*, of Athens. So too the numerous riders on the frieze, taking up about two-thirds of the total, have no place in the Panathenaia as nearly as we can determine.

Ultimately, trying to reconcile the meaning of the frieze with the sources is cut short by the problem that we cannot even identify the gender of one of the main figures, making any certainty of interpretation through iconographic analysis problematic. One could argue that the Panathenaia is not being represented, but rather that the frieze is an epitome of the many processions of the Athenians. This, however, sets up a curious problem for iconography methodologically, in that it would suggest that various elements of the frieze are meant to evoke associations with several different festivals, such as the folded garment with the presentation of the peplos to Athena. We would be suggesting that the frieze is intentionally ambiguous in terms of a unified subject matter. This suggests the potential for a multiplicity of meanings that is counter to the assumption in iconography of a unified, inherent meaning within the work that is put there by its maker.

Indeed, one could argue that many scenes are intentionally ambiguous or unspecific in character, and are susceptible to more than one specific interpretation based on the viewing circumstances. A change in setting or viewer could, in theory, produce two plausible but different interpretations of the image. In such situations, and in others for which there are iconographic difficulties, we can look at other means to fill in the gap, as we see in the rest of this chapter.

Semiotics and Structural Analysis

An alternative approach to interpretation would be to look at the imagery as a language, as a collection of signs and structures that generate meaning by the interaction of the image and viewer and the broader culture. Semiotics, the theory of signs, was developed concurrently in the late nineteenth and early twentieth centuries by Ferdinand de Saussure and Charles Sanders Peirce as a means for explaining language. Their related ideas look at a sign as being divided into several parts, but differ on their number, terminology, and interaction. This presents an issue for using semiotics and other theories developed in conjunction with spoken and written language for the analysis of art. Even though pictures are like a language, there are differences in the way that words and images work. Verbal and written communication takes place as a defined sequence of words that can take a considerable amount of time to complete. In contrast, pictures are more open in the order in which the whole and the details are perceived, and they are usually experienced much more quickly than a long poem or text. The challenge in looking to semiotics and other literary theories for the analysis of art is to adapt the concepts and vocabulary to work with the properties of pictures and visual perception. To do this, one may need to rely on one or more version of the theory, and then redefine the terms to suit the nature of visual language. In the following discussion, we will be adapting the work of Saussure and Roland Barthes, but other possibilities would be available depending on the nature of the project.

Semiotics

Saussure essentially defined a *sign* as a unit that represents or signifies something. For example, the written word "vase" is a collection of letters that would signify the object in Figure 33. Spoken aloud, it is a composite sound that signifies the same object. Both the written and spoken forms of the word are *signifiers*; the object is the *signified*, and together, signifier and signified make up the sign. The signifiers in both cases are arbitrary forms or sounds that users of English would recognize. Although the same letters in French or German would signify the same object, their oral form would be different. So, too, what is signified can be varied. The word "vase" not only signifies the object in Figure 33, but would also signify a tall glass cylinder used to hold flowers, a type of object that would not be found in ancient Greece. Both a flower vase and a Greek amphora are tall containers that could hold a number of different things, but the meaning generated by the written or spoken word "vase" could be quite different, depending on the speaker and the reader or listener. By focusing on the system of signs and the shared code that links the creator of the sign and the recipient, **semiotics** can provide a way of showing how meaning is generated and, of particular interest, how several plausible interpretations might coexist within the same image.

The utility of semiotics for the interpretation of meaning in Greek art was demonstrated in a series of articles on pursuit scenes by Christiane Sourvinou-Inwood.[10] She examined whether pursuit scenes such as the one in Figure 30 have an erotic meaning to them and whether two different types of pursuit scenes, one in which a young man pursues a woman while holding a spear and the other in which he carries a sword, have the same basic meaning.

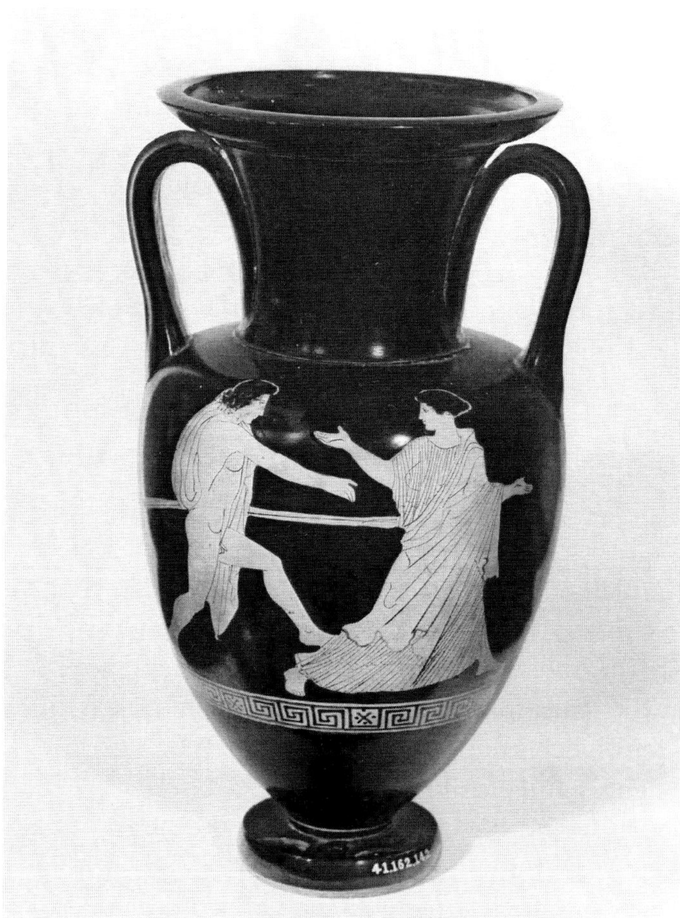

Figure 30. Attic red-figure Nolan amphora attributed to the Phiale Painter, c. 440–430 BCE. *Youth with spears pursuing woman. New York, Metropolitan Museum of Art,* 41.162.142. *Image Copyright © The Metropolitan Museum of Art/Art Resource, New York.*

In the first example, we could identify both figures as signs that in turn are made up of smaller signs. The young man is nude, which would signify his being an extraordinary, not everyday, type of figure. Although nudity in athletic performances would have been a normal experience, naked men chasing women would not have been. Nudity would further signify an idealized type of male figure, and would be a sign appropriate to a god or mythological hero, or to a more generic idealized type. So, too, the spears he carries would signify male activities such as hunting or warfare, so this sign reinforces the almost full nudity as a cultural male ideal.

In the second example (Figure 31), we have a nearly identical, mostly nude male figure. The cloak is draped completely over his left arm, and his

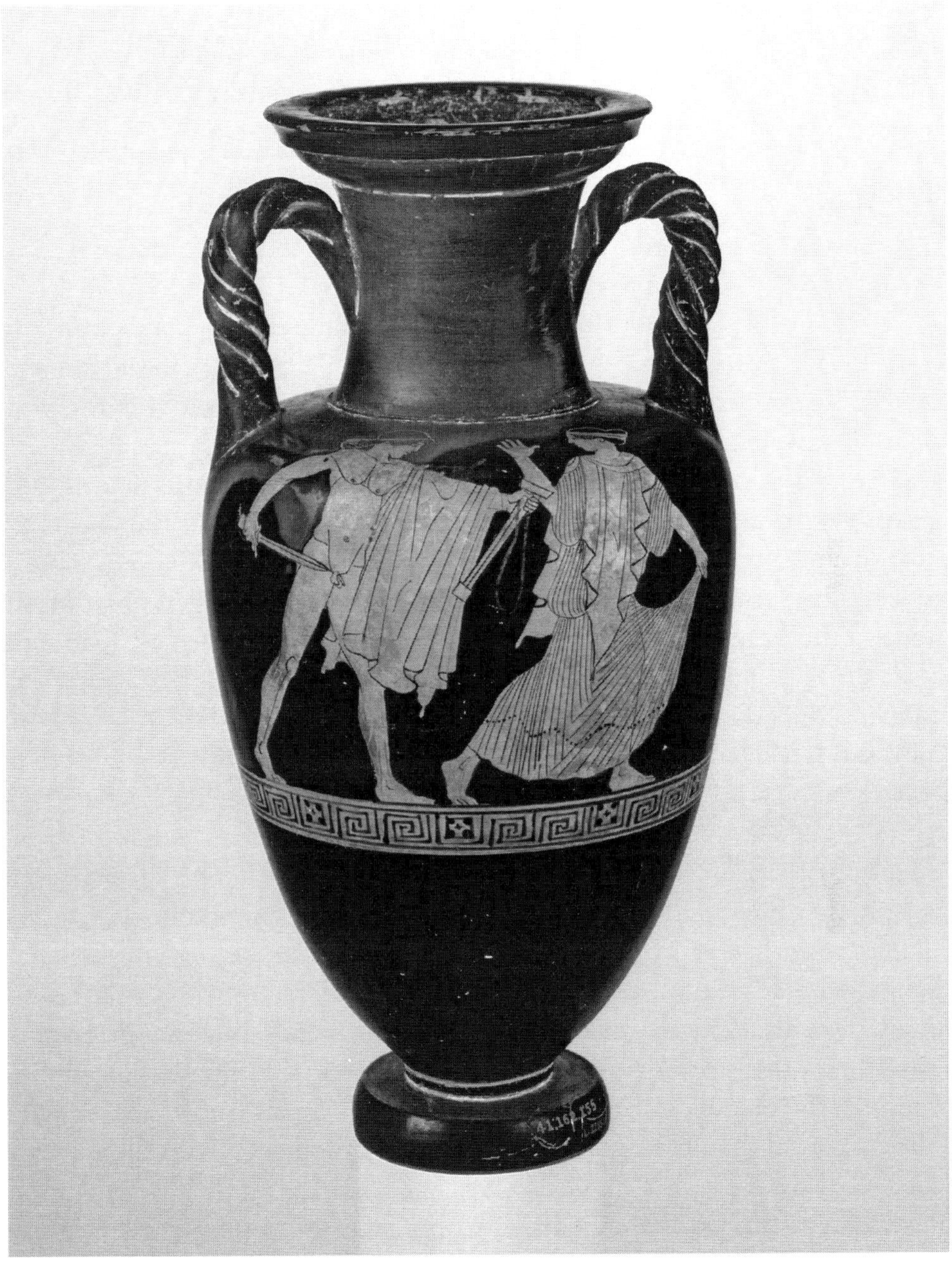

Figure 31. Attic red-figure Nolan amphora attributed to the Painter of the Yale Oinochoe, c. 475–450 BCE. Youth with sword pursuing woman. New York, Metropolitan Museum of Art, 41.162.155. Image Copyright © The Metropolitan Museum of Art/Art Resource, NY.

hand holds a scabbard; he does not reach out toward the woman like the first man. His lower hand holds a sword rather than a spear, but he, too, chases after a woman. The women on both vases wear thin chitons and heavier mantles, a more normative type of female dress in art. Both run from their pursuers while looking back, and both raise an arm toward their pursuers. The position of each woman's back hand is different: upturned versus turned out. Gestures, like words, can be very culturally specific, so these gestures should also be regarded as different signs.

To return to Sourvinou-Inwood's question, should both these scenes be regarded as erotic pursuits, with the idealized male figure intent on possessing, raping, or having sex with the female figure? Sourvinou-Inwood pointed to a key semiotic difference between the two: the signification of spear versus sword. As she pointed out, an unsheathed sword held in such a position conveys an intention to act with it. In contrast, the spears are held in a position meant to carry them, and not to drive them into a body. Indeed, the spears are held in the left hand and their points go behind the body of the woman, so they are not in a position to be used at all. The spear is a sign that signifies the idealized type of male, but it is not a sign that connects directly to the object of the pursuit in this case. The drawn sword, on the other hand, signifies an intention to use it, for otherwise it would be left in the scabbard to be carried. Thus both the drawn sword and the carried spears can denote an idealized male type, but they signify different intentions toward the victim. Although one could read the spear-bearer's pursuit as erotic, the sword-bearer has a more lethal connotation.

The sword-bearer is often identified as Theseus and the woman as Medea, who attempted to poison him after he arrived in Athens to claim his patrimony from his father Aegeus, who had married Medea. Sourvinou-Inwood's "reading" of the images, however, does not depend on that identification to interpret the picture, and not all pursuers with swords can be identified as Theseus. As a formula, we find it in other mythological scenes such as Ajax pursuing Kassandra or Odysseus charging Kirke; in these cases the story is about a rape or erotic encounter. Other signs in these pictures serve to combine and modify the reading of the sword threat. Thus, the picture in Figure 31 need not be Theseus pursuing Medea, but could be interpreted as such, or more broadly as an aggressive pursuit that could signify a response to any dangerous or deceptive woman. This would be consistent with the gestures of the women in the two pictures. The woman pursued by the spear-bearing man holds her hand up and toward the chin of the man, a

Table 2. Semiotic terms

Sign	Unit of meaning = signifier + signified
Signifier	The form that represents an object or concept (man with lionskin)
Signified	The object or concept that is represented (Herakles)
Symbolic level	Internal relationship of signifier and signified (man with lionskin is Herakles)
Syntagmatic level	Relationship to other signs in a semantic field (Herakles + lion is story of the Nemean lion, lack of weapon shows lion's invulnerability, etc.)
Paradigmatic level	Associative or homological relationship to signs in the reservoir of signs, connection on principle (Herakles is a hero, Herakles killing the Nemean lion is like Theseus slaying the Minotaur; wrestling pose of Herakles links to wrestling as athletic activity, etc.)
Metonym	A sign that refers to a figure, category, or idea and is a part of that whole (a helmet as symbol of a warrior)
Metaphor	A sign that refers to a figure, category, or idea to which it is not directly related (Boreas chasing Oreithyia as a symbol of the god's aid to Athens at the Battle of Salamis)

gesture that suggests pleading. The gesture of the hand held out in Figure 31 is interpreted as surprise or alarm, which would certainly be an appropriate response to a lethal threat.

As these two examples point out, to explore the range of meanings semiotically, one needs to look closely at the way in which signs work collectively. Barthes defined three levels at which signs work: symbolic, syntagmatic, and paradigmatic (see Table 2). The *symbolic* level is the internal and vertical relationship between the sign and the signified that we have been discussing. For images, it can be a result of the resemblance between the signifier and signified, as in the case of a portrait, but it can also encompass an array of attributes, such as the lionskin that Herakles wears or the trident of Poseidon, often derived from an action or quality of the figure. The other two levels are external and involve the relationship between different signs. The *syntagmatic* level is the connection between the signs collected in a field. Thus, for example, the combination of nudity + weapon + youth in both male figures is a syntagmatic combination; each signifies an idealized type of male figure, but together they convey that idea more strongly. Were we to add another element, such as a lionskin, we would add to the syntagmatic combination in a way that would then identify the idealized figure as a particular hero, Herakles. The generalized signification would still apply, but the interpretive range would be narrower.

The *paradigmatic* level is also an external relationship of the sign, but one that is homological or associative and connects the sign to other signs in the visual language outside the picture. For example, a figure wearing a lionskin would imply that the wearer of the skin had some type of encounter with a live lion. Herakles' prototypical deed was the fight with the Nemean lion, so the lionskin references that deed, even while appearing in a different story such as that of the battle at Troy (see Figure 19) or his apotheosis (see Figure 43).

More broadly, we can look at signs such as nudity in the picture. By representing the pursuer as nude, the intention is to associate the pursuit as heroic or ideal in quality, and the generic pursuit becomes associated with all other specific pursuits, such as Poseidon chasing Amymone, Zeus pursuing Aegina, or Peleus chasing Thetis, most of which ended in unions that produced heroic offspring and help to associate pursuits with erotic actions. However, a figure pursuing with a sword also associates that scene with battles and fights. Thus a change of sign within the picture changes the relationship of the image by shifting the associations that a viewer would make, leading to a different interpretation for the pursuit with a sword than the pursuit with spears. In the case of the youth with sword in Figure 31, the pose mimics that of the figure of Harmodios in the Tyrannicides, a pair of bronze figures set up in the Agora in 477 that commemorated the pair of men who, in 511, killed Hipparchos, brother of the tyrant Hippias (see the stone copies in Figure 50). As a political symbol of the city, this pose would be entirely appropriate for a local hero such as Theseus or any other type of heroic figure. This paradigmatic association further weakens the erotic connotations of pursuit beyond the internal, symbolic level of the picture itself.

There are two particular types of paradigmatic relationships that bear mentioning: metonymy and metaphor. A *metonym* is an attribute that represents the whole, such as a spear as a sign for a hero or warrior. Real warriors did not fight nude with just a spear and shield, but either sign is sufficient to represent the type of the warrior, whether heroic or contemporary. A *metaphor* is a sign that is unrelated directly to the concept but symbolizes it. So, for example, the siren at the top of the mirror in Figure 2 can function as a metaphor for the alluring beauty of the woman; as the sirens' song drew men irresistibly toward them, the beauty of the mirror's owner could do the same. The use of the Amazonomachy as a metaphor for the Greek wars against the Persians has been widely recognized on public monuments as well as smaller objects, such as vases. Curiously, the actual battles against the Persians, which loomed so large in the events of the fifth century BCE, were only rarely represented in art, and metaphors such as the Amazonomachy, Centauromachy, and Ilioupersis were far more common.

Structural Analysis

Semiotics can help to explain the web of associations and meanings that a sign can generate, but to understand narrative and action, we need to turn to a related approach, **structural analysis** (see terms in Table 3). One might say that this approach looks at how the signs of a picture work as parts of speech, focusing particularly on the subject–action–recipient or noun–verb–object combination that is the basic building block of action. As developed by Roland Barthes in relationship to the analysis of film narratives, these subject–action–recipient clusters are called *syntagmatic functions* because they connect together within the picture. These functions serve to move the action of the story forward and come in two forms: nucleus and catalyst. A *nucleus* is a function or action on which the narrative hinges, a climactic or decisive action that changes or defines the direction of the action. A *catalyst* is an action that amplifies or contributes to the action, but is not essential to it. The test of whether an action is a catalyst or a nucleus would be to imagine it deleted from the narrative. If the end result of the episode (say, someone dies) would be roughly the same, then the function would be a

Table 3. Structural analysis terms

Function (Relationship)	Definition
Nucleus (syntagmatic)	The essential action and its participants on which a narrative hinges (subject–action–object)
Catalyst (syntagmatic)	Pictorial action or figure that elaborates on the nucleus, but is not essential to the main action
Informant (paradigmatic)	Pictorial element that identifies participants or locates the narrative in time or place
Index (paradigmatic)	Pictorial element that refers to an action, event, idea, or person outside the immediate setting

catalyst. If removing the figure and/or action would conceivably change the result, then the action is a nucleus.

Translating this from movies to single, still images requires some adaptation and can best be explained by looking at a picture that we have already examined, the scene of Neoptolemos attacking Priam in Figure 27. Most of the figures are engaged in some action, but our attention is drawn to the figure of Neoptolemos wielding the boy Astyanax as a club, both because of its central location and by the open form of the figure. Neoptolemos's action has an object – the prone figure of Priam on the altar. This cluster, Neoptolemos striking Priam, forms a function in the picture and can be readily seen as a nucleus of the composition, because removing it would change the distinctiveness of the action and its result. The women to either side also act, holding out one or both arms, and the figure on the right also grabs at her hair in a gesture associated with grief, tearing the hair and drawing blood from the scalp. The two figures clearly react to what is taking place and signal the importance of the figures in the nucleus, but if we remove them from the picture, there would not be a change in the course of the story. They are therefore catalysts, as are the figures of the nude youth and man who run away from the scene in the background. One might think of them as Trojan men who will fall later in the story. The mantled man on the far right does not act at all, and is neither a catalyst nor a nucleus.

If syntagmatic functions can be thought of as nouns, verbs, and objects, one can look at the other types of functions as modifiers, such as adjectives, adverbs, or prepositional phrases. These *paradigmatic functions* link the action to a specific setting or to other actions and stories outside the narrative. These consist of two types: *informants*, which serve to identify characters, time, or location of the story, and *indexes*, which work semiotically to link the narrative to other scenes or actions. Turning back to the Ilioupersis picture in Figure 27, the altar on which Priam lies is an informant, indicating the palace altar of Zeus Herceius, where Priam was killed. The use of a boy as a club also serves as an informant by serving as an attribute for the scene in identifying Neoptolemos. The additional figures of both men and women not only expand the scene, but also serve to locate the central action within a populated place such as a city, and not an isolated sanctuary. The running men can index future moments of the carnage and the grieving women signal the death of the men and the lamentation of their survivors that follows. The spectator to the right is most likely an index referring to the contemporary viewer and city, linking the mythological and heroic past

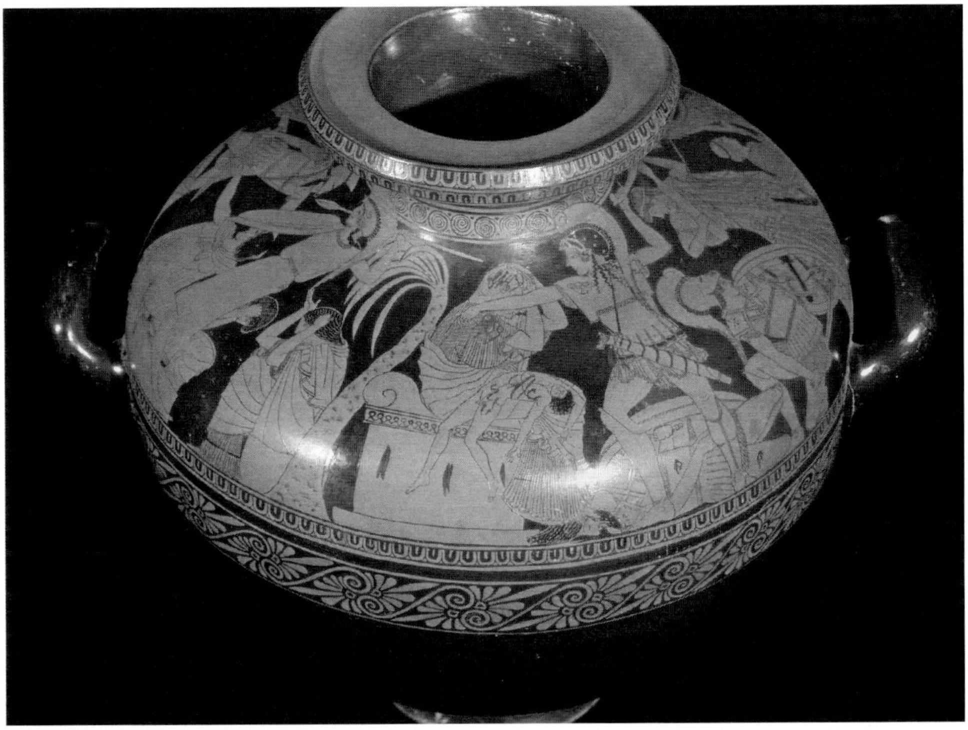

Figure 32. Attic red-figure kalpis attributed to the Kleophrades Painter, around 480 BCE. *Neoptolemos attacking Priam. Naples, Museo Archeologico Nazionale, 2422. Photo: Scala/Art Resource, NY.*

to the present. Thus we can see that some visual elements can perform a double or even triple duty structurally within a pictorial narrative. Indeed, the unique action of a boy as a club makes the nucleus itself into an informant, quickly identifying the scene for the viewer.

So far, our structural analysis of the Ilioupersis scene confirms much of the understanding that we developed earlier by using iconography, although the emphasis is first placed more on the internal function and relationship of the pictorial elements. We can see the difference in approaches if we look at another representation of the subject on a later *kalpis,* or water pitcher, attributed to the Kleophrades Painter in Naples (Figure 32). Here a slightly later moment has been chosen, with Astyanax lying dead on his grandfather's lap. Rather than using the boy as a weapon, it is probable that Neoptolemos has already stabbed the boy (with the blood as an index for that earlier moment) and is now poised to bring his sword down on Priam. In most representations of this scene, Priam is already collapsing as if struck once, as in Figure 27, or reaches out his hands toward the chin of Neoptolemos in a gesture of pleading for his life. Priam's pleading would constitute an appropriate reaction to the attack, one that not only acknowledges the lethal threat of Neoptolemos but also acknowledges that Priam does not have the right to oppose him. After all, Priam acquiesced in the abduction of Helen by sheltering her and Paris, and now he is guilty before the avenging Greek. Pleading is, in essence, an acknowledgment of guilt, and the victim's only hope for survival is by begging. Curiously, in the Kleophrades Painter's version, Priam is instead shown in extreme grief, with shorn or torn hair and blood on his scalp that is likely from his own actions as he mourns his dead grandson. Priam here does not react to his attacker, and his action is independent of the main nucleus of "Neoptolemos attacking Priam." Indeed, removing Neoptolemos does not alter this action of Priam grieving over his grandson, thus showing it to be a second nucleus in its own right.

The consequence of this shift in the narrative structure is that the main nucleus is now about an armed warrior attacking an unarmed elder who is acting appropriately to the death of a child. Showing Priam this way, and not resisting or begging, is to make the action of the warrior decidedly less heroic, in that a hero's opponent should be strong, wicked, or both. In other words, a heroic action needs an appropriate reaction from the recipient, which is now missing. Structurally, we can see that the main functional units create an asymmetry that takes this narrative in a significantly different direction from other versions, regardless of the specific identity of the figures or story subject. We might consider this as significant in the same way as the modern distinction between justifiable homicide or self-defense on the one hand and the heinous murder of an innocent victim on the other. Death is the result in both cases, but the story is quite different.

Another useful application of semiotics and structural analysis is to scenes that are not specifically mythological in their subject. Early study of pictorial narrative divided action scenes into categories of either myth or genre. As a narrative must be specific according to these approaches, genre scenes could not be narrative because they did not have a definite, specific content put into them by the artist. However, semiotics and structural analysis put emphasis on the viewer's perception and recognize that multiple viewers could create different but plausible interpretations of the same set of signs. In this approach, narrative and its meaning exist not in the specificity of a scene, but in the potential of an action to prompt a sequence of actions or story in the mind of the viewer.

To see this, we can look at a common scene found over the course of a couple of centuries in vase painting: the warrior leaving home. On an amphora from about 530 BCE and related to the workshop that produced the Ilioupersis scene in Figure 27, we see a warrior in the center-right of the main body (Figure 33). He is almost fully armed for battle with helmet, cuirass, greaves, and shield; all that is missing is a spear. He is shown striding toward our right while looking back at the woman and bearded man. The other three figures all wear mantles and are watching and reacting to the warrior's departure. The older man to the left raises an arm in salute or acknowledgment, and the youth to the right is passive. The woman holds her arms at different angles, in a position that suggests distress. The nucleus of the scene is the warrior leaving, whereas the other three figures are catalysts and represent three distinct civic groups that are potentially found in a household: women, adult men, and youthful men. This is not a snapshot from daily life, but a construction that epitomizes events that happen in both the "real" world and in the "imaginary" world of myth.

The social or familial relationship among the figures is ambiguous. The woman shows no sign of age, as is typical of the period, so she could be a new bride of fifteen, a wife and mother at twenty-five, or the mother of the warrior and in her thirties or forties. The older man to the left is almost certainly the warrior's father, and the red circle on his head may indicate that he is balding and elderly. The youth to the right might be a son or a younger brother of the warrior. There is no sure way to tell, but making a decision about the relationship would cast this collection of actions within a more specific narrative framework. For example, if a viewer were to identify the warrior as an adult father who left home to fight, then one could see the mantled youth as the warrior's son, the woman as his wife, and the older man as his elderly father. If one were to see the warrior as a younger figure, then the older man and woman could be his father and mother and the mantled youth a younger brother remaining at home. The consequences of going into battle would be hazardous in either case, but the impact on the family would be different. In short, it depends on a decision of the viewer to see what is most likely and construct a scenario for the perception of the picture. If the viewer had lost a husband in battle, then the first interpretation would be more meaningful, but a mother who had lost a son in battle would see the second interpretation as more relevant. Each "reading" would be consistent and logical, but the course and consequence of the story would be different, and each viewer's scenario would be influenced by his or her own situation or experience.

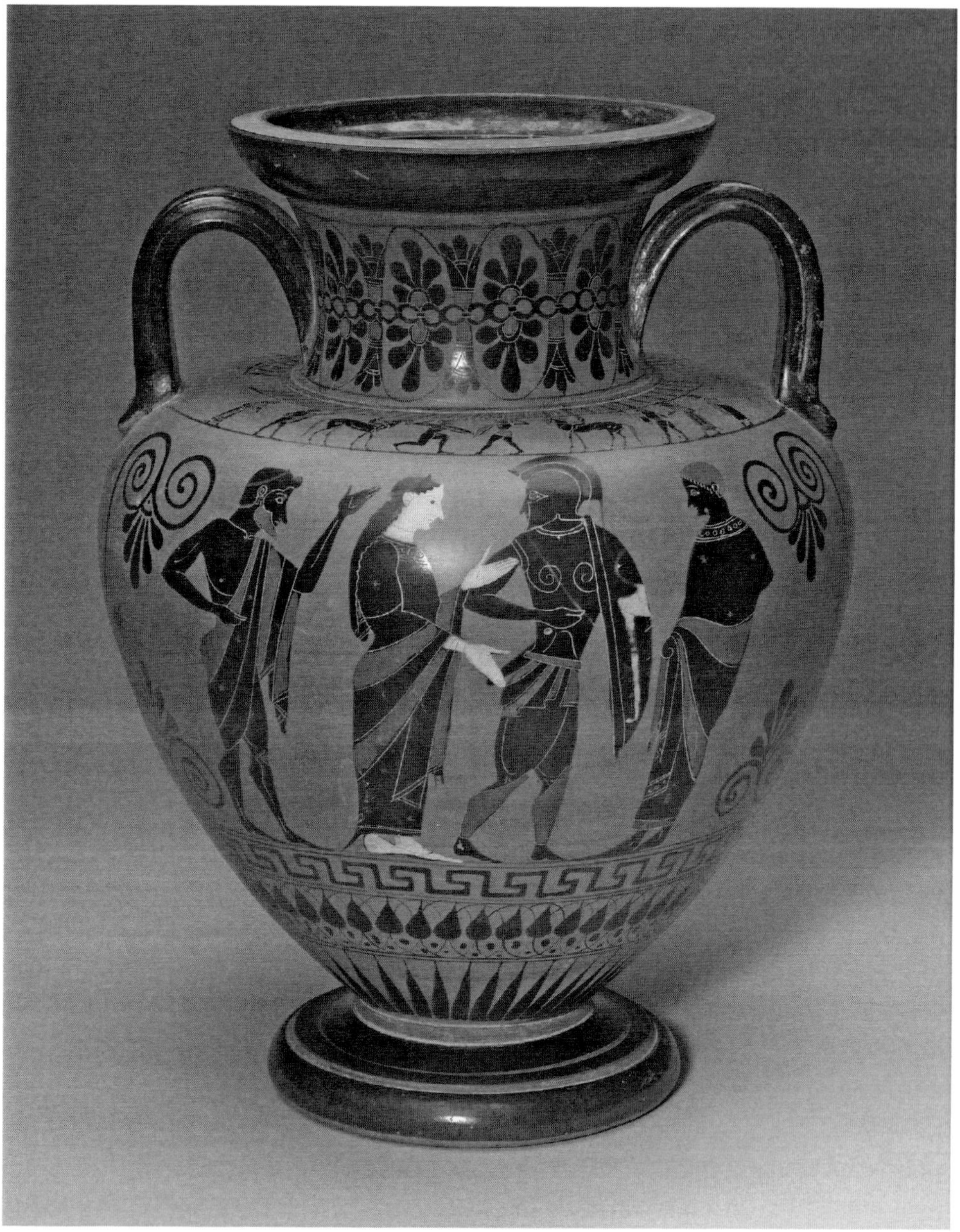

Figure 33. Attic black-figure amphora attributed to the Painter of Vatican G357, c. 530 BCE. Warrior departing. Minneapolis Institute of Arts, The Ethel Morrison Van Derlip Fund, 57.1. Photo: Museum.

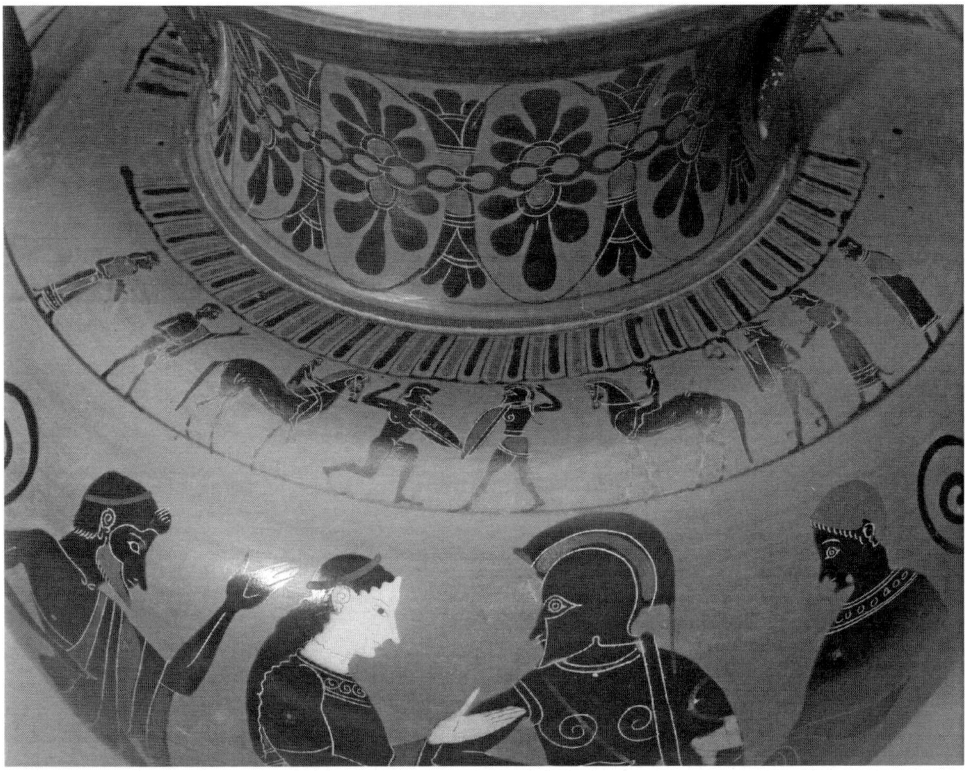

Figure 34. Detail of shoulder of Figure 33. Warriors Fighting. Minneapolis Institute of Arts, The Ethel Morrison Van Derlip Fund, 57.1. Photo: Museum.

In the frieze above the main scene, we see the warrior repeated and now fighting a second, nude warrior (Figure 34). In each picture, then, the armored warrior is not only the nucleus of the picture, but also an index that links the two scenes together, as is the repetition of the mantled youth and female in the two scenes. Hermes, holding his kerkyion, stands on the right side of the upper frieze behind the armored warrior. His presence is an index for the death of one of the warriors, because he will bear the psyche of the deceased to the underworld. The question is, to whom do we link Hermes? In most Greek battle scenes the victor is on the left; because Hermes is behind the right-hand warrior, we could see the god as ready to take the armored warrior's soul to the underworld. However, the left, nude warrior is bent to one knee, in a position suggesting disadvantage in the battle. In that case, Hermes would be behind the victor, ready to take the psyche of his opponent. The armored warrior may be on the right to align him with his appearance in the departure scene below, strengthening the narrative connection: warrior leaves, warrior fights.

What this discussion points out is that there are several structural possibilities for "reading" this narrative, and that the painter has in fact left the scene ambiguous (and without spears). This does not mean, however, that it is without narrative intention. Rather than judge such scenes in a binary of mythological versus genre scenes based on content, structural analysis makes the viewer part of the storytelling process. After seeing the main outline of the action, the viewer makes a series of interpretive choices that shape the direction of the narrative, as we shall discuss later with the viewer response approach. This approach sees the picture as a broader type of narrative that relies on recognizable formulas that permit specific solutions on the part of the viewer. Several terms, such as "generalized heroic" or "generic narrative," have been proposed for such narrative types, suggesting that even though the scenes lack the specificity of mythological narrative, there is a specific intention in these pictures to elevate the status of the figures to a heroic level. The coincidence of these terms with "genre scenes," however, is probably confusing. Perhaps "universal narratives" would be less confusing, and would also signal that a specific reading would be but one potential interpretation of a narrative scene.

This distinction is also important for considering the development of narrative art outside of the myth versus genre categories. Anthony Snodgrass first coined the term *generalized heroic* for describing the intention of the first action scenes in Middle and Late Geometric art, such as the frieze on a monumental krater in the Metropolitan Museum of Art (Figure 35).[11] Some of the early studies of Geometric figural art sought to find specific mythological figures in some of these scenes, making them narratives or protonarratives. The simplicity of the scenes makes it impossible for them to be convincingly mythological, but could they still be narratives? On the back of the ship, for example, are two warriors fighting. At shoulder level, the warrior on the right appears to have grabbed the forearm of the other warrior with a hand, and at waist level each has thrust a sword whose tip meets the silhouette of the opposing figure. It would seem that we have a stalemate, with one or both of the figures likely to die as a result of the symmetrical nucleus (warrior attacking warrior). Another pair of warriors once fought at the prow of the ship. This entire ship battle is repeated on the other side of the krater with a few variations, connected by the warriors marching with shields and spears from left to right.

That a viewer might read a story from such a simple scene becomes plausible on two accounts. One is that there is a funerary scene on the top of the krater, which could plausibly link to the fight below; a nude geometric

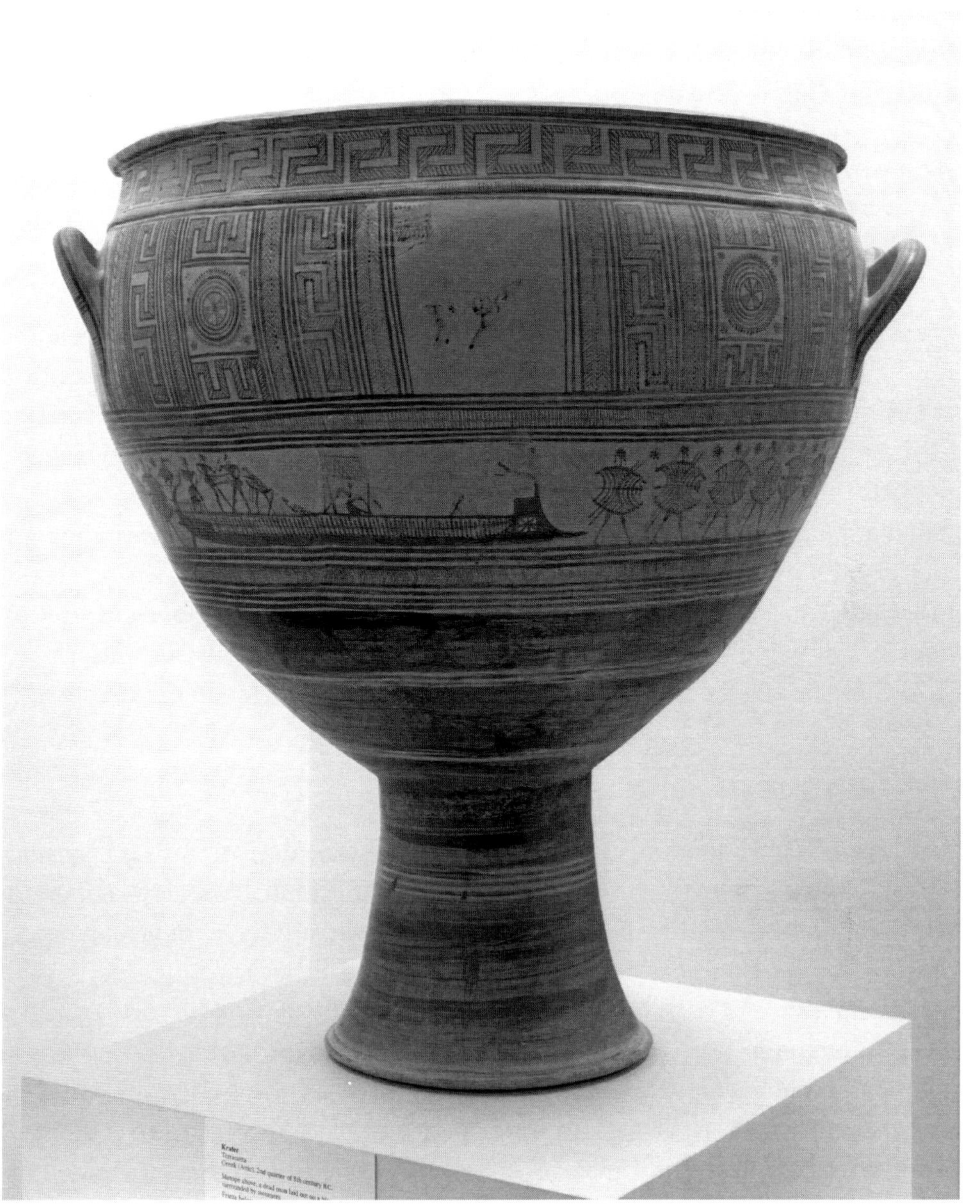

Figure 35. Middle Geometric krater, c. 770 BCE. Battle on a ship and warriors marching. New York, Metropolitan Museum of Art, 34.11.2. Image Copyright © The Metropolitan Museum of Art/Art Resource, New York.

figure on a bier would be a repeated sign and index. Second, the vase itself is an elaborate funerary marker for its time, so the setting would also suggest the potential for looking at the scene as being typical of what an elite male of the community would do, either dying in battle, or leading in battle and dying much later. In either case, ships, warfare, and elaborate funerals are the common threads for the biography of an elite male, or of a hero, so either reading is possible.

Structurally, the eighth-century BCE duels on this krater are not very different from the scene of warriors fighting on the Siphnian Treasury frieze about 250 years later (Figure 1). Here, too, one has an equal match. Identifying Achilles on the right allows us to know who is the victor, but typically the victor is on the left. Indeed, we can recall that early iconographic interpretations of the frieze had a different subject; the only difference is that now inscriptions have been found to identify the figures. But inscriptions are informants, not primary functions like a nucleus, which describes action. Structural analysis would argue that the main element of narrative is the nucleus, not the identification of the figures. Indeed, after the inscriptions faded at Delphi, it may not have been possible for even an ancient viewer to identify the protagonists decisively on the Siphnian Treasury frieze. Applying a label narrows the range of interpretive possibilities, but storytelling does not depend on labels; a viewer could plausibly construct alternative stories for the frieze directly on the basis of the pictorial elements.

Repetition and Information Theory

An approach that dovetails with semiotics and structural analysis is *information theory*, which examines how messages are communicated from sender to recipient. Whether with spoken language, written language, or visual images, messages must compete for attention against the background "noise" that makes up the audio or visual environment – the *entropy* or disorder that exists. Language uses codes to create an ordered message that competes against the background entropy, but an important strategy for signaling the intentionality of a message and the clarity of its communication is through repetition. A repeated signal or sign brings an order that a viewer can observe both to recognize the existence of a message and to help decipher its meaning.

Repetition in information theory has been developed by Ann Steiner to explore how visual images and their associated inscriptions can be read in a systematic manner. Looking at repetition is key to understanding the development of a visual language, in that it is the repeated use of motifs and specific combinations of signs that allows a man with lionskin to be recognized instantly as Herakles.

Steiner defines some key terms to recognize the forms and variations of repetition.[12] Basic repetition is the reproduction of something – such as a

Table 4. Information theory terms

Term	Definition
Verbatim repetition	Exact repetition, allowing for differences of style
Duplication	Intentionally identical to the original
Reduplication	Repetition with a variation or inflection on the original
Redundancy	Repetition of all parts
Synonymy	Reiteration or substitution of a related item with equivalent meaning
Antonymy	Reiteration with the substitution of an opposite term

motif, figure, or action – that one can observe directly within the work of art. There are different forms of repetition, including *verbatim repetition* (an exact repetition allowing for differences of style); *duplication* (repetition intentionally identical to the original); *reduplication* (repetition with a variation or inflection on the original); and *redundancy* (repetition of all parts to ensure alternative paths for the message). There are also two forms of repetition that introduce more variation from the first to the second image: *synonymy* (reiteration or substitution of a related item with equivalent meaning) and *antonymy* (reiteration with the substitution of an opposite term, such as front and back). These terms are listed in Table 4.

If we turn back to the amphora in Figure 33, we see that the warrior, woman, and youth are repeated in the main image and on the frieze above. The youth and woman are verbatim repetitions, whereas the warrior can be seen as a reduplication; he is the same except that his action has changed from departure to fighting. The verbatim repetitions signal to the viewer that the two messages are related, whereas the variation provides a sequence that establishes a two-part message, from one picture to the next.

If we look at the other side of the same vase (Figure 36), we can see that there is nearly a *duplication* of the scene on the shoulder in Figure 34: two warriors fighting and watched by riders, Hermes, a youth, and two women; only the mantled youth is missing. We can think of this repetition as a redundancy, ensuring that the subject of warriors fighting, even if on a smaller scale, is a message that is conveyed to the viewer regardless of which side of the vase he or she will see. Its role as a duplication would also signal to the viewer who received both messages that the two sides of the vases were intended to be understood together, thereby linking the two large-scale pictures. Interestingly, both of these are departure scenes, but different in many ways, and so should be seen as synonymous (synonymy).

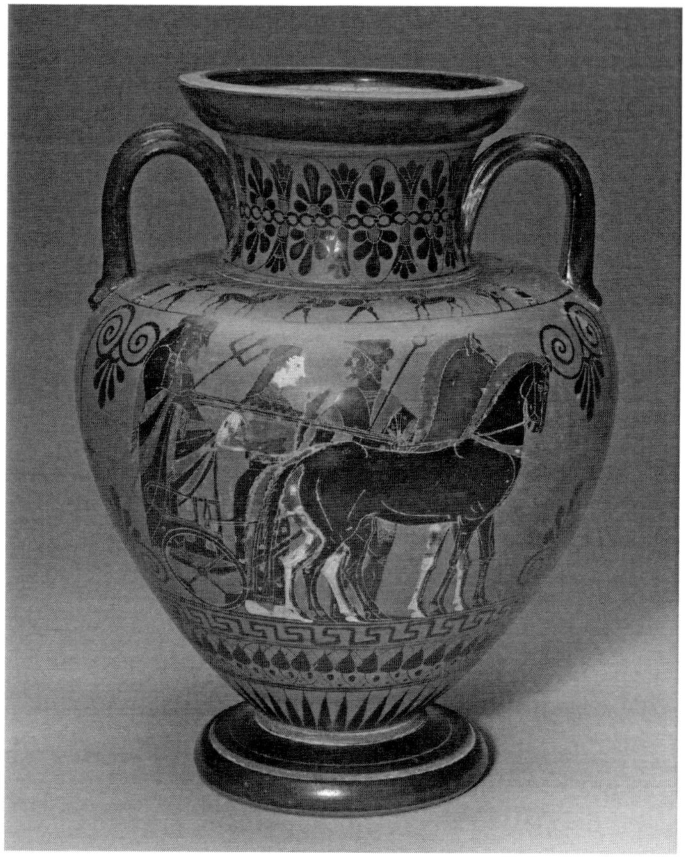

Figure 36. Attic black-figure amphora attributed to the Painter of Vatican G357, c. 530 BCE. Departure of the Gods. Minneapolis Institute of Arts, The Ethel Morrison Van Derlip Fund, 57.1. Photo: Museum.

Understanding how repetition works helps us to see the development of a visual language and the establishment of "types" that can be used broadly by artists. Two further and important consequences for interpreting images result from this approach. The first is to understand the role of images as establishing paradigms for the viewer – that is, "comparisons between a present situation or individual and (usually) a mythical precedent."[13] In the amphora with the departure scenes, one is a type that epitomizes the general events that happen in the world of the viewer: warriors leave (and warriors fight). Members of a family leave the household and act within the greater realm of the city and culture. The gods, too, leave their abodes; they become involved in the affairs of the world, overseeing and influencing them. Their behavior becomes a model for the living mortals; the vase establishes a paradigm that conveys a message about the order of the household, city,

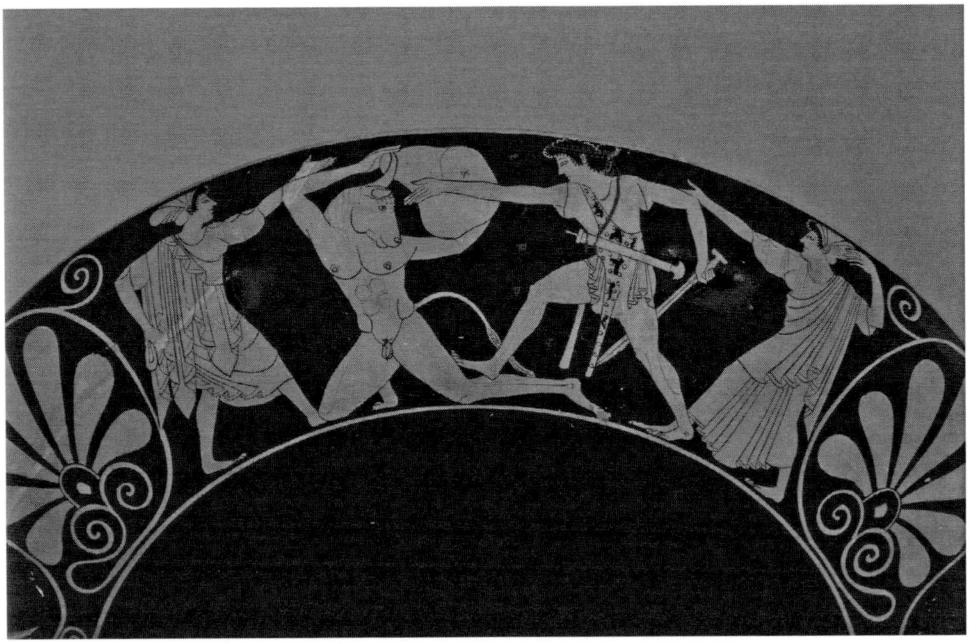

Figure 37. Attic red-figure kylix signed by Epiktetos, c. 520–490 BCE. Theseus and the Minotaur. London, British Museum, E37. Photo: © Trustees of the British Museum.

and world beyond. One could go further and see the actions and dress of the prototypical mortals on the vase as models for the behavior of the viewer, a third iteration that acts out the message on the vase.

A second useful consequence of this approach is to analyze *parody*, an imitation of a serious subject for comic effect. For an imitation to be effective

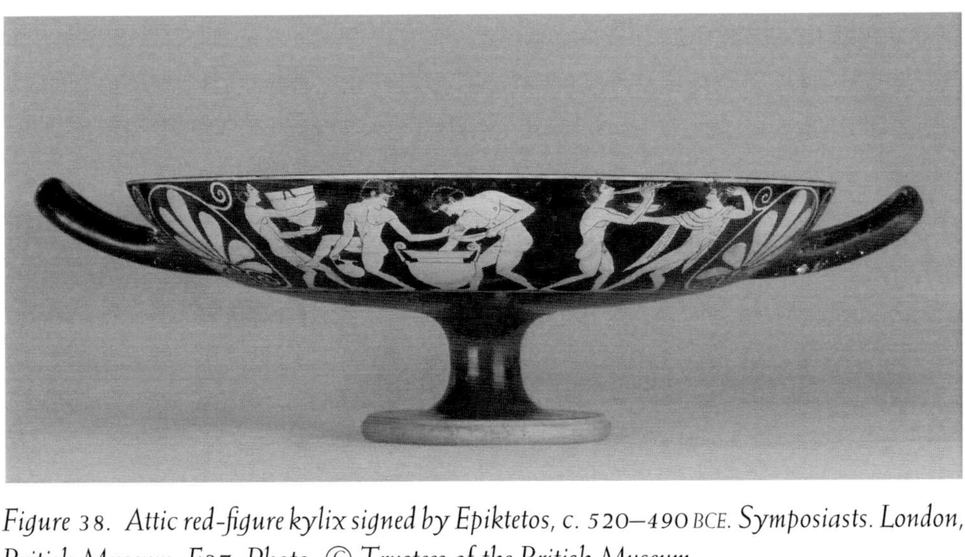

Figure 38. Attic red-figure kylix signed by Epiktetos, c. 520–490 BCE. Symposiasts. London, British Museum, E37. Photo: © Trustees of the British Museum.

as humor, the viewer must recognize or remember the original and realize, through the disparities between the two images, the incongruities that make the work amusing.[14] Steiner uses the example of a cup signed by Epiktetos that shows Theseus attacking the Minotaur on one side, with two of the Athenian maidens who were to have been victims of the Minotaur looking on and gesturing in acknowledgment of the hero (Figure 37). Theseus is the ideal youth, and a paradigmatic model for the youth of Athens. The latter appear on the other side of the cup, which shows five of them at a *symposion* or drinking party (Figure 38). Their physiques and forms are variations on the figure of Theseus on the other side, so they are reiterations of the hero. Unlike Theseus, they are nude, but this makes them heroic on one level. However, their poses are like those of the women on the other side of the cup, and not like the heroic stride of Theseus. Further, their actions include balancing or filling cups and, in the second figure from the left, urinating into a pitcher. One might call the symposiasts merely rowdy if seen by themselves, but the form of repetition used on the cup makes a parodic interpretation more likely. Whether the symposiasts are being ridiculed, as would be the nature of satire, or are shown as merely amusing, gets to the question of intent. For this, one must look to context for an answer, as we will explore in the next section.

Poststructuralism, Hermeneutics, and Viewer Response

Semiotics and structural analysis can expand our ability to interpret subject matter and to see how complex meaning can be generated by the way in which images work as a visual language. It also opens up the possibility of multiple meanings or interpretations that have validity. This is not without its problems, though. Semiotics assumes the existence of some type of perfect reader or viewer who would be aware of the almost infinite permutations of signs and their relationships and would be able to decode them readily. It is doubtful that such a viewer existed in Greece, and given the limitations of our knowledge, even more doubtful in our day. Our experience today also suggests that just because a meaning is possible, this does not mean it existed. There can be a common interpretation that the vast majority of viewers would agree on without much debate, even if other interpretations are theoretically possible. Structural analysis, as it looked at the level of narration, also tended to clump large collections of stories from many different cultures or periods into relatively few categories or types, such as "heroic journey" or "struggle." The inference is that these different stories have basically the same meaning based on their category, although the number of these categories varied by theorist.

Critics of semiotics and structural analysis would argue that interpretation cannot be separated from context, and that the study of unchanging structure is artificial when compared to the more varying and changing use of signs in spoken language or visual art. We will turn our attention to these "poststructural" approaches in the remainder of this chapter.

Hermeneutics

Hermeneutics is an approach that was originally associated with scriptural interpretation, but more broadly refers to the science of interpretation. As developed from the philosophy of Martin Heidegger, it recognizes that interpretation is inextricably linked to both time and history, and to the history of interpretation itself. On one hand, hermeneutics would recognize, like iconography, that an artist invested a certain meaning into a work that is inherent to it. On the other hand, it would also recognize that the meaning or significance of the work can differ over time or place, but these would be added layers to the original core of meaning in the work. Further, these shifts in meaning or reinterpretations will be the result of the new culture, which might be quite different from that of the work's creator. As Hans-Georg Gadamer saw it, the meaning of a work of art is a dialogue between the original producer of the work and its audiences, including contemporary scholars. Within the "hermeneutic circle," one strives toward a full knowledge of a work by examining all elements of it, including the history of previous interpretations.

We might consider, as an example of this, a sculpture in Munich that shows an older woman sitting on the ground and holding a large vase (Figure 39). Another example of this subject is found in the Capitoline Museum in Rome; both are generally thought to have been carved in the Roman era and were found in the vicinity of Rome. However, whether the work before us is an original work of Roman patronage, or a copy of a Hellenistic Greek original, or a transformation of a small-scale subject popular in terracotta figurines, is much disputed. The work is usually titled the "Drunken Old Woman," but as several scholars have pointed out, this is misleading. She wears a buckled tunic similar to one worn in a festival, indicating that she is of a higher social class and is engaged in a ritual activity. The vase that she holds is a *lagynos*, used in an Alexandrian Dionysiac festival. The tendency of an average modern viewer is perhaps to look on this figure with some mixture of scorn and sympathy – indeed, a drunken old woman. However, one can find in art depictions of a drunken and staggering Dionysos; surely these would not be critical of the god. As we should look at the woman within a ritual context, one might consider her state as in some way transcendent, rather than debased.

The interpretive problem that this work presents is difficult and perhaps unsolvable, but it points to the importance of context in guiding interpretation. For example, the medium and scale affect our understanding: a small terracotta work of this same subject might well have a satiric or sarcastic intention, but a life-size work in marble is too monumental in scale and cost to be a simple lampoon.

The motive for the work is also an important interpretive factor. As a votive statue in a public or religious setting, it would recognize the giver's involvement in the cult and its activities. As a privately commissioned work for a private setting, though, it and other "genre figures" might be purely decorative, or perhaps a reflection of a philosophical type of rustic simplicity. Even the question of originality influences our analysis. If the original is indeed a Hellenistic work, whether votive or private, the motivation behind the production of the copies might be different, as the patrons and cultural context for the copies would be Roman, not Alexandrian.

The interpretive issue is further complicated by the problem of looking for Greek originals through Roman copies, treating works as Roman copies rather than Roman originals to recover lost Greek copies, as we saw in Chapter Two. Although it is undoubtedly true that Romans did purchase some replicas of Greek works and placed Greek originals in their buildings and gardens, the meaning that they derived from them would have varied from the original work and from what a Greek viewer might have thought.

Poststructuralism

We may never be able to arrive at a full understanding of the old woman, but it is a good example of the hermeneutic idea that meaning will shift with the change in historical circumstances and that context is critical in narrowing the range of likely interpretations. This is the stance taken by **poststructuralism**, which developed in reaction to the virtually limitless possibilities of semiotic interpretation and the tendency of structuralism to relegate the wide variety of individual stories or motifs to a small number of broad categories.

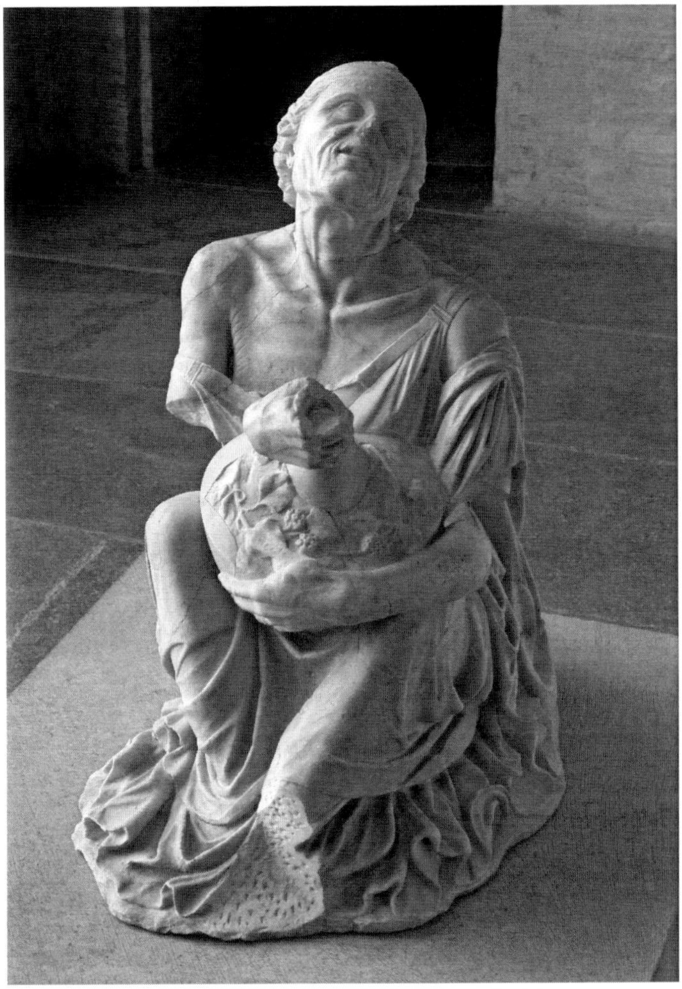

Figure 39. "Drunken Old Woman." Probably Roman copy of Hellenistic original of uncertain date. Munich, Glyptothek, GL437. Photo: Renate Kühling. Staatliche Antikensammlungen und Glyptothek München.

We can see the importance of a contextual approach to meaning by considering the problem of interpreting a vase (Figure 40) with Boreas, god of the north wind, chasing Oreithyia, an Athenian maiden who was the daughter of Erechtheus and later bore to Boreas two sons with wings, Zetes and Calais. Iconographically, the scene has been interpreted along two lines. The subject became very popular in Athenian art during the Early Classical period, very likely as a result of the Athenian victory over the Persians at the Battle of Salamis in 480 BCE, when the north wind aided the city's fleet by wrecking the Persian fleet at Artemision. Boreas's pursuit of an Athenian woman and fathering children with her shows his prior

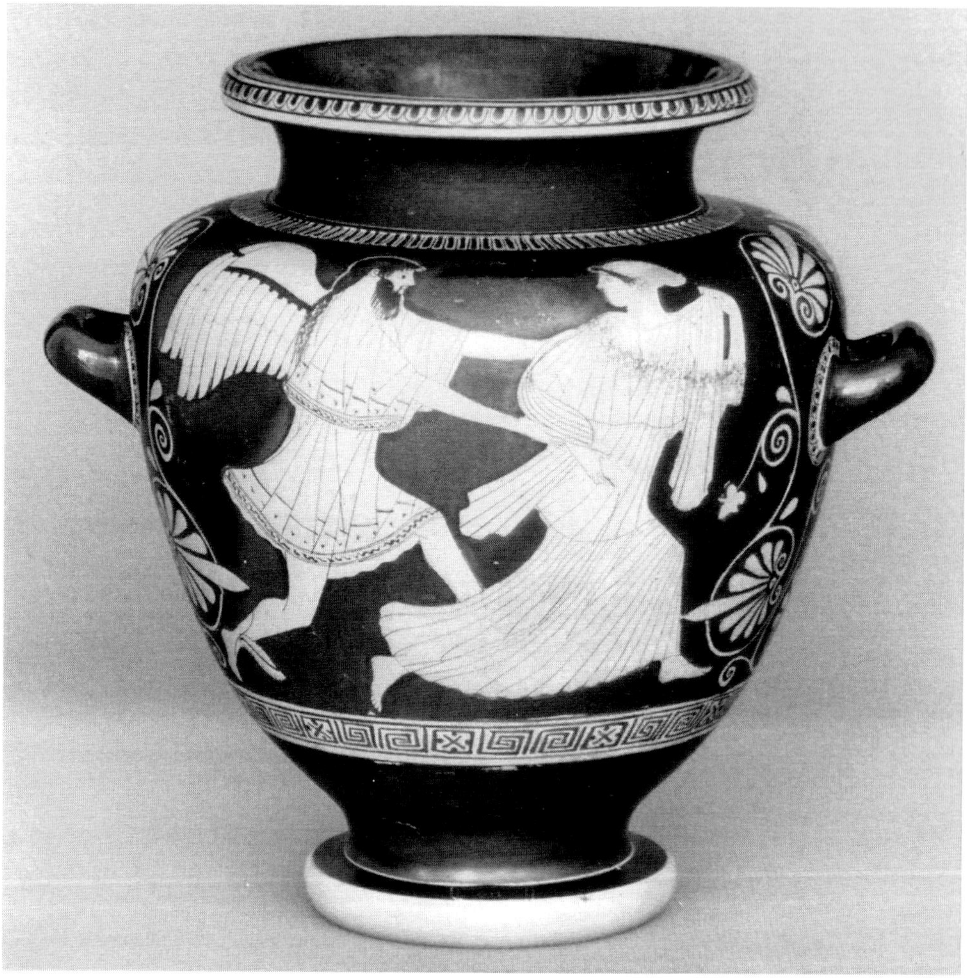

Figure 40. Attic red-figure stamnos attributed to the Deepdene Painter, c. 470–460 BCE. *Boreas chasing Oreithyia. Karlsruhe, Badisches Landesmuseum, B1904. Photo: Badisches Landesmuseum.*

connection to Athens, so the scenes of the pursuit are metaphors for the god's aid and good will at Salamis. The theme is one of several in which male gods (especially Zeus, Poseidon, and Hermes) pursue mortal women; they have been interpreted as analogies for men's possession of women through abduction and marriage, and, more generally, male dominance of the world itself. There have been some recent challenges to this line of interpretation, however. One thought is that the themes are, in the words of Sian Lewis, "imagery of the rite of passage . . . whether it be funerary, nuptial, or initiatory."[15] Mary Lefkowitz points, more specifically, to the funerary connotations of the subject by noting that the gods' pursuit takes

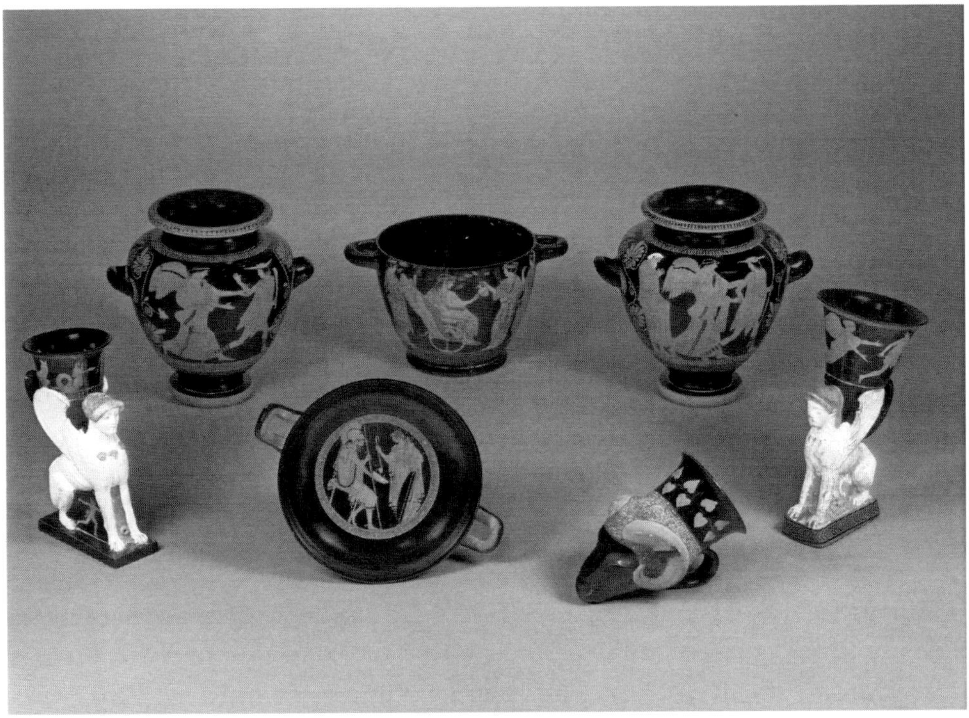

Figure 41. Vases from Brygos Tomb. London, British Museum (also Karlsruhe, Badisches Landesmuseum and New York, Metropolitan Museum of Art). Photo: © Trustees of the British Museum.

their victims away from their families and confirms the power of the gods generally over mortals.

One difficulty of interpretation here is the assumption that a series of works with the same subject must have a very similar meaning. Context, however, would suggest that there is more variation possible. A theme such as pursuit could have multiple possibilities for meaning that would be narrowed through the action of the viewer.

In the case of the Boreas stamnos, it was one of seven vases from a tomb in Capua discovered in the nineteenth century; the vases have been reassembled by Dyfri Williams (Figure 41).[16] The Boreas stamnos was one of two in the assemblage by the same artist, the Deepdene Painter. All the vases are Attic and belong to the same general time frame. Some, such as two large sphinx rhytoi, were almost certainly funerary in their intention. Other vases, such as the stamnoi and two drinking cups, were not necessarily funereal in their intention, and could have been used ritualistically, domestically, or in a symposion. One factor that unites both funerary and general-use vessels from the tomb is that pursuit themes are quite plentiful among the vases. Three vases show the goddess Eos, who pursues the young hunter Kephalos on the two stamnoi and the young shepherd Tithonos on a rhyton. Satyrs pursue Hera on one side of the kylix and Iris on the other. With the Boreas pursuit, this makes a total of six pursuit scenes on four of the seven vases.

Because the vases were from several different workshops and not created as a set in Athens, their selection for the tomb in Italy was the result of action on the part of the family who organized the funeral and collected the grave goods. This would suggest that the vase with Boreas was selected for a funerary context, and that pursuit themes generally were appropriate subject matter for that purpose in this particular assemblage.

However, this does not mean that the Boreas stamnos was intended solely for that purpose. The Deepdene Painter decorated a number of stamnoi, and the decoration needed to appeal to a wide range of potential purchasers. For example, a stamnos is frequently seen in pictures of Dionysiac ritual. In a ritualistic context, one could look at the pursuit pictures as showing the gods having close relationships with with mortals, rather than taking them away forever. Indeed, on another stamnos by the same painter, the Boreas pursuit is paired with Dionysos and a maenad. Generally, the workshop's vases feature a mixture of subjects: pursuit, ritual activity, domestic scenes, and warriors arming and departing. Most of the painter's vases for which we have findspots are scattered through both Greek and Etruscan areas of Italy, so it would appear to have been a practical approach for the painter to put a variety of scenes with broad appeal on the vases. This would allow purchasers to make their own selection based on the purchase circumstances; a vase for a tomb would make the funerary implications of the theme become the determined interpretation. If we had found the Boreas vase in a different context, such as Athens, we might instead focus on the specifically Athenian elements of the picture, making its selection by a purchaser a reflection of civic feeling or patriotism in the decades during which Athens continued to fight with the Persians.

The implication of a poststructural approach is that meaning is determined by both the creation of a work and its use, and these meanings are not necessarily the same. It allows for multiple meanings to be possible for an image, but limits their range on the basis of the contextual circumstances. Thus the same subject would have potentially different meanings if placed on a sympotic vessel, a gem set into a ring, a tomb, a votive gift, or a temple relief, whether for local consumption or export, and so on. In other words, we need to think about the *agenda* behind the creation, selection, or viewing

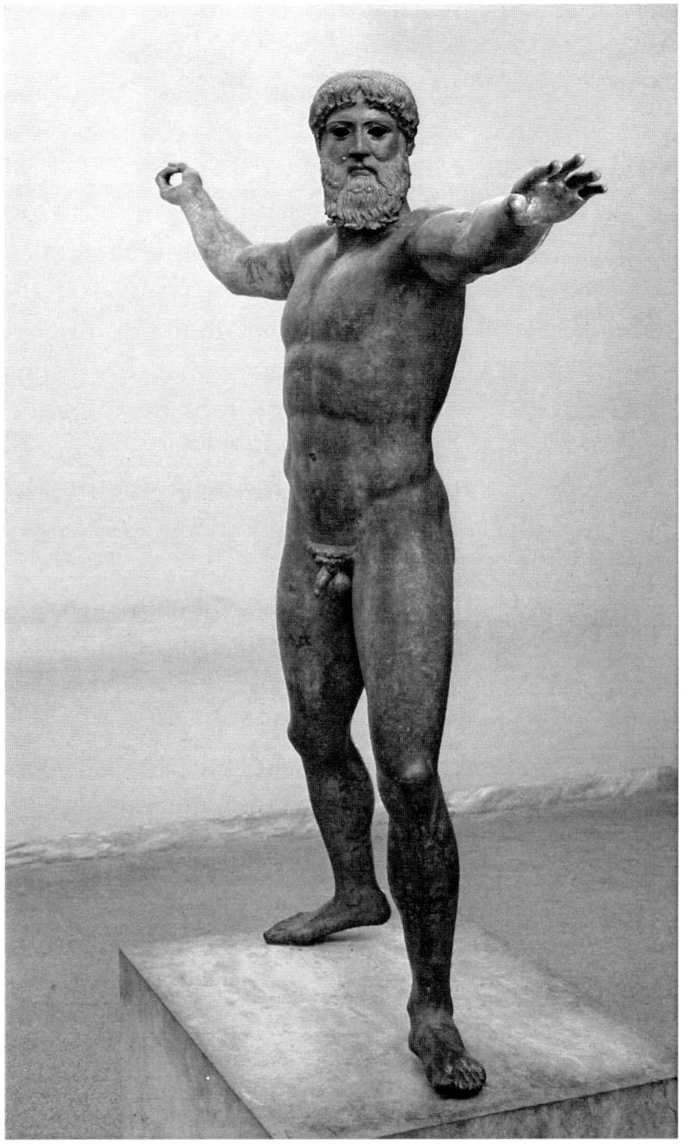

Figure 42. Bronze god found off Cape Artemision, c. 460–450 BCE. Athens, National Archaeological Museum, Br. 15161. Photo: Erich Lessing/Art Resource, New York.

of a work, and how this affects its interpretation. We will review these contexts in more detail in Chapter Four.

Unfortunately, precise knowledge of the context for a specific work of art is frequently difficult to obtain. For example, the statue of the god found off Cape Artemision has an archaeological context, but we do not know what its original context was (Figure 42). Given the scale and medium, it is likely to have been a significant public work, perhaps a dedication in a sanctuary or agora of a city. In the absence of a weapon, we are not even sure whether the god is Zeus or Poseidon. Still, we can think about what the original viewing circumstances would have been like and how a viewer was meant to confront the work in its original setting. The work is shown in profile in the middle of its gallery today and in most illustrations in books. The arms of the statue are much too long to be lifelike in that view, but such formal problems disappear if we look at the statue from the front. From this vantage point, the difficulties of the too-long arm disappear owing to the foreshortened angle, which would suggest that this is the proper view. From here, one can also see that the god is looking straight at the viewer and, more menacing, is sighting the viewer with his left hand while pointing the missing weapon in his right hand at the same spot. In other words, the viewer becomes the potential target of the god and confronts the power of the god directly.

Looking ahead at the representation of the Tyrannicides on an oinochoe fragment in Boston (see Figure 51), we can see that such a viewing point in front is intended for that sculpture group by the small pillar with beveled top in front of the group. Inscriptions, generally, are written on the front side of statues, usually on their base, so this aspect could be considered as a likely vantage point for a sculpture unless the composition of the statue contradicts this assumption. If a viewer were, therefore, reading the inscription for the Tyrannicides, then he or she would be in the position of Hipparchos, and thus making the viewer the target of the attack as well. One can further understand the dynamic nature of a viewer looking at a work of art by noting that a viewer is also meant to read inscriptions aloud, thus activating the work verbally as well as visually.

This more dynamic consideration of viewing and its context could also be applied to vases, which were not meant to be static objects in display cases, but objects moving through space as they were used. The picture on the interior of a kylix filled with wine will be glimpsed only in the act of drinking, and then only briefly before the wine would spill over the side. The pictures on the exterior of drinking cups are as much for fellow drinkers, if not more so, as they cannot be seen by the drinker while imbibing. In other words, one aspect of context is to consider the mechanics of the viewing experience and how it limits, frames, or gives a sequence to the viewing experience, and thereby can direct our understanding of the meaning and impact of the work. We will explore aspects of context in Chapter Four.

Viewer Response

Another approach that is often included in discussions of hermeneutic or poststructural approaches is reader response theory. Here, one focuses not on the writer or the text per se, but on the interaction between the text and the reader. From the opening sentences of a story, a reader must try to make sense of the information and actions described in the text and examine how it might be symptomatic of the story as a whole. Readers select details that they think are significant and form what Umberto Eco called "macro-propositions" – that is, how these details will fit into the larger story. As they read, further details are added that may contradict the initial macro-propositions, necessitating their reformulation. As all works of literature are selective in what they recount, an engaged reader will have to consider not only the information that is received from reading, but also account for the omissions.

Viewer response follows a similar process, as can be seen in descriptions of real works in literary sources, or of imaginary works in poetic *ekphrasis*. If we analyze the structure of these accounts, one sees that the first stage of the viewing process is the identification of the subject matter. If the subject is familiar to the viewer, such as Neoptolemos killing Priam or Herakles wrestling the lion, the viewer can resort to a shorthand identification that corresponds to his or her experience or knowledge of the visual language before moving on to look at the details of the picture. However, if the viewer has trouble recognizing the subject matter quickly, there is a more detailed examination of the significant elements to identify a potential subject. Such difficulty could be a result of the story being obscure and not commonly found in art, or because the action is unfamiliar, or because a key element of the picture seems to contradict the normal formula for what the viewer might have guessed from first glance. What we have called the nucleus in the discussion of structural analysis appears to be the major concern in these accounts, along with any details of the figures in that nucleus.

Once the subject has been identified, the viewer, if looking further, seems to identify the main figures and their actions, noting attributes, costumes, attitude, expression, or inscriptions. What seems to attract additional attention from the viewer, in particular, are scenes that depart from standard representations. If the viewer engages even deeper with the work, the next step includes taking note of visual elements that seem to have symbolic or referential value, corresponding most closely to the indexes mentioned earlier. In these secondary and tertiary stages the viewer is frequently selective, picking out details that have direct, personal associations, such as gods from one's own city.

Following this process, one can see that each engagement with a work has the potential to be different based on the level of engagement and experience on the part of the viewer. It is possible for a viewer to construct a plausible and consistent interpretation of a work that contradicts the intended subject matter, but this interpretation may still be valid. Further, thinking about the viewing circumstances and process can help us to understand the complexity of the interpretive process.

An example of both a poststructural approach and one incorporating viewer response would be to look again at the Siphnian Treasury frieze (Figure 1). In hermeneutical terms, it is already an instructive example of a poststructural approach in that early explanations of the subject matter based on iconographic analysis proposed a subject (Sarpedon and Patroklos) based on a literary source that was shown to be incorrect based on the recovered inscriptions (Memnon and Achilles). We can also consider how it would have been presented to a viewer in its original context, on the "back" side of the building along the Sacred Way (see Figure 4). As the reconstruction drawing shows, the view of the building was initially obscured by another treasury. At first, only the northeast corner of the building would have been viewable, and viewers would have seen the right half of the frieze as a self-contained composition of warriors fighting before they saw the council of the gods on the left.

In iconographic studies, this left half was the key in identifying the subject because of the *psychostasis* (weighing of the fates/souls) by Zeus. However, it would be more likely for a viewer to have already made a guess about the subject matter before seeing that detail, based on the right half of the composition that he or she saw first. The frieze has inscriptions in letters about 3 cm in height. At that size, the legible viewing distance is less than 10 m. However, the viewer would be about 14 m away from the frieze on the Sacred Way at the point where he or she would have been able to see the nucleus of the scene, and would have been further away when first able to see the building at the east entrance to the precinct. There are no large details at that point distinguishing the frieze's specific subject from any of a number of warrior fights, so both Sarpedon versus Patroklos or Achilles versus Memnon are plausible hypotheses for a first glance. Whatever subject might be identified, it is likely that the viewer would have placed the victor on the left, as would be the convention in Greek art.

Continuing a few paces until the inscriptions could be read (and assuming the viewer could read and that the inscriptions were still legible), the viewer might then reformulate the identification and also note that the victor, Achilles, is on the right side. This is not a rare rearrangement, but one may wonder why. Here, one would consider the placement of the viewer relative to the frieze. By reversing the typical placement of the victor and the vanquished, the viewer is now on the same side as the victor in the composition, creating a spatial association between the narrative and viewer. Interestingly, the victorious figures in the north frieze (see Figure 5) along the Sacred Way go back to the left-to-right convention, but they are now moving in the same direction as the visitor proceeding to the Temple of Apollo. Thus the movement in both friezes is oriented to the viewer, suggesting a deliberate effort of engagement.

Proceeding a few steps further, the viewer would see, in its entirety, the remaining half of the composition, the council of the gods and the weighing of the souls. Zeus is on the left side, in a position in which he would be facing the viewer on the path below and in which the bronze scales would be clearly visible. With this detail, we might now consider that the gods control the fate of all mortals, even Achilles. Considering that a viewer coming to Delphi is seeking guidance from the oracle or is offering thanks to the gods for their benevolence, this reminder of mortality is nicely framed by the arrangement of the frieze's composition.

Poststructural Synthesis

How, then, might one construct a poststructural analysis? In some ways, one might argue that one must be both iconographer and semiotician and be cognizant of the history of interpretation. Unlike iconography, poststructuralism sees the potential for multiple meanings within the work, and regards the early hypothesis about the subject as plausible for a modern viewer as well as for an ancient visitor. Unlike semiotics, however, it looks at the details of the context to see how the range of interpretive possibilities was limited by the physical arrangement of the elements and the sequence of the viewing experience, and gives consideration to the habits of the ancient viewer. One might start, then, with the identification of the main subject matter, but noting all the potential ambiguities that might lead to alternative hypotheses. Next, one could consider all the elements of the viewing context: distance, legibility, framing, viewing circumstances and environment, timing, and others that may arise in individual cases. Even if the exact context is unknown, such as a drinking cup or the Artemision god in Figure 42, one can reconstruct at least some of the viewing context based on internal information. This would next require a reexamination of the initial hypothesis, either to replace or to supplement it and to consider the potential range of plausible interpretations.

We will conclude by looking at an Attic black-figure hydria showing the apotheosis of Herakles (Figure 43). The basic scene could be described as a chariot procession; Athena is readily identified by her aegis, helmet, and spear, Herakles by his club and lionskin, and Hermes behind the horse by his hat and winged boots. An unidentified woman stands mostly hidden by the head of the lead horse. Following his death, Herakles was granted immortal existence and a goddess, Hebe, as a new wife for his assistance to the gods; this scene represents his being brought to Olympos.

A more political interpretation of this subject for black-figure vases of the later sixth century BCE has been offered by John Boardman, who sees the basic scene as symbolizing the entrance of Peisistratos into Athens, probably some time in the 550s.[17] Peisistratos successfully became the tyrant of Athens from 546 until his death in 528, when he was succeeded by his sons Hippias and Hipparchos (who was killed by the Tyrannicides; see Figure 50). Before this, he had attempted to come to power through an elaborate entry by chariot into Athens. According to Herodotos, Peisistratos had Phye, an extraordinarily tall woman from the countryside, dressed up in armor. She then drove a chariot into town, with Peisistratos at her side. Heralds had preceded them into the city, proclaiming that Peisistratos was returning to Athens and that Athena herself was bringing him as her chosen one. Peisistratos did seem to have a temporary success at gaining power in Athens, but was soon expelled from the city. Boardman's hypothesis is that the scene of the apotheosis of Herakles became popular in Attic vase-painting as a result of this spectacle, following his final, successful return to power in 546.

Boardman's theory has met some resistance, particularly because such political symbolism is hard to find in the sixth century BCE, although it did exist in the fifth century. On iconographic grounds, his theory seems to have much against it. Many of the vases with the apotheosis of Herakles, as well as some other themes that Boardman also interprets with a Peisistratid gloss, were exported to Etruria. It is hard to imagine that an Etruscan viewer would be equipped to decode the subtext of a local Attic event a quarter-century after it happened. However, as we saw with pursuit scenes, it is possible to construct a local Athenian reading based on the selection of criteria that

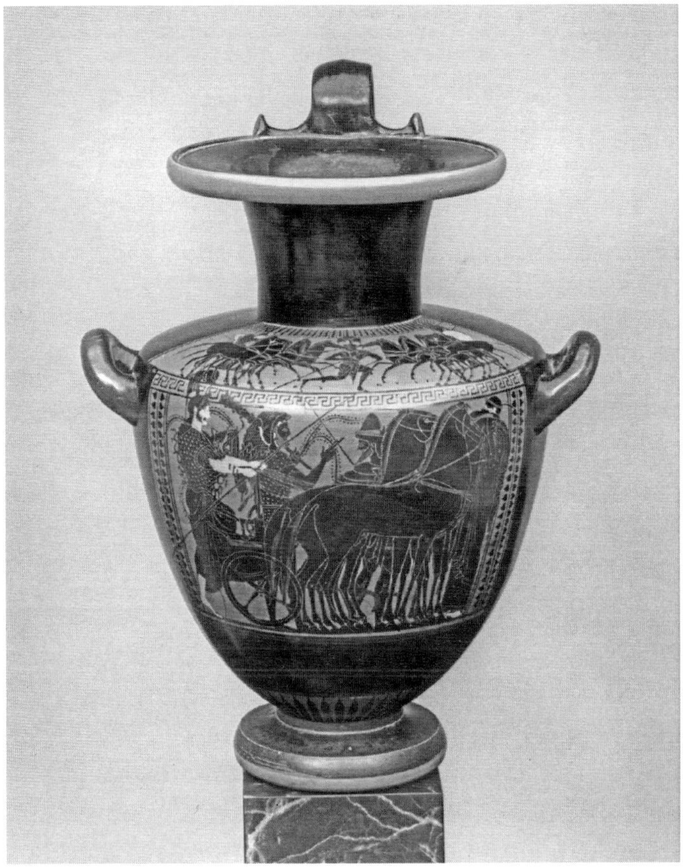

Figure 43. Attic black-figure hydria attributed to the Priam Painter, c. 510 BCE. Apotheosis of Herakles. Chazen Museum of Art, University of Wisconsin-Madison, Gift of Mr. and Mrs. Arthur J. Frank, 68.14.1. Photo: Museum.

could differ from the meaning to an Etruscan. Theoretically, it would be entirely possible that an Athenian would have been able to glimpse a double meaning in the subject that would be lost on a non-Athenian viewer, not unlike the way humor does not always translate well into another language.

Even if the Herakles-as-Peisistratos symbolism is plausible on semiotic grounds, we must consider whether the context makes it likely. In describing the incident, Herodotos comments that the Athenians, normally astute and realistic people, were utter fools in being duped by Peisistratos. The event is thus one that, in his mind, did not reflect well on the Athenians. It seems unlikely, in this light, that an Athenian would look at a picture of the apotheosis of Herakles as a positive piece of political propaganda unless he or she was a supporter of Peisistratos. Even in that case, though, the subject would represent a failed political effort; Peisistratos finally had to succeed in 546 through more traditional political means: armed troops. In these circumstances, it is hard to see that the apotheosis of Herakles would naturally meet the agenda of either pro- or anti-tyrant viewers.

One also must consider the means by which the scene would have been selected. For a political agenda to be conveyed, there needs to be control of the means of artistic or visual production, an issue we will consider further in discussing a Marxist approach in the next chapter. Outside of Panathenaic amphorae, commissioned for the prize oil in the quadrennial competitions, there is little evidence of political control of pottery production. Indeed, suitability for export was probably of greater concern for the producers of pottery, and on the vase here we also see a scene of warriors fighting, which could, like processions of gods or scenes with Herakles, have a universal appeal.

One argument against the Herakles–Peisistratos symbolism finds such politically symbolic meaning improbable for archaic Athens. However, thinking about the event suggests that political symbolism was indeed possible. It is unlikely that the Athenians were really duped. Rather, it seems more likely that Peisistratos had carefully prepared for his return by negotiations with powers inside the city, and that he chose a dramatic means for symbolizing his return. As political theater, it makes sense; Herodotos indicates that it also met without resistance, testimony to careful planning. That Peisistratos was expelled sometime afterward is more likely to have been the result of a falling out with his allies, rather than that Athenian citizens finally saw through the deception. This shows that sixth-century Athenians could and did get the symbolism of mythological metaphors, and the code that the heralds provided confirms this. However, for the apotheosis scenes on vases two or three decades later, it is harder to see the contextual circumstances that would suggest the intention that these scenes be read with a strongly Peisistratid agenda. Indeed, for a vase such as the one in Figure 43, dated around 510 BCE and likely done after the death of Peisistratos, one might see it more as subversive toward his son Hippias by mocking the successor's father, if one were to read it politically. On the whole, one needs to accept the plausibility of interpreting the apotheosis with a Peisistratid gloss, but in the absence of a stronger contextual framework, one would see it as improbable.

Developing a poststructural approach to meaning, therefore, depends much more strongly on a contextual analysis. The economics of artistic production and distribution, the ritualistic nature of its use or deployment, the ideology and social systems of its makers and users, and other elements of context will be the subject of the next chapter.

Further Reading

Iconography

On iconography, see Panofsky 1955 and D'Alleva 2005, 20–8.

The *Lexicon Iconographicum Mythologiae Classicae* (*LIMC*) is a fundamental source for any study of meaning. For overviews, see also Carpenter 1991, Shapiro 1994, and Woodford 2003.

There are many iconographic studies of Greek art, but two recent studies that are very clear as models for the approach are Neils 2001 and Oakley 2004. See also the essays in Moon 1983.

Narrative

On narrative, see Weitzmann 1947, Snodgrass 1982, Holliday 1993, Stansbury-O'Donnell 1999, and Steiner 2007.

On myth and genre, see Kannicht 1982 and Ferrari 2003.

On the relationship of literature and art, see Small 2003.

Semiotics

See generally Eagleton 1996, 84–109; D'Alleva 2006, 28–43; Barthes 1982, 211–7; and Eco 1979.

On the application to Greek art, see Sourvinou-Inwood 1991, esp. 29–98, and Ferrari 2002.

On gestures, see McNiven 1982 and 2000, Boegehold 1999, and Stansbury-O'Donnell 2006, 128–229.

Structural Analysis

See Barthes 1982, 251–95.

On the application of structural analysis and structuralism to Greek art, see Stewart 1983 and 1987, Stansbury-O'Donnell 1999, 18–53, and Stansbury-O'Donnell 2006, 12–24.

On the interpretation of early Greek narrative, see Snodgrass 1980b, 1987, and 1998.

Information Theory

On information theory and its application to Greek art, see Steiner 2007, esp. 17–73.

Parody and Humor

There has been much recent discussion of this area. See Mitchell 2004 and 2009; Steiner 2007, 194–211; Walsh 2009; and Stansbury-O'Donnell 2009.

Hermeneutics

See generally Eagleton 1996, 53–64; D'Alleva 2005, 122–31; and Gadamer 1989.

On the hermeneutics of vase paintings, see Schmidt and Oakley 2009, and the overview of Lissarrague 2009 in that volume. See also, in German, Junker 2005.

On Roman originals and copies, Greek originals, and the issues of interpretation see Marvin 1989 and 2008, esp. 121–247.

Poststructuralism

See generally Eagleton 1996, 110–30 and D'Alleva 2005, 136–49. Bérard et al. 1989 have been influential in applying new models to the study of Greek art. See also Osborne 1991 and 1994 and Stansbury-O'Donnell 1999, 54–117.

On reading inscriptions see generally Svenbro 1993; also Steiner 2007, 68–73, with recent discussions.

Reader/Viewer Response

See Eagleton 1996, 64–77 and D'Alleva 2005, 113–6. See also Eco 1979.

On applications of this approach to Greek art see Castriota 1992, esp. 15–16, and Stansbury-O'Donnell 1999, 54–70.

On Peisistratos and Herakles, see Boardman 1972 and 1975, 1978a, 1978b for other political interpretations. Contra see Moon 1983 and Cook 1987. See also Sinos 1998 for a ritualistic interpretation of the same subject matter.

General Studies

A number of other recent books that explore specific subjects and place them within a broader context are useful starting points for developing interpretive models; some of these are also the result of exhibitions. See, for example, Barringer 2001, Buitron and Cohen 1992, Bundrick 2005, Hedreen 1992 and 2001, Kaltsas and Shapiro 2008, Neils 1992, Neils and Oakley 2003, Oakley and Sinos 1993, Reeder 1995, and Vermeule 1979.

Four

Context

In the previous two chapters, we considered the style and meaning of an artwork. In the approaches that we outlined, the starting point was the object or artifact itself, which we then placed within a broader realm of objects, workshops, or systems of symbols and interpretation. As the discussion of poststructuralism indicated, however, context has a strong effect on the meaning of a work. In this chapter we will reverse the direction of analysis by considering the broader context that produces an object or provides the setting in which it is used. Indeed, one can think of an artwork as a commodity or functional thing: something that is made, exchanged, used, and potentially reexchanged and reused; something that maps out economic, social, and religious practices and relationships.

To begin, we focus on a Marxist or materialist approach to the work of art, considering broadly the economic factors that provide the infrastructure for the making of art, and then examine a few case studies. Following this is a generalized description of some of the main categories of contexts and a discussion of how these can affect our understanding of a work's appearance, meaning, and importance. We then consider some case studies about how politics – the systems of government and ideology – can play a role in the production and message of art, and then we consider ritual and religion. We also look at two more recent approaches that bring these broader issues of production, distribution, use, and the like back to the specific object: agency and object biography.

Marxism: Production and Distribution

The focus on the economic aspects of art has generally come under the heading of Marxist art history, although other terms, such as socioeconomic or social historical analysis, have been used. Although known for his ideological arguments for communism, Karl Marx himself discussed the production of art and the relationship between the maker and the patron, including how the control of production exerted control over the content and ideology of art. Social and political systems develop their authority by their control over production, making art a social and political, as well as an economic, product. Although the use of the term *Marxism* as a theoretical approach is sometimes clouded by associations with the politics of the Cold War, its consideration of the broad role of the economy in shaping social and political systems makes it a convenient term of reference.

As an approach for art history, we look at the range of factors or questions that help us to understand the economic factors behind the work of art. These will be divided into four broad categories: production, patronage, value, and distribution. We then look at several case studies to outline how the questions might be considered in broad terms and how concrete data might be developed to answer them. It should be remembered, however, that the actual, individual circumstances are always more varied and complicated than we can now determine, just as individual economic decisions are sometimes different from national economic trends today. As more data become available from excavations and other studies, we will be able to develop a more nuanced understanding of the economic context of Greek art in the future.

Production

First, we should consider the factors involved in the physical production of a work. Broadly speaking, one needs to consider raw materials, manufacturing and technical processes that transform raw materials into the finished product, the facilities that are necessary for these, and, finally, the labor and skill needed to carry them out.

Regarding *materials*, we should consider whether they are available locally or need to be imported. Producing marble sculpture, for example, is easier and cheaper if a marble quarry is close at hand, whereas shipping marble overseas or up to a remote location will make it considerably more expensive as a medium. In such a case, a locally available limestone might serve the purpose just as well and be more affordable. Clay is generally available throughout the Mediterranean, so much ceramic production is usually local, but the quality of clay and the final product will vary widely.

Even though clay may be a common and easily accessible material, it, like most materials used to make art, requires *refinement* to make it usable. Clay must be dug and then sedimented and refined before it can be used. This is not very demanding technologically, but other raw materials, such as metal ores, require more complicated mining, smelting, and treatment. Mining is a hazardous occupation, and the amount of metal that is yielded from ore is small. These factors, combined with the limited number of places that have usable quantities of ore, make metal very expensive as a medium and gives it a higher intrinsic cost than clay. Metal can also be reused by melting it down, whereas clay, once it has been fired, has far more limited potential for reuse, making metal more valuable after it has been refined. Ivory and bone as materials do not require so much in the way of transformation to be used, but the limited and distant sources of ivory, as well as its durable qualities, make it a more expensive medium for a small plaque, for instance, than bone or wood. Supply as well as visual qualities, then, create a hierarchy of values among the media used to make art.

After the raw source has been refined into useful material, *manufacturing and technical processes* transform the material into the finished product. For each material, there is a variety of processes that have an impact on the production and final form of the work. For example, ceramic vessels can be shaped by hand from clay using coils, but the use of a wheel (whether slow or fast) speeds production and can allow for more intricate and thinner shapes. Firing the vessels requires a kiln, but the control of temperature and airflow can produce very different effects, such as red-figure and black-figure pottery. Bronze sculpture has several processes, from small, solid-cast objects to molds, hammered sheets, and lost-wax processes. In the case of bronze sculpture, new techniques such as lost wax provided the opportunity to create monumental figural sculpture that would have been impossible with the solid-cast techniques of the Geometric period. The earliest large bronze figures, however, do not differ dramatically from their contemporary stone or terracotta counterparts in the Archaic period. As we saw in Chapter Two, the earliest red-figure vases are very similar in style to contemporary black-figure works. The value of a change in material and process, then, is not necessarily a result of stylistic development. Rather, it may be that the material costs of a monumental bronze sculpture, compared with the costs of a stone counterpart, gave it a higher economic and/or social value for the artist and patron. So, too, the initial uniqueness of a new medium may have created a value in the market for its producer ahead of its stylistic potential.

Facilities and infrastructure are also important to consider. The production of small-scale metalwork, for example, does not require a substantial and permanent physical workshop, and some metalwork production might work well in temporary spaces or small spaces, such as a room in a house. This would make some media and objects less tied to a specific place, whereas large-scale stone or bronze work would require larger amounts of space, open as well as covered, to accommodate production. Kilns can be built in a variety of locations, but it is more efficient to have a dedicated place to build and rebuild them. Pottery production would require a significant amount of storage space for the greenware before firing, and for the fired ware before any finishing work. In none of these cases does one need a vast amount of space, such as a modern factory. However, the need for a dedicated space with ample working and storage areas, as well as access to open spaces for kilns or forges, lends itself to stability in terms of places of production, at least over the short run. In some sense, any operation could be relocated, but smaller-scale production could be more fluid in its setup.

Labor has been a key element in all of the aspects of production that we have considered so far; in a Marxist analysis, we need to consider how the artistic workshop was organized and the role of *skill* in the production of objects. Large workshops were assembled for some monumental building projects. For example, Andrew Stewart has estimated that there could have been a little more than fifty workers employed on the Parthenon pediments at one time.[1] Such large-scale projects were not normal, however,and much smaller workshops of a few individuals would have been more typical for production. It is likely that there was a mixture of skilled workers, who made the molds, carved the stone, or painted the pots, and some unskilled labor, probably in many cases slaves, who performed the heavier tasks of moving stone, tending the forge, digging the clay, and so on. In some cases, as we saw with artists' signatures in Chapter Two, there seems to have been some division of labor, such as making the vase and decorating it. Such small workshops could also add labor as needed for specific projects that were too large to complete on a schedule. The owner of the workshop was probably also the head artist, and would train new artists in a master–apprentice system. In many cases these would have been family members who would continue the workshop into a new generation.

Artists, with their tools and skills, were also movable. Sculptors could set up temporary workshops for large civic projects such as the Parthenon or the Temple of Asklepios in Epidauros, or emigrate to set up a more permanent workshop in a new territory with good local sources of materials. Many of the painters and potters in Athens were apparently immigrants or metics, to judge by their names, such as Lydos (the Lydian). Other evidence shows that metalworkers from the Near East worked in Crete and elsewhere in Greece, and written sources mention artists traveling for commissions. This mobility would help to spread techniques, styles, and visual ideas through the Greek world. The small size of a workshop would facilitate flexibility in meeting needs, but it also complicates identifying the work of individuals and their working conditions or history.

Patronage

The starving artist, though a romantic stereotype, would not be considered a successful artist. We need to consider how artists were compensated for their work and how the structure of payment could affect their production. In general, we can refer to the person paying for the artwork as the patron, but this is a broad term that covers a wide range of potential relationships to the artist. First, we can consider the range of patrons and types, which would include civic entities such as a city and its government, groups with a common purpose such as traders, or individuals. Patrons would also vary widely in their wealth and control of political resources, so a king as a patron would be both an individual and a civic authority.

This is fairly straightforward, but considering the patron and his or her resources also means that there is a variety of potential relationships between artist and patron. For example, were artworks made on *commission*, or sold *over-the-counter* by the artist, either individually as in a direct retail sale, or in batches to a wholesaler or trader? In an over-the-counter sale, the artist would be assuming more of the risk of production, as there was no guarantee of a patron or customer for the finished product. The artist would need to be aware of the market demand and calculate what might attract a purchaser. Would an innovative technique, style, subject, or shape distinguish the artist's production in the marketplace, or would these be wasted efforts if no buyer emerged for the wares? Should an artist keep the work simple, keeping labor and material costs low, and sell in large quantities for lower prices? Or should the artist devote more time and skill to create a more distinctive work that could fetch a higher price, while keeping material costs relatively low? This would make a larger profit margin on a single work, but the artist would be making and selling fewer works overall.

There was, in some ways, less risk involved with commissions. Even though a commission might have a greater financial guarantee, it also meant that the artist had to be more directly accommodating to the desires of the patron. Content and composition could well be determined by the patron's wishes, and if the patron were insisting on a deadline for production, this could impose restrictive conditions on the artist to meet these needs. Commissions were probably necessary for work in more expensive materials, as it is less likely that most workshops would have had sufficient capital to have large stocks of materials such as gold and silver, and limited quantities of less precious materials, such as imported marble and bronze, on hand.

In addition to these models, it is also possible that artists could be retained – that is, paid a salary or *retainer* for their services. This would be the case in large, state-controlled workshops or in employment as a court artist for a royal household. In the latter case, this might be a lucrative and prestigious appointment, but artists in large workshops were probably compensated at a relatively normative salary and would have had less control over their production than in the other two models.

These three broad models of economic relationships between patron and artist are not mutually exclusive. The retainer model was relatively rare in the Greek world, but it might be an option for short periods of time, particularly because labor was relatively mobile. Small workshops could do work on both commissions and over-the-counter products, perhaps adding extra labor to meet the increased demand from a commission or an especially large batch sale to a wholesaler/trader. Indeed, we should probably regard the organization of labor and workshops as both fluid and complex, responding to opportunities and both competing and cooperating with other workshops in different situations.

Value

Studies of other periods of art history have explored the relative proportion of materials, labor (the hours of work in production), and the skill level in the value of a work of art. Luxury materials, such as gold, silver, and ivory, will always command a high value, both monetarily as well as in the impression made on the viewer. The inventories of sanctuaries such as Delphi were filled with precious dedications, such as the six gold kraters sent by King Gyges of Lydia (reigned c. 685–657 BCE) and kept in the Corinthian Treasury at Delphi. Herodotos (1.14) records that these weighed thirty talents, and that they were called "Gygian by the people in honor of the donor."[2] The value of dedications of gold are often expressed in terms of their material value and the name of the donor, but only rarely in terms of the name of the artist. With precious metals, material would seem to be more highly valued than labor or skill, although Herodotos does note that a silver krater in the pronaos of the Temple of Apollo at Delphi is said to be the work of Theodoros of Samos, and that "it impresses me as a work of more than average quality." Still, the huge size of the krater (reputedly more than 4,000 gallons) and its material are the first qualities noted by Herodotos.

Materials, however, were not the sole determinants of value. Textiles, according to the literary sources, were also highly valued. Some pigments might have been more expensive, but the value of the textiles lay in the quality and fineness of their work, both in the labor used to refine and dye the raw materials and in the labor taken to weave the cloth into the final product. Plutarch records that Alexander the Great had a mantle that was fancier than his armor, a work of the artist Hellikon and a gift of the city of Rhodes. It would seem, then, that there was sometimes recognition of skill that made a work special and that might bring a great value to the work beyond its materials and labor. Certainly some Classical painters and sculptors were reputed to be noted for both their skill and their wealth, suggesting that in some cases skill might bring financial recognition and enhanced value for a work. Given the relative scarcity of our sources, though, we should probably regard these cases of extreme artistic worth as the exceptions rather than the rule. Most often, skillful labor probably achieved a greater value than unskillful labor, but the premium would have been fairly modest.

A work is valuable only if someone commissions or purchases it, and we might well ask what value a work of art might have for its owner compared with a plain, undecorated version. Michael Baxandall nicely summarized some of the reasons for owning art in fifteenth-century Italy that we may adapt here.[3] A major reason for investing in art would be the glory and honor that it would confer, whether to the gods, to the city, or to one's self and family (or all of these). A second reason would be the status that it could convey because of its value, rarity, splendor, and the like. A third would be personal pleasure, an appreciation of beauty and what is finely made and designed. Finally, the utility of the work would also give it value, particularly for works, such as pottery and textiles, that have a function. These reasons can overlap with one another, and to the degree that they do, we can consider the greater willingness of a patron to invest more heavily in a work.

Distribution

Last, we should consider the distribution of art and its eventual contexts. We have already noted the mobility of some materials for the production of art and of artists themselves to places where large projects or markets would provide employment, but the artwork, too, could be mobile. One of the first aspects of distribution to consider would be whether the artwork was distributed locally or exported. In the former case, the workshop might have sold directly to the public, either at the workplace or at the agora or marketplace in the town. It is also possible that local merchants or agents sold the work of several shops in the same place, either on consignment or retail, having paid a wholesale price. Locally consumed wares would have several general types of contexts as their ultimate destinations: work for the household, including the symposion; goods and markers to go with graves and funerary practices; works given as votive offerings in sanctuaries; works used publicly in sanctuaries and their rituals; and works for the civic areas of the city, such as memorials or civic decoration. Patronage for these could vary widely, from modest to rich individuals and civic or religious groups for larger-scale projects.

Exported works would fulfill many of the same types of functions: domestic, funerary, votive, ritualistic, or civic. The expense of transportation, whether by land or by sea, would be magnified by the loss of goods from accidents and wrecks, all of which would add to the cost of the work compared with those in the local market. Whether exported work was valued at its destination for its exoticism; the quality of its materials, style, or content; or its artistry and skill, the value is likely to have varied. In the past, for example, it was thought that Etruscans valued Athenian pottery because of its great artistry. It seems more probable that the Etruscans may have been eclectic in their taste and that Athenian pottery was collected as part of an expression of cosmopolitanism.[4] In some cases, it is the taste of an export market that would seem to have driven the choices of artists at the production centers. Shapes such as the Attic Nikosthenic amphora imitate Etruscan bucchero ware, and some types of pottery, such as Tyrrhenian amphorae, were made in Athens mostly for the Etruscan market.

To consider this relationship of the artist to a distant customer, we must consider how the artist's production reached the market.[5] Merchants and traders would have controlled most of this trade, as they had access to shipping. Further, they would have been in a position to trade the product for a range of goods to ship back to Athens, potentially turning a profit on both ends of the transaction. Indeed, we should consider that art was one of many commodities traded and that the pattern of distribution would vary by the itinerary of the trader. In some cases, it would seem that there were batches of artwork that were distributed *point-to-point* for sale in one place. In such cases, the trader would have purchased a large consignment from a workshop, selecting what would likely sell in the market, which might have been limited to a narrow range of goods, such as drinking cups or lekythoi.

Other traders would seem to have been more *itinerant*, buying and selling wares at a series of stops. Given the potential variety of customers, such a trader would have considered a wider range of works for stock, keeping in mind the varied tastes and needs of the communities being visited. The means by which such traders acquired their goods was also likely to have varied. It is reasonable to expect that some traders had continuing and repeated relationships with specific workshops, especially if they came to a production center like Athens regularly. Other, less regular traders might have shopped at workshops, but there is also evidence that there were large emporia in Piraeus, the port of Athens. It is entirely possible, given the seasonal pattern of trading, that these emporia could have been held at regular intervals and that workshops would bring samples or works there to appeal to traders. Smaller and lighter goods would fit most readily into this model, whereas trade in large stone and bronze work would have a closer relationship between the trader and workshop.

There were other wares that were distributed throughout the ancient world, such as Corinthian pottery, terracotta figures, and even marble sculpture during the Hellenistic period. The same general considerations about the structure of distribution and its potential variables would apply.

Some Case Studies

The generalities sketched in the previous sections need some concrete data to arrive at some specific answers about how the economic context shaped the production of art. Unfortunately, such information – such as sales records, inventories, and correspondence – that helps historians of more recent periods to develop their analyses is notably lacking for Greek art when compared with modern art. The scarcity of such information also leads to the risk of creating too simple a picture, masking what was likely a more fluid and complex matrix in which art was made and distributed. With that warning, we can still look at a few situations to make a preliminary sketch of the market that might serve as a model as more information becomes available. We begin by considering the payments for the reliefs on the frieze of the Erechtheion in Athens from the later fifth century BCE, and then turn to the production of a slightly later grave relief from the same city. We then consider the potential value of red-figure pottery from Athens.

To begin, we can look at some of the sculptural work on the Acropolis in Athens. As a public project using funds from the city, the accounts of the building program were inscribed on marble slabs, which survive in fragmentary and weathered form. Of particular interest are the payments made in 408/7–407/6 BCE for marble figures of the Erechtheion frieze:

> . . . the man holding the spear: 60 drachmas.
> Phyromachos of Kephisia for the young man with the breastplate: 60 drachmas.
> Praxias living in Melite, for the horse and the man who is visible behind it and who strikes its flank: 120 drachmas.
> Antiphanes from Kerameis, the chariot, the young man, and the horse being harnessed: 240 drachmas.
> Mynnion living in Argyle, the horse and the man striking it and the stele which he added later: 127 drachmas.
> Sosklos living in Alopeke, the man holding the bridle: 60 drachmas.
> Hiasos of Kollytos, the woman and the small girl pressed against her: 80 drachmas.
> Total sum for the making of the images: 3,315 drachmas.[6]

The individual figures are about 49 cm high and were made as high reliefs set onto the darker limestone background of the frieze, rather than being part of the frieze block itself (Figure 44). This would mean that the figures would not necessarily need to have been carved on the site itself, but could have been made in a local workshop on specification and then brought to the site.

The names of the sculptors who received payment indicate that they included both Attic citizens, as indicated by the genitive phrasing "of Kephisia" (or "from Kerameis"), the name of their *deme* or ancestral home. Others are metics, foreign workers in Athens, who are indicated by the expression "living in Melite" (or Argyle or Alopeke) – that is, resident in a deme but not belonging to it as a citizen. In other sections of the Erechtheion accounts, slaves are indicated by association with the name of their master. The payments for the sculptors, though, do not distinguish between citizen and metic status. Each sculptor is paid according to the size of the relief at the basic rate of sixty drachmas for a single adult figure. A figure with a horse, which would have some overlap, gets a double amount of 120 drachmas; a woman with a child fetches a one-and-one-third payment. The scale of the works, about one-third of life-size, would project to about one-sixth of the labor for a full statue in the round, which has been generally estimated to take about a full year's work.[7] At that amount of labor, it would appear that the sculptors were paid about one drachma for a day's work. As sources for the period indicate, this would have been about standard for craft wages during the fifth century BCE. As they were paid a set amount based on size, it would be possible for a more efficient or skillful sculptor to work more quickly and take on additional projects, such as a gravestone, simultaneously, thereby generating some additional income over the course of a year.

Although the Erechtheion accounts are silent on the timing of the contracts, as part of a building project there was likely a deadline for completion of the work. In the case of another Erechtheion tablet that records payment to the encaustic painters working on the interior moldings of the building, the rate was calculated at five obols per foot. With six obols equaling one drachma, this works out to almost a drachma, and the contractor, a metic named Dionysiodoros living in Melite, was paid thirty drachmas for the project.[8] However, the account mentions a citizen, Herakleides of Oa, as the guarantor of the contract. This was an individual who would essentially provide an insurance policy in case the work was not completed according to schedule or to specifications, in which case the city would be reimbursed and another artist hired to complete the work without cost to the patron. What kind of premium the guarantor would ask from the artist is not known, but it would certainly add to the cost of the work for the artist, while leaving the payment from the patron fixed. Other sites, such as Delphi and Epidauros, had similar arrangements; this could have been a practice for private commissions, too. The guarantee placed limitations on the artist and potential fines for not meeting the terms of the contract, demonstrating some of the control that a patron could exert.

One final note of interest is the payment to Mynnion of 127 drachmas for a horse and human. The additional seven drachmas would appear to result from the addition of a stele to the relief, apparently after the work was completed. An adjustment requested by a patron is not unusual, although it is more difficult to accomplish in stone. This could be done by adding material to a block through inserting a slab with a pinion or dowel into a socket, or by removing additional material and reworking figures while not damaging the existing work. Based on the additional payment of seven

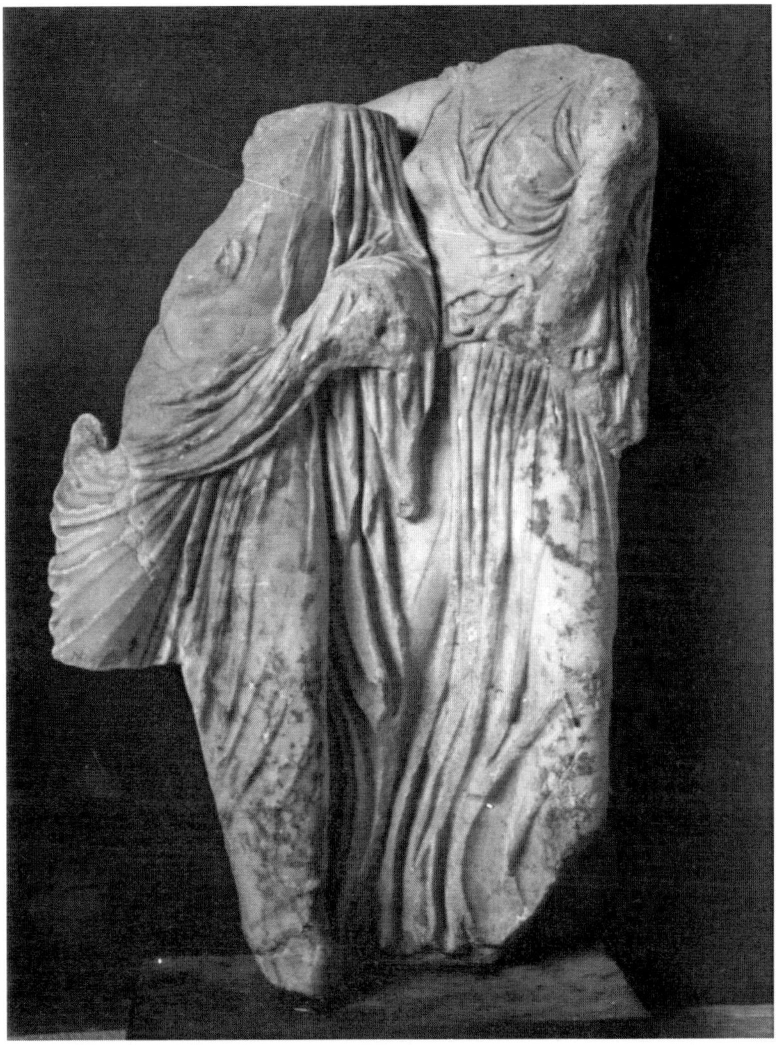

Figure 44. Figure from the frieze of the Erechtheum in Athens, c. 410–407 BCE. Athens, Akropolis Museum. Photo Copyright Deutsches Archäologisches Institut Athen, Neg. Nr. D-DAI-ATH-Akropolis 1071. Photo: G. Welter.

drachmas, it seems that the change required about a week's additional work to carry out the modification.

This sketch of the relative wages for architectural sculpture is consistent with accounts of payments for the Parthenon and the Temple of Asklepios at Epidauros. We can use it to get an idea of another type of sculptural product in the Classical period, the grave stele. More than 1,000 grave reliefs from Athens survive, and are found in museums throughout the world. A relatively early example from around 400 BCE is the grave stele of Hegeso, which

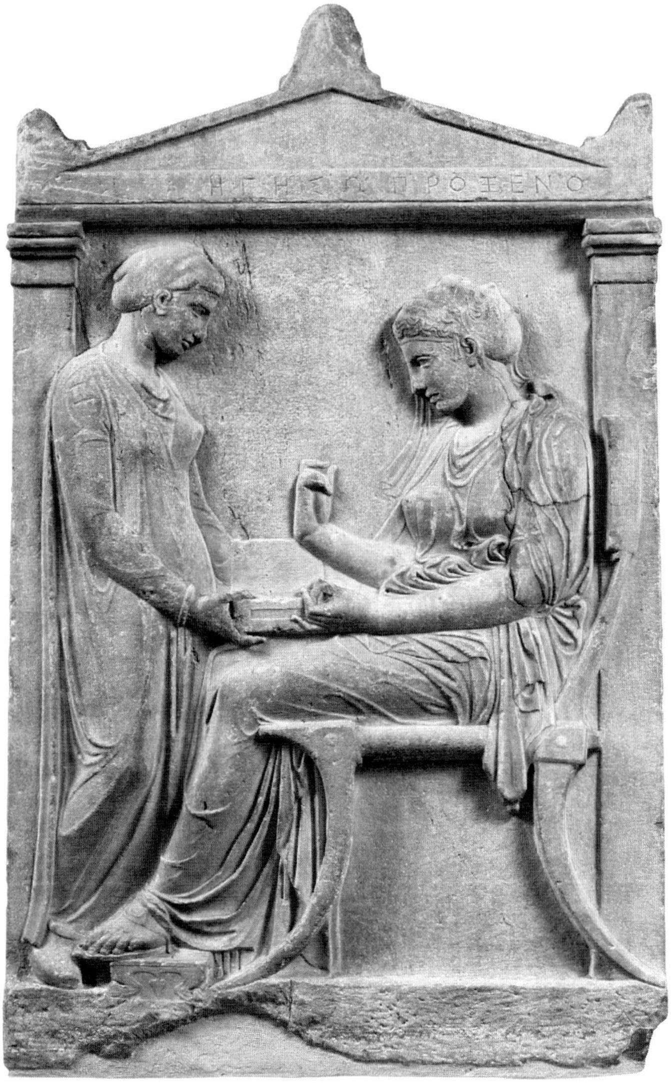

Figure 45. Grave stele of Hegeso from the Kerameikos Cemetery, c. 400 BCE. Athens, National Archaeological Museum, 3624. Photo: National Archaeological Museum, Athens. © Hellenic Ministry of Culture/Archaeological Receipts Fund.

was excavated in the Kerameikos cemetery and is today in the National Archaeological Museum in Athens (Figure 45).[9] On the right sits Hegeso, identified by inscription as "Hegeso [daughter of] Proxenos." In front of her is a slave girl holding a jewelry box. The grave stele was one of three that belonged to a family and occupied a prominent bastion along the Street of the Tombs in the Kerameikos. The bastion was originally a bit larger and its components were rearranged after the late fourth century. It is this state that is seen in the reconstruction in the Kerameikos today (Figure 46).

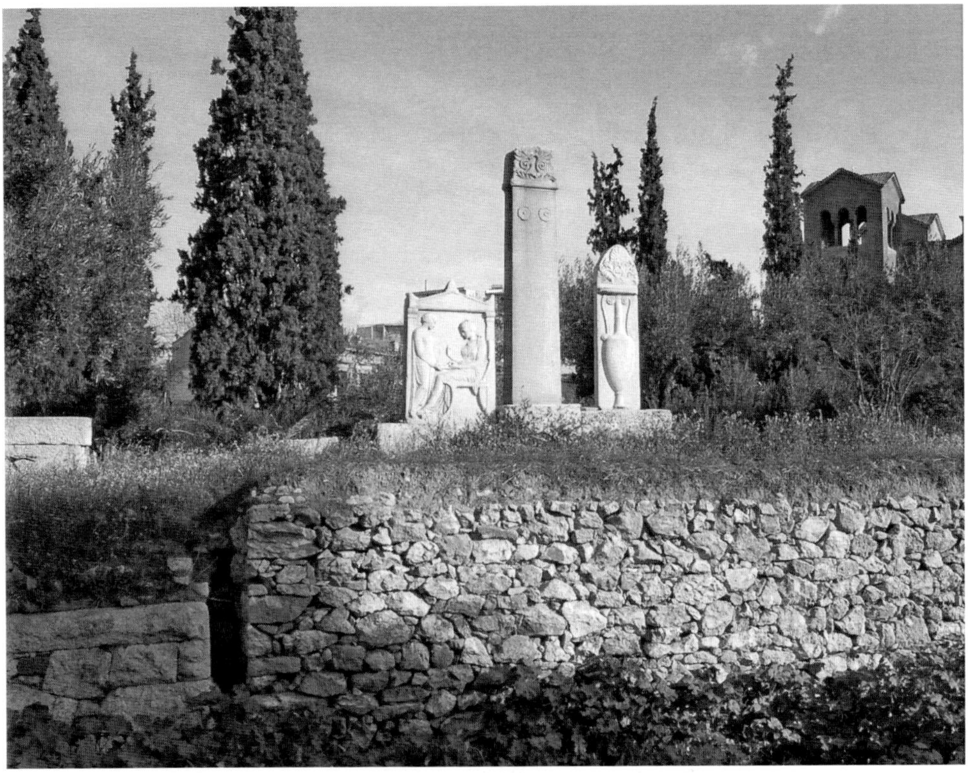

Figure 46. Tombs of Hegeso and Family in the Kerameikos (reconstruction). Photo: author.

The tall stele with a palmette top in Figure 46 lists three generations of the male members of the family:

> Koroibos son of Kleidemides, of Melite;
> Kleimedes son of Koroibos, of Melite;
> Koroibos son of Kleimedes, of Melite.

The first name was original with the stele, c. 370, and the latter two names, his son (Kleimedes) and grandson (Koroibos II, following the reuse of names in alternating generations), were added later by different hands. The third stele with the relief loutrophoros (a vessel for water used in ritual washing for funerals or weddings) commemorated a brother of Koroibos I, who apparently died virtuously in battle, but without having married. Whether Hegeso was the wife of Koroibos I is unclear, but her monument is thirty years older than his, so she would have died early in marriage. Whether she left a child (Kleimedes?) and died in childbirth is also unknown from the evidence, but she is shown as the matron of a prominent household, and it seems clear that the work is intended to commemorate the family and the virtues of its male and female members as much as the individual.

The relief itself is 1.58 m in height, about three times the height of the Erechtheion figures. Coming from the same decade, we could use the Erechtheion accounts to suggest that a work such as this double-figured stele should cost about 360 drachmas, given its greater width as well as height, or perhaps a bit less. This would represent more than a year's wages for a skilled worker, and would be a conspicuous display of wealth on the part of the patron, set prominently on a busy street leading out of the city of Athens. Such a work would have to be done on commission, and completed well after the death of the individual, given the time for labor.

The relief is not a portrait as we think of it, but a portrayal of the deceased as a type that represents a social ideal. We do not know how the specific content, seated matron and slave girl with jewelry box, was determined, but the reliance on models that were well established in the visual language of the fifth century would have made an agreement between artist and patron relatively straightforward to negotiate. Social expectations, then, would have constrained both the artist and patron, but in different ways. The patron would want to convey the family's status without being arrogant, whereas the artist would strive to meet a social need and would limit the range of content to meet the interests of the patron. The artist might distinguish the work and increase the total income through the quality of the carving, composition, and rendering, and thereby seek additional commissions. Indeed, as the grave stele market starts up only in the last few decades of the fifth century, it is thought that its producers may well have been sculptors working on the Acropolis and other civic projects who may have found new sources of employment as those projects began to decline. Grave reliefs come in a range of sizes and depth of relief, so that it would be possible for a family of more modest means to commission a work costing closer to thirty to sixty drachmas, still a significant outlay but one that could be afforded if desired.

An economic analysis does not preclude artistic innovation or effort, but it does show that in a medium such as sculpture, and for contexts that are very public and limited by social expectations, innovation or individuality would have to be more subtle. Furthermore, objects such as grave stelai are constrained by ritual practices, and we should be cautious about a purely market-based explanation for the relatively sudden appearance of grave stelai. Such works had been absent from Attic cemeteries for almost a century, so their reappearance reflects a change in ritual funerary practices that had to coincide with, if not precede, the production of stelai. In making a stele, the artist would have been necessarily subject to the needs and demands of the patron in creating the work, as it would have to follow more of a commission model. Other media, such as pottery, would have had a more entrepreneurial model and with somewhat different results for artistic license and innovation.

Given that the modern prices for museum-quality Greek vases are well in excess of $100,000, or even $1 million in some cases, getting some idea of their original value is important for understanding ancient values and usage. Unlike public projects, with contracts and accounting, there is virtually no documentation of inventories and contracts for vases. Some vases are labeled with the name of their maker or painter, but this is only a small proportion of the total. A very small number of vases also have "trademarks" on them, usually on the base or underside, that provide some hints about the pottery market.

In the most thorough study of these, A. W. Johnston notes that these trademarks were locally applied in Athens where the vessels were made, in some cases before firing, even though the works ended up being exported to Italy or elsewhere. The recorded prices are likely, then, to be wholesale prices for sale in Athens to traders, who would then mark up the price at the destination to realize their profit after factoring in their shipping costs and risks. Among other conclusions, Johnston suggests that figural decoration on a vase raised the price of a work by one-third, and that there was some variation in prices over the course of the fifth century BCE. For example, prices on kraters during the first quarter of the fifth century range between four and six obols (two-thirds to one drachma), whereas around the year 440 the range is twelve to eighteen obols. Prices decline in the late fifth century to three and one-half to seven obols, or returning to near the price at the beginning of the century.

One thing that can be noted from this is that the prices are expressed in obols rather than drachmas, which immediately tells us that pottery was less expensive than sculpture. The difficulty for a Marxist analysis is to figure out what these prices can mean in terms of the market, and particularly whether these works were bought by the elite at relatively expensive prices, or were cheap, discount goods. To think about this question, we can look at an amphora attributed to the Berlin Painter and dating to the first quarter of the fifth century (Figure 47). Under its foot, this vase has a mark of seven obols, indicating the price of the vase in Athens. The vase itself ended up in the Etruscan cemetery at Vulci (and is today in the Louvre), as did many other vases by the painter, so we will use this example as a test case for considering the value of painted figural pottery.

To understand the ancient market through modern equivalences, Vickers and Gill tried to calculate the current purchasing power of the drachma and other units of Greek money by looking at the price of similar weights of gold and silver today and their relative ratios in antiquity and in the current market in British pounds. Their calculation in 1992 determined that 1 drachma = 6 obols = £1.80. Thus, in this formulation, a vase by the Berlin Painter marked at 7 obols would be worth £2.10, or about $3.80 at 2009 exchange rates.[10] In their opinion, this would make the vase a very cheap good indeed. However, this would have meant that a sculptor being paid for the Erechtheion reliefs would have received $228 for two months of work on a single figure, which would be an absurd living wage today.

Another way to look at value would be to consider that a drachma was considered to be a standard wage for a day's work in the fifth century. Jury pay in Athens was set at one-half drachma (or three obols) to make it possible for citizens to serve on a jury without being severely burdened by the loss of wages, so the purchasing power of a drachma in goods and services must have been considerably higher than $3.80 in contemporary money. If we were to consider that the median Athenian worker received one drachma per day, we could look at this as equivalent to the median household income then and compare that to the median household income today. In 2007 for the United States, this was about $50,000 a year, roughly equivalent to $25 an hour for a 38.5-hour workweek (2,000 hours per year), or about $192.50 a day. If we use this as the contemporary equivalent of one drachma, then the Berlin Painter's amphora would have cost about $225.

To think of a modern equivalent, this would be about the price of a five-piece place setting of Royal Doulton "Tennyson" pattern of "heirloom-quality china." Clearly this would be too expensive for everyday ware, but it is the kind of china that might be found in a median-income household and used for holiday dinners. It, too, is something that might have been passed down from parents or grandparents and might be part of the family history as well. Even though Greek pottery does not seem to have been acquired as matching sets in the same way as modern china, there were multiple pieces in any given household to equip guests for an occasion such as a symposion. To afford a set of modern china, a household today often depends on gifts at a wedding, with a number of friends and families each buying one setting to make up a full service. If matching by style and size were not a concern, one could collect a group of vases over the course of years, replacing pieces that

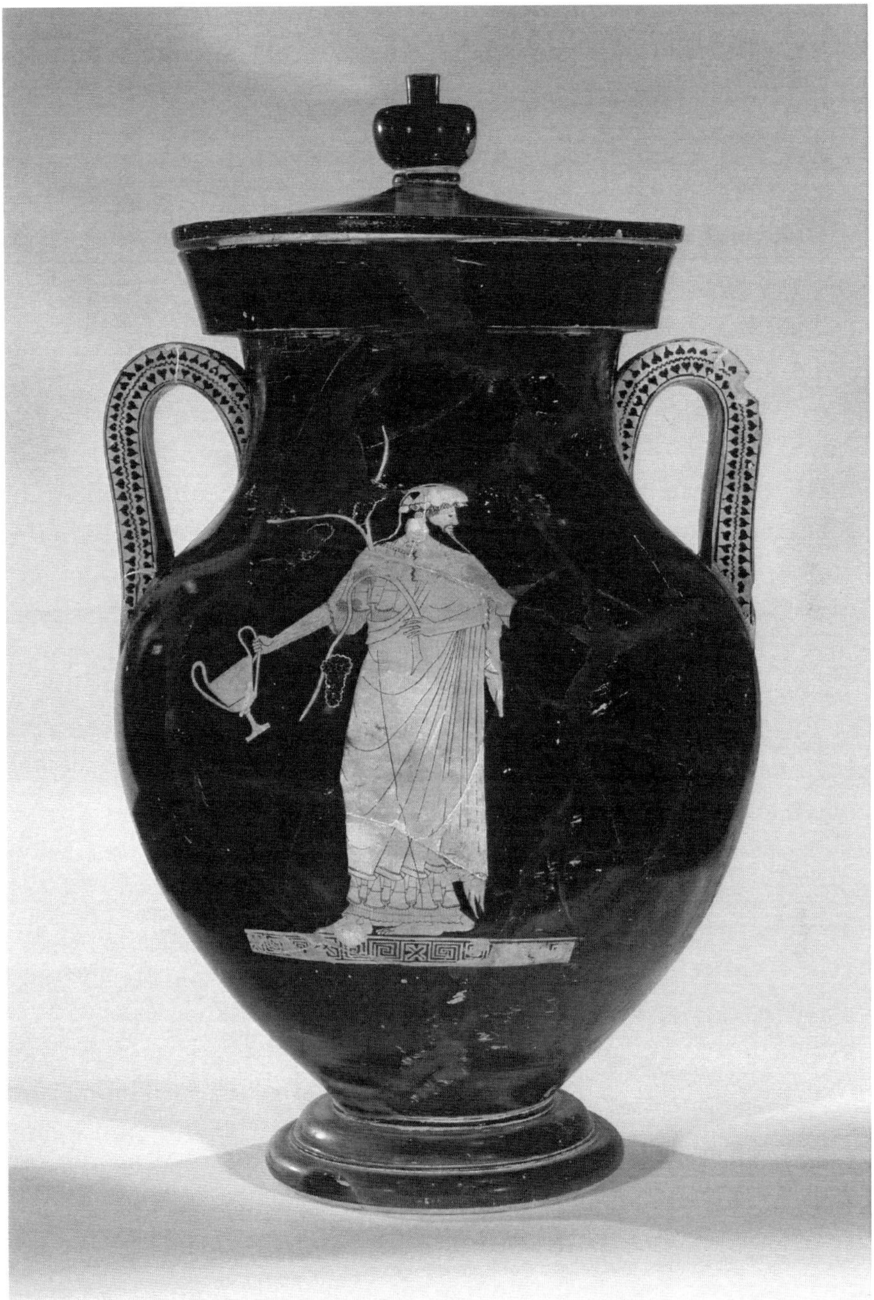

Figure 47. Attic red-figure amphora attributed to the Berlin Painter, c. 490 BCE. Dionysos with Kantharos. Paris, Musée du Louvre, CA2981. Photo: Réunion des Musées Nationaux/Art Resource, NY.

got broken as necessary. If we think about this, then, figured pottery would be something special, but not out of the realm of possibility for someone earning a drachma per day. They would not be cheap goods, but they would have a modest value that undecorated pots would not and would be in some sense special, although not priceless.

The Berlin Painter's amphora is a median work in terms of size and the amount of decoration. One must think that a larger and more complicated shape, such as a volute krater with multiple scenes and complex pictures, would fetch a higher price. In this scenario, an unusual or elaborate scene might be a worthwhile risk for a vase painter, in that the material cost remains relatively fixed and one could get a higher return on one's labor by presenting a more distinctive product for the purchaser. Because the Berlin Painter's artistic quality is high, we would have to expect that the prices for these larger or more ambitious vases would not be much more than three or four times the price of this pot, and still probably less than a week's wages. Still, a week's wages are an investment, and if being used for a funerary gift or votive offering, would be an expenditure without a continuing functional return.

The distinctiveness of a product can also have an interest for a patron, in that it can distinguish him or her from others. This could work at the individual level of choosing a vase for a household, but it would also work at a wider scale of production. Corinthian pottery of the early seventh century, for example, has long been distinguished by its style. Its vases, such as the small pointed aryballos in Figure 48, have a number of innovations of style and subject matter, including a miniature but highly precise painting technique that opened up the representational possibilities of Greek art. Why did Corinthian potters and painters develop this new style and content? Contact with Near Eastern art can certainly explain the sources of subject matter, composition, shapes, and even the engraving-like, black-figure technique, but is it just a question of an artistic model creating this change? Or is there a socioeconomic factor that helps to explain not only the development of the style, but also its widespread adoption and distribution?

Tom Rasmussen has speculated that the appearance of the new Corinthian Orientalizing style "may have been designed specifically to draw attention to, in fact to advertise, the exotic substances within," that is, the perfume and scented oil that came from the Near East and was rebottled and shipped from Corinth.[11] Thus, we could look at the development of this new style and content as a commercial decision, creating a brand identity that would be recognizable and distinct from other pottery. The growth of the Corinthian

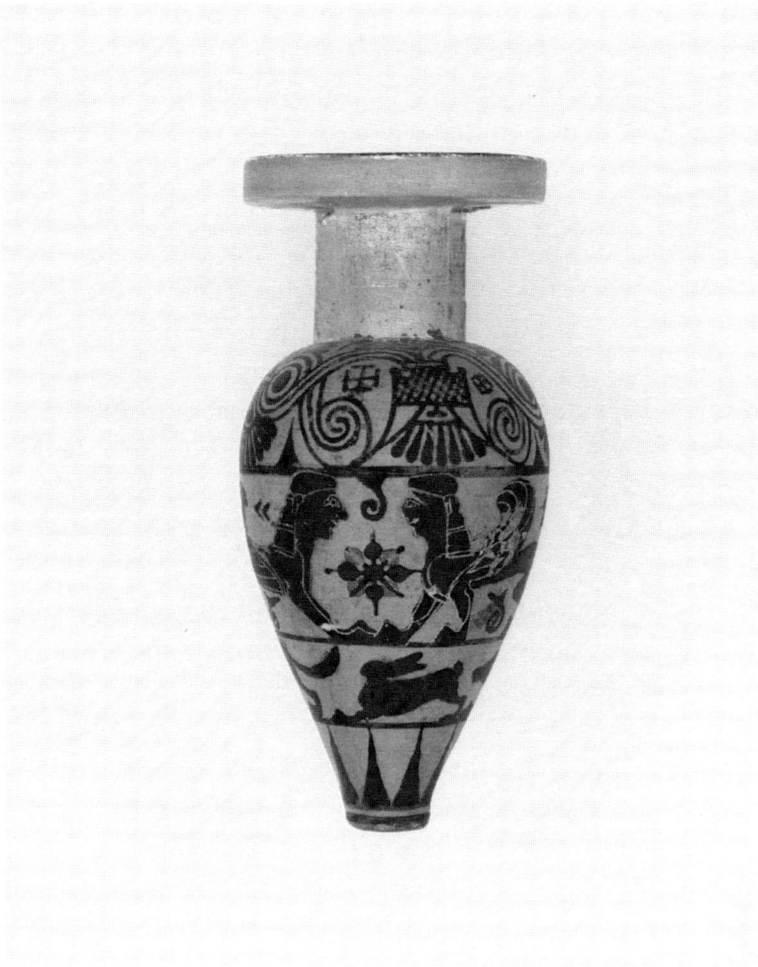

Figure 48. Proto-Corinthian aryballos with sphinxes attributed to the Fighting Rams Group, c. 670–630 BCE. Malibu, Getty Villa, 86.AE.40. Photo: The J. Paul Getty Museum. Villa Collection. Malibu, California.

pottery industry in the seventh century would be an extension of this initial stimulus, as potters and painters would seek additional markets for their wares. Indeed, the development of the *olpe* or wine pitcher can also be traced to Corinth in the mid-seventh century, but the popularity of this shape as an export would have been a result of expanding the market for Corinthian pottery from perfume containers to sympotic or ritual vessels. These olpai offer a larger surface for more complex decoration, but their precision and style would have benefited from the associations with luxury goods of the same "brand" identity.

Much of later Corinthian pottery, from the end of the seventh century into the sixth, shows a continuation of technique, subjects, and shapes, but a distinct change in terms of the precision of the style (Figure 49). The vessels themselves are well made, but the decoration shows less labor invested. The incised lines defining internal details do not always align or match well with the silhouette boundaries, and the silhouette forms are more asymmetrical. The large number of vases produced shows that there continued to be a demand for this type of container, so we should not suspect a decline in artistic skill, as the vessels are well made. Rather, the traders may have been less willing to pay for the packaging, or perhaps the demand became too great to meet with the additional time and labor that more precise decoration would require. Given the continued quality of the vessels themselves, the "decline" in decorative style, if we wish to call it that, is not a question of skill or artistic ability, but one of market and need that the potter and painter had to face.

In conclusion, we can think about the style and content of a work not only in terms of artistic decisions, as we have tended to do in the previous chapters, but also as the result of economic conditions that controlled the production and distribution of artwork. As we have seen, this is a complicated and fluid situation, and no single hypothesis can explain all, or even most, aspects of manufacture. Control over production was, in most situations, a negotiation, with the impetus shifting according to the circumstances and nature of the project. Because concrete data are hard to find, one must generalize from the information that we have, but it is still possible to consider the following when thinking about how a work was made:

- What were the value and availability of the materials?
- How much labor was required to make the work?
- What special skills or techniques would have been used that might add value or distinctiveness to the work?
- Was the work made for over-the-counter sale, or on commission or retainer?
- What type of workshop or facilities was needed to produce the work?
- Where were the eventual clients or patrons located, and how was the artwork distributed to its destination?

Politics

One other aspect of Marxist art history is politics and ideology. As Anne D'Alleva has explained, "from a Marxist perspective, art is an 'ideological form' that dominant classes may use to perpetuate class relations that benefit

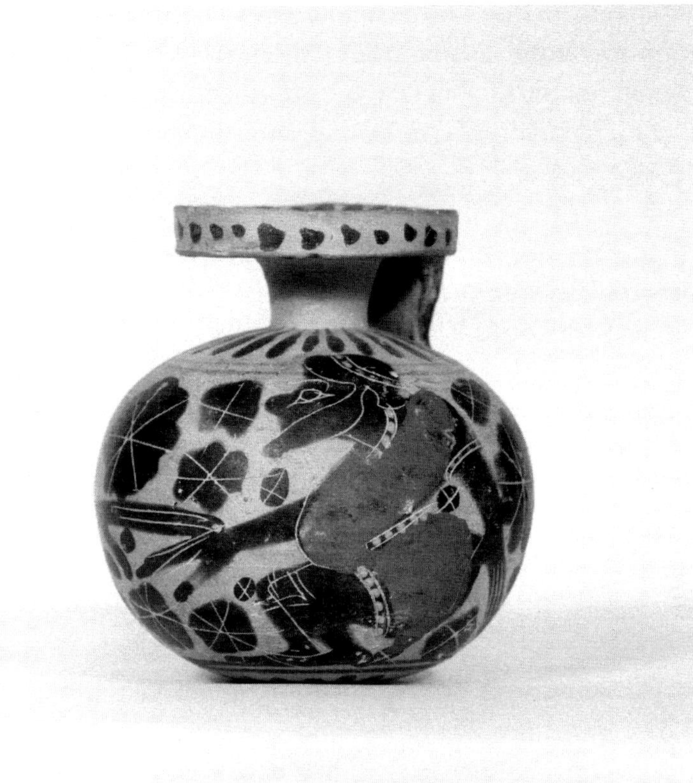

Figure 49. Early Corinthian aryballos from Camirus, Rhodes, c. 625–600 BCE. Padded Dancer. London, British Museum 1860.4–4.22. Photo: © Trustees of the British Museum.

them – or that revolutionaries may use to undermine the power of the dominant class."[12] By control of the production of art, a group can use art to convey messages that support their program and seek agreement or acquiescence from the larger population. Construction of buildings brings not only employment, but also an expression of the power and control of the patron, whether public, governmental, or private. Artwork is also the mass visual medium of its time, so the content of art can serve as propaganda, articulating or supporting an ideology or claim. Portraits of rulers, for example, became common in the Hellenistic period and were intended not simply to record or commemorate their likeness, but also to assert their prerogative to rule.

Demonstrating a specific political or ideological agenda in a work of art depends on several factors that are often hard to document. Perhaps the most difficult to demonstrate is control over the production of the work, which provides the opportunity for a group to choose the artists, the content, and the delivery of the work. In the case of the Parthenon, for example, the use of public funds, some from Athens but some appropriated from the defense budget of the Delian League, provided the patronage opportunity for Perikles to hire Pheidias as an overseer to direct the project and determine its scope and content. In addition to showing control of production, a second factor in exploring political context is to be able to identify the agenda that is being promoted and to connect it to the choice of form and subject matter. Because much of the content of Greek art is mythological or typological, this means that the ideas are expressed metaphorically or metonymically, rather than directly. For example, showing that an Amazon is metaphorically equivalent to a Persian with the idea that an Amazonomachy is a metaphor for a Greek victory over the Persians requires demonstrating that the ideological message was sufficiently clear and widespread in the visual language to make it effective. It is more difficult to demonstrate a specific political agenda than a broader and more generic ideological view.

A study of the Siphnian Treasury by Richard Neer demonstrates how one can approach a work within a political context.[13] Dedications at Panhellenic sanctuaries such as Delphi included monuments to individuals that celebrated their virtues, triumphs, and greatness without reference to their hometowns. The sanctuaries also included civic dedications, such as the Siphnian Treasury, that were the result of collective patronage. Not only is Herodotos's record of the building of the Siphnian Treasury important for dating that building, but it also serves contextually to tell us who dedicated it and why:

> [T]hey [the Siphnians] were the richest of the islanders, because they had gold and silver mines on the island; so much so that, from the tenth part of the money being produced in that place, a treasury is dedicated at Delphi that is equal to the richest of them.[14]

So, in thanks to the gods for their good fortune, the Siphnians used a tithe to build a treasury at Delphi that would be pleasing to the gods (see Figures 1 and 4). They also built it in a particularly prominent location, clearly visible from the new entryway at the southeast corner of the sanctuary. As one of the first buildings constructed after the fire of 548 BCE destroyed the sanctuary, it would have been a prominent sight to any visitor to the sanctuary. In addition, its use of marble from Siphnos and Naxos and the lavish Ionic decoration and rich sculptural program made the building quite distinctive visually from the other existing buildings at the site. Thus, we could argue that the Siphnians were not simply content to make a gift to acknowledge their good fortune, but they also wanted the building itself to be a visualization of the extent of their collective wealth and polity. Neer links this assertion of collective over individual identity to a broader ideological struggle in the archaic period.

As Ian Morris has suggested, this pitted an "elitist" group advocating traditional, aristocratic, and Panhellenic values that favored the individual against an emerging "middling" group that was anchored in the polis and the subordination of the individual to the authority of the state.[15] We have already mentioned that King Gyges of Lydia dedicated a golden krater weighing thirty talents at Delphi, and that the Delphians referred to such works as Gygian in type, further perpetuating the celebration of an elite individual. How, then, does a civic or "middling" dedication such as the Siphnian Treasury function in the midst of such elitist gifts? As Neer explains, the treasury becomes a frame for all dedications from the people at Siphnos. The revenue from the mines there, rather than being controlled by wealthy landowners, was distributed to the citizens of the island. With the riches of a territory belonging to the middling class rather than the elite, the treasury becomes an expression of the power of the polis to control offerings to the gods.

Turning to the content of the sculptural decoration of the Siphnian Treasury, Neer offers an alternative interpretation to the struggle of Herakles and Apollo over the tripod (Figure 1). Earlier interpretations suggested that the subject was linked to Peisistratid politics in Athens or to the First Sacred War at Delphi.[16] Within the political context of middling versus elite, Neer proposes that the theme expresses the authority of the polis to mediate disputes between individuals. As the tripod is central to the oracle at Delphi, the subject also asserts that access to the sanctuary is open to all. The tripod does remain an elite symbol, but one that is now placed within a civic as well as individual context.

Although all these readings might well have occurred to various visitors to the sanctuary, a political and contextual approach would focus on how the control of the production and content developed the ideological agenda of the patron. The challenge is developing the information that illuminates both production and ideology for a specific monument.

Contexts

Before looking at some additional approaches for contextual analysis, we shall review the general qualities of the main contexts for Greek art. We begin by looking at the most public types of settings, and then turn to more individualized situations.

Civic Setting: Agora and Sanctuary

Large public buildings were found primarily in two places: sanctuaries and civic centers. The agora is an open area in the city where markets, as well as civic offices, would be found. Stoas, long buildings open on one long side and enclosed on the other three, served a variety of civic purposes for administrative offices, markets, and gatherings, including dining rooms, and these often stood at the boundaries of a central open area in the city. Other types of buildings, including mints, assemblies, shrines, and temples, could also be part of the agora. In most cases, these buildings seem to have restricted their decoration to architectural elements, but some, such as the Stoa Poikile in Athens, could have large-scale paintings, sculptures, or trophies from military victories. The open areas were also filled with sculpture, including herms as boundary markers and statues dedicated by the city or civic groups.

One such example is the sculpture of Harmodios and Aristogeiton, originally made in bronze by Kritios and Nesiotes and dedicated in the Agora in 477/6 BCE. Now known only through copies in vase painting or stone, such as the figures in the Naples Museum (Figure 50), the original statue group commemorated two Athenian men who, in 514, killed Hipparchos, brother of the tyrant Hippias and son of the tyrant Peisistratos. From the literary sources we learn that the reason for the slaying was the dishonor that had fallen on the sister of Harmodios, whose chastity had been slandered by Hipparchos after his efforts to woo Harmodios had been unsuccessful. To avenge the dishonor, Aristogeiton, the successful suitor and wearing a beard as the older man in the statue group, and Harmodios leapt out during a religious procession and killed Hipparchos, only to be slain by the bodyguards. Four years later a democratic revolution ousted the tyrant, and Harmodios and Aristogeiton were rebranded as Tyrannicides, "Tyrant-Killers," for their attack on Hipparchos, and were commemorated by a bronze statue group made by Antenor. When this sculpture was looted by the Persians in 480 BCE, a new group by Kritios and Nesiotes was commissioned by the city to replace it.

In the marble copy of the second bronze group, we see the two figures poised to strike with their weapons as they stride forward. One vase painting fragment shows the statue group on a base (Figure 51). Placed prominently

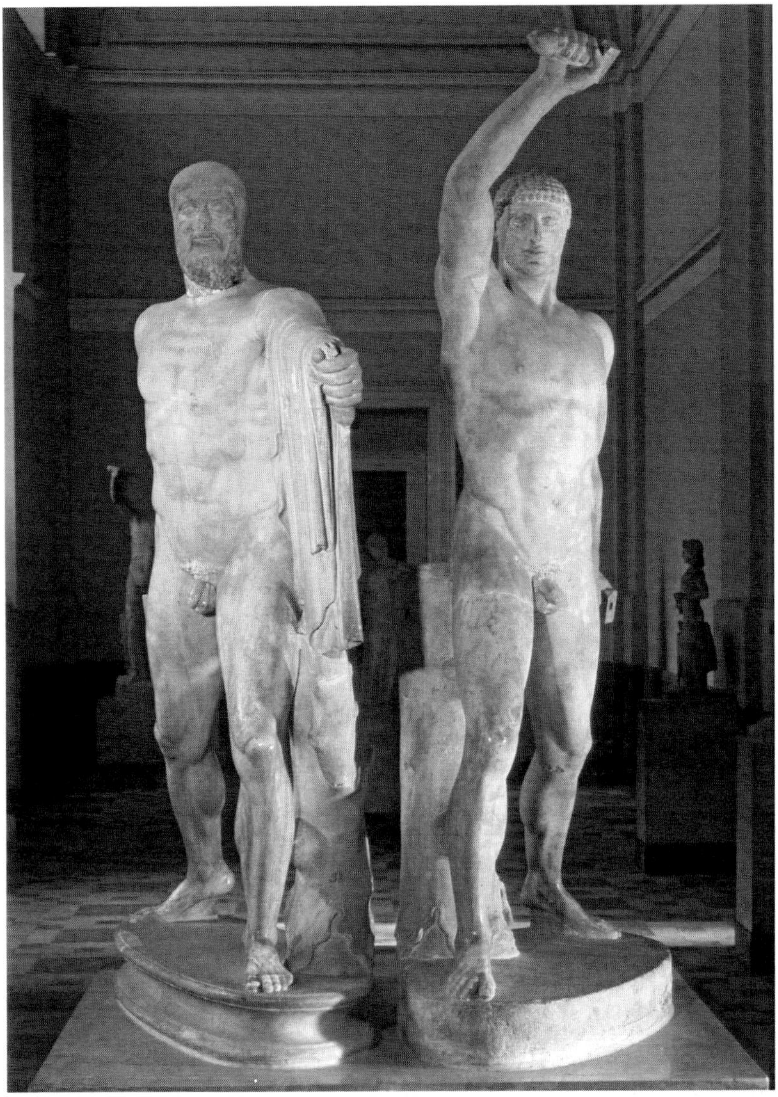

Figure 50. Tyrannicides (Aristogeiton and Harmodios) by Kritios and Nesiotes. Roman copies of Greek originals, c. 477/476 BCE. Naples, National Archaeological Museum. Photo: Scala/Art Resource, New York.

near the center of the Agora and the Panathenaic Way, the avenue used for the Panathenaic procession that was the occasion for the murder, the statue group became a well-known symbol of Athens and its democratic government. Stopping to read the inscription on its base, which would have been spoken aloud rather than silently read, viewers would have actively commemorated the figures and their deed, but would also be standing in the place of the murdered Hipparchos as potentially active participants

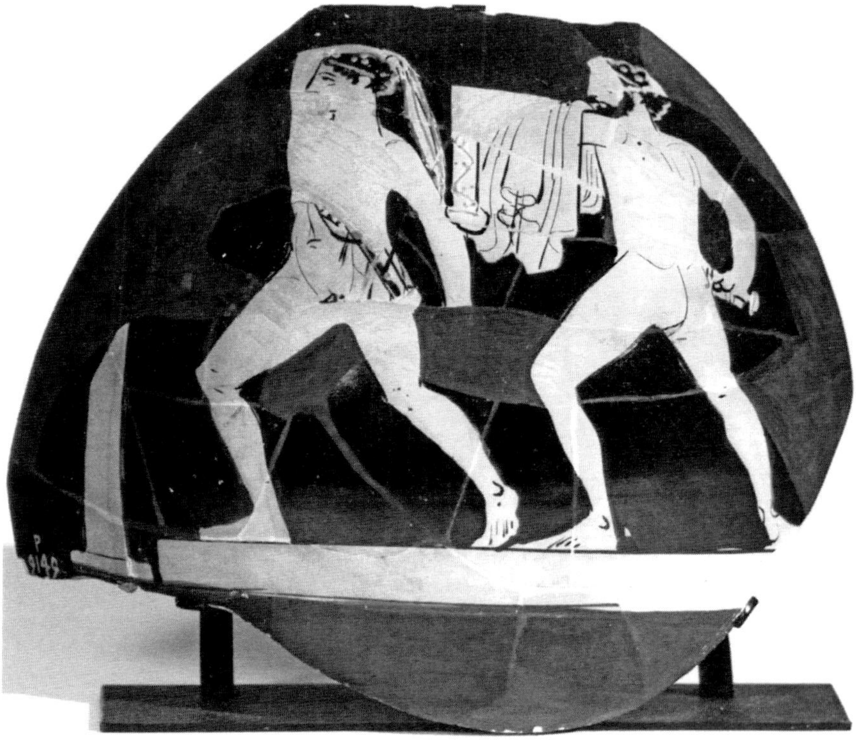

Figure 51. Fragment of an Attic red-figure oinochoe, c. 400 BCE. Tyrannicide sculpture group (left: *Harmodios*; right: *Aristogeiton*). *Boston, Museum of Fine Arts, Henry Lillie Pierce Fund, 98.936. Photo: © 2011 Museum of Fine Arts, Boston.*

themselves. Although we tend to read inscriptions silently and think of them more as labels, in reading aloud, the viewer in effect proclaims and acknowledges the subject.[17] The setting and inscription guide viewers into considering their own positions within the city.

A similar situation exists in sanctuaries, which had more elaborate architectural settings. The temple, as a building, was larger than other structures in the city. Placed in an open setting and often on elevated ground, it created an impressive visual spectacle. Sanctuaries could also have stoas as functional buildings; the more famous sanctuaries also had small treasuries, such as the Siphnian Treasury, that housed many of the dedications to the gods. Both temples and treasuries could be lavishly decorated with sculpture. The pediment of the Temple of Zeus at Olympia, for example, had a larger-than-life-size sculptural ensemble in each of its pediments, including the battle of the Lapiths and Centaurs on its west end (Figure 52).

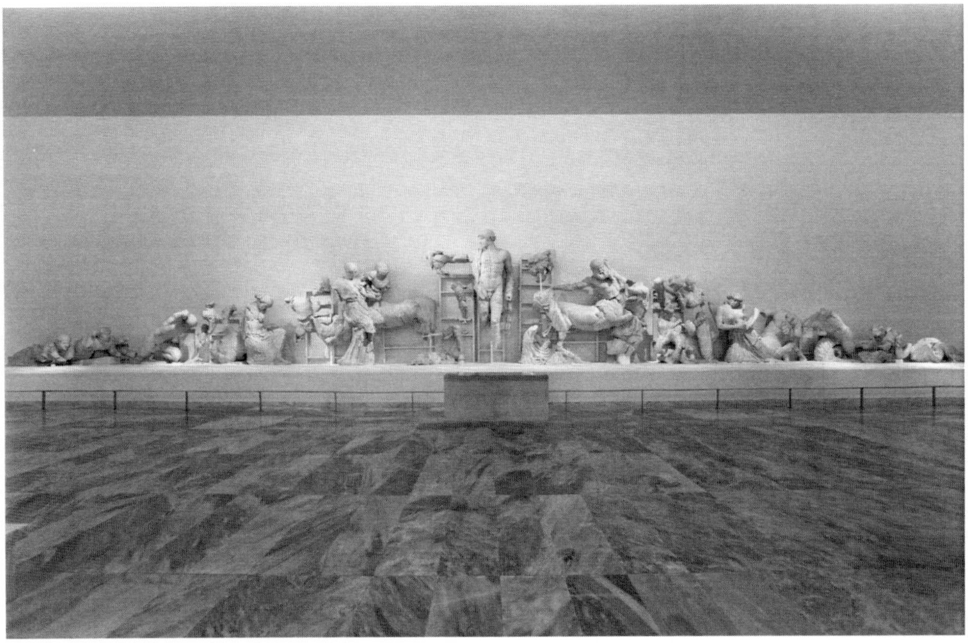

Figure 52. West pediment of the Temple of Zeus at Olympia, 470–457 BCE. *Olympia, Archaeological Museum. Photo: Vanni/Art Resource, New York.*

In the center of the pediment is Apollo, watching over the action but not directly involved in it. To his left and right are Theseus and Peirithoös, each attacking a centaur who has attacked a Lapith woman. One can note that their poses, striding forward with the right arm held bent back over their heads and holding a sword, imitate the pose of Aristogeiton in the Tyrannicides sculpture, done about a decade or more earlier. The Tyrannicide poses are also used as a formula in other works, and we should consider that such poses must have quickly conveyed a general heroic meaning to a viewer of the time.

The religious context, though, must be considered as giving the figure a different significance than the original use of the pose in the agora at Athens. The original Tyrannicide statue must be seen as more political and specifically Athenian. A visitor to Olympia, who may never have been to Athens or been aware of the model, would see the striding and resolute figure as a more general model of behavior that aligns with the will of the gods. One would view the pediment while performing ritual or devotional acts at the sanctuary. The lofty, monumental, and sacred setting at Olympia would have had a different impact on a viewer than the Tyrannicide group, which was set at ground level off a busy street in the heart of the city.

Votive Offerings and Dedications

Although both agora and sanctuary are contexts for monumental works, each frames the experience in different ways and helps to determine the compositional and interpretive choices of artist and viewer. There is also a more personal dimension to these civic contexts in the form of votive offerings and dedications, objects left at a place to fulfill a vow or acknowledge a benefit. They are far more numerous and would have littered the landscape in both places. For example, the archaic Acropolis in Athens had dozens of kore statues dedicated on it, such as the one in Figure 53. The statue, which is over life-size in scale, is associated by most scholars with the base that is inscribed:

> Nearchos the potter dedicated first fruits of his works to Athena.
> Antenor the son of Eumares made the *agalma*.

The right side of the inscription is missing and is restored, and there is some debate over whether the restored word "kerameus" refers to the occupation of Nearchos as a potter or to his coming from the Attic deme Kerameis, which also housed much of the potting industry in Athens. There was an Attic potter named Nearchos who signed some surviving vases, but these are dated in the second quarter of the sixth century, whereas this statue is generally dated to the last quarter of the same century, at least twenty-five years later. If this Nearchos were a potter, it would be significant evidence that at least some potters could make a significant livelihood to be able to dedicate almost a year's wages for such a statue, but the chronology prevents us from relying on that identification.

Whatever the case about which Nearchos this was, the inscription focuses on the name of the dedicator, or patron, and the reason for the dedication; this inscription also includes the name of the sculptor. The term *agalma* is often used for sculpture, and in this context it signifies a pleasing gift to the recipient or god, which is the basic idea of a votive offering. As Catherine Keesling has explained, the work can be seen more broadly as an *anathema*, the act of setting something up for the gods.[18]

The reasons for a votive dedication vary. In the case of Nearchos's kore, it is an offering that is equivalent to a portion of the first proceeds, whether from a crop (first fruit, or *aparche*) or, in this case, his trade. A votive could also

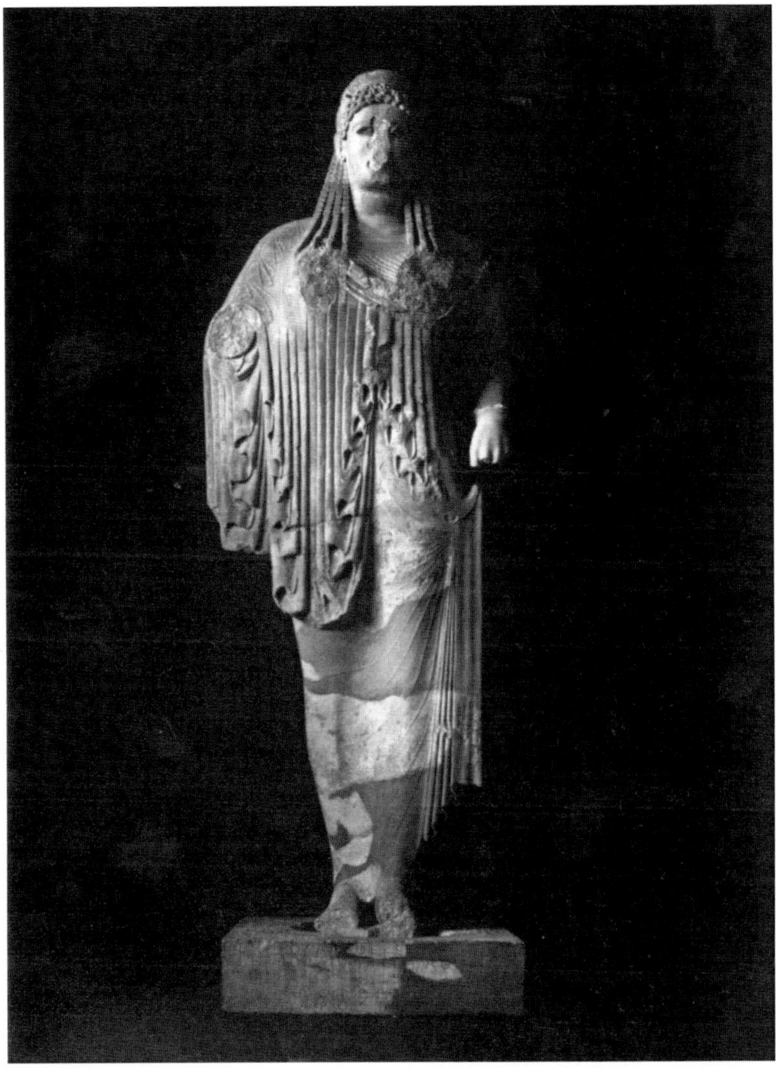

Figure 53. Kore dedicated by potter Nearchos and signed by Antenor son of Eumares, c. 530–520 BCE. Athens, Akropolis Museum, 681. Photo: Copyright Deutsches Archäologisches Institut Athen, Neg. Nr. D-DAI-ATH-Akropolis 272.

be a tithe offering (*dekate*), which would represent a longer-term valuation of the benefit that the goddess had conferred on the dedicator. Other votives were the result of vows made in exchange for or in recognition of a benefit from the gods, such as recovery from an illness or disaster, success in an endeavor, or victory or honors received. Rites of passage, such as marriage or childbirth and celebrations of religious festivals, could also be causes for making a votive offering to the gods.

The importance of the patron, and the benefit to him or her from the gift, is seen in the formula that goes with these dedications, "X dedicated . . ." The name of the artist is sometimes included, as it is with Nearchos's kore, but more typically it is not, pointing to the potential control that the patron would have over the creation of an expensive work. The name of the patron was meant to be read out loud, whether by a guide or the viewer, reiterating again the deed of the dedicator for posterity. Votive statues such as this would have been set up together in a densely packed manner within the sanctuary, and would have competed against other dedications through their size, splendor, height, or other visual qualities. An agalma should be pleasing to the gods, but it should also convey the status and piety of its dedicator.

Not all votives, however, were so expensive or carried inscriptions. Sanctuaries and shrines of far more modest size were a feature of the Greek city and countryside. One such shrine, named Stele Shrine A, was found in the potters' quarter in Corinth. The shrine consisted of two stelai set to the east of a wall; the stelai faced east.[19] The stelai were made of limestone and had a recessed central panel with a stucco covering. Below the earth floor on the front, east side of the stelai was a roughly meter-square hole about 60 cm deep containing 120 vases, 215 miniature vases, and 55 figurines (Figure 54). The vessels date mostly to 500–450 BCE and may have been placed there as an offering when the shrine was set up; the vases themselves were stacked on top of and inside each other. Some additional small cups belonging to the later fifth century may be from a second offering.

No inscription tells us about the nature of the shrine, but the offerings and the location would suggest some association with the neighborhood and its activities. Rather than commemorate an individual, the votives should be seen as gaining their power through their collective action. Here the quantity of offerings can serve to signify the importance of the gods and their potential impact on the welfare of a community. Although in museums and excavation publications these terracotta votives are spaced so that a viewer can see them individually and study them, most of them would have been part of "deposits," groups of works set next to and on top of one another, with the emphasis on the aggregate rather than the individual effect.

The purposes for such modest votive offerings are similar to those of their more monumental counterparts. Most people, however, could not afford dedications of metal and stone, and therefore turned to cheaper media that could be produced in greater quantities. As can be seen from the examples in Corinth, there is a great deal of repetitiveness in the formulas of form, decoration, scale, and the like in these, but it is interesting that there is not

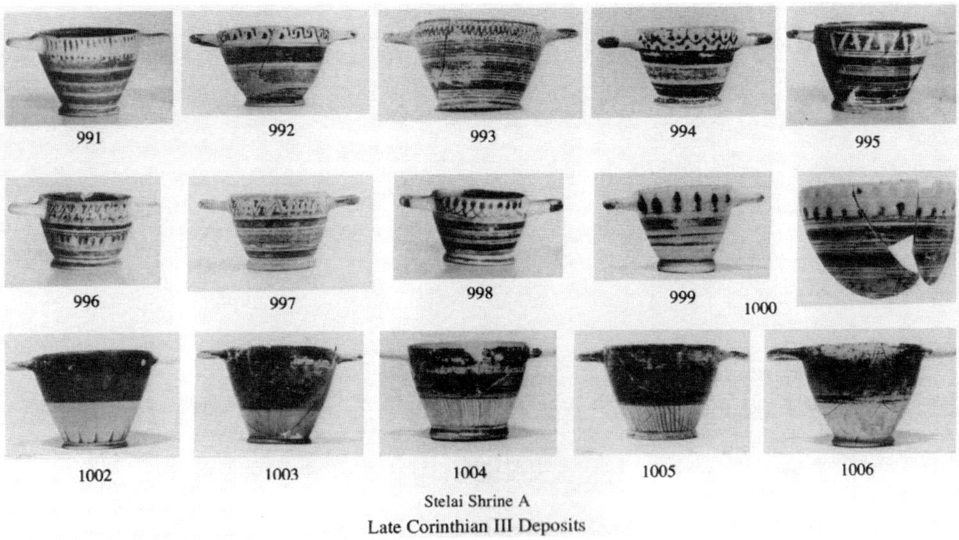

Figure 54. Pottery from Corinth Stele Shrine A, c. 500–450 BCE. Corinth, Archaeological Museum. After A. N. Stillwell and J. L. Benson, The Potters' Quarter: The Pottery *(Corinth XV.3) (Princeton, 1984), pl. 44: 991–1000, 1002–1006. Courtesy of the Trustees of the American School of Classical Studies at Athens.*

much in the way of outright duplication. Although their variations might be relatively slight, we should also remember that the kouros and kore statues were also formulaic and that their form and decoration were meant to serve a purpose that confined both the patron and the artist within broader social and religious expectations. Even though the artists may have produced the miniature vases for direct sale to the dedicator, having nominally more control over production, they still had to work within the demands not only of the patron, but of ritual and religion as well.

Graves

Graves are a major market for the ancient artist and an important investment for the Greek patron, as we saw earlier in the grave stele of Hegeso (Figure 45). Objects were placed inside the tomb as *grave goods* (Figure 55), as well as on top of the tomb after the burial as *grave offerings*. Grave goods often consisted of pottery vessels that could contain food or drink offerings for the deceased, as well as objects such as drinking cups for the "use" of the deceased in the afterlife. In some periods, precious offerings in the form of jewelry and textiles could be placed in the graves; such offerings were certainly an expression of wealth and status, as this valuable material was

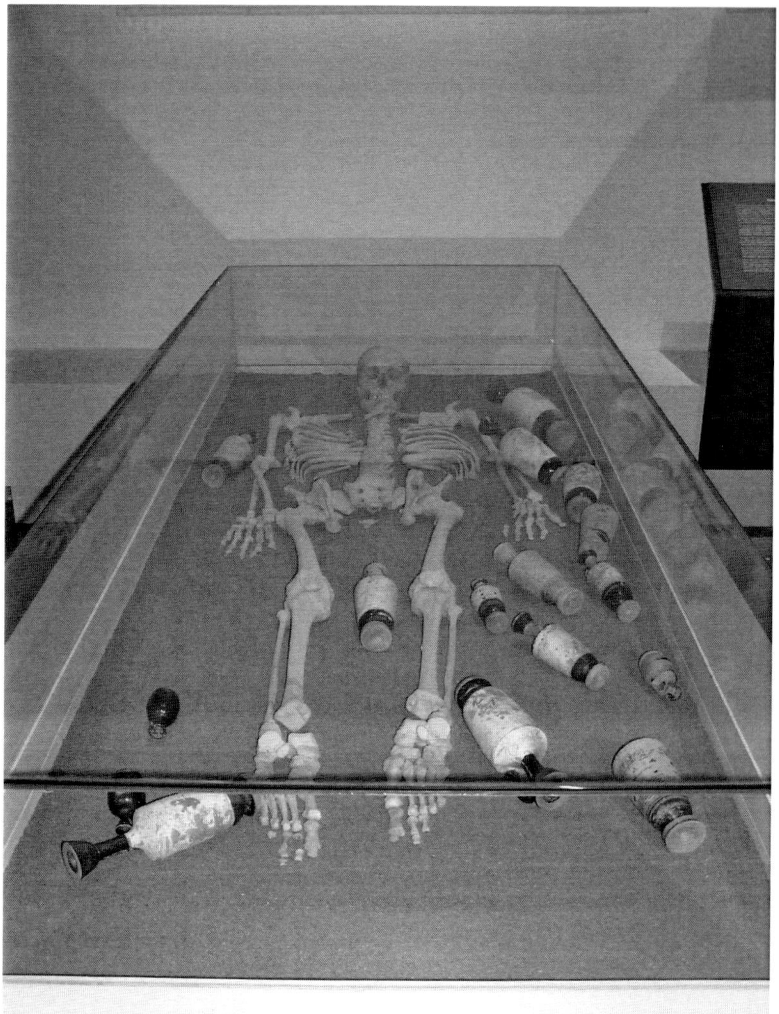

Figure 55. Reconstructed grave with lekythoi as grave offerings. Athens, National Museum. Photo: National Archaeological Museum, Athens. © Hellenic Ministry of Culture/Archaeological Receipts Fund.

literally being discarded. Offerings for the deceased were intended to comfort and show respect for the dead, but as with votive offerings, the elite would often indulge in more lavish offerings within the general limitations of the time and place.

It is important to remember that grave goods within a tomb would need to be readily at hand, as the burial would be taking place within a few days of death at most. Grave goods would have to be objects already in the household or available for quick purchase. Given the time necessary for making and firing clay, pottery placed in a grave would almost certainly

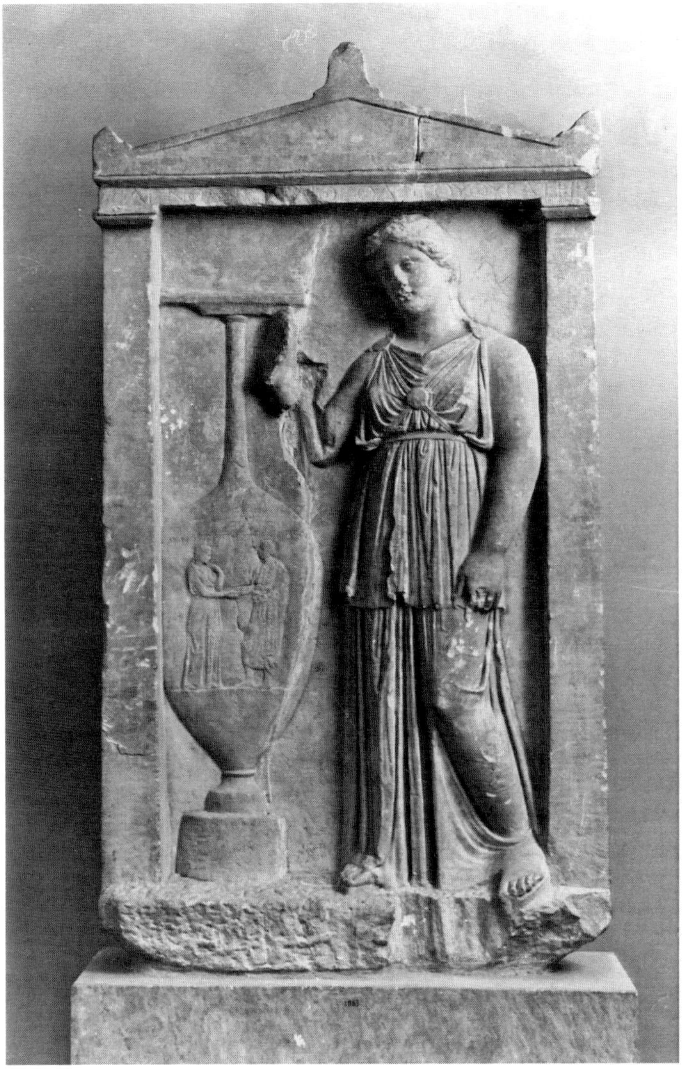

Figure 56. Grave stele of Hagnostrate, daughter of Theodotos, c. 320 BCE. Athens, National Archaeological Museum, 1863. Photo: National Archaeological Museum, Athens. © Hellenic Ministry of Culture/Archaeological Receipts Fund.

have been previously made and not commissioned for the funeral. Potters and painters would then need to have on hand a stock of vessels for funerary purposes, such as lekythoi, whose subjects would be readily adaptable or appropriate to the particular circumstances.

Above the tomb would be a marker of some sort. These markers, whether slabs, statues, or structures, did not just show the location of the burial, but also served in a sense as shrines and places for later grave offerings by the surviving family. The material, type, and size of markers vary over the course of time. In every period there is both a broad set of parameters that narrows the range of possibilities and a range of variations that would allow some individualization of the memorial.

The grave stele of Hagnostrate, daughter of Theodotos, shows a woman standing in front of a stone loutrophoros that itself is a grave marker (Figure 56). Because the main inscription at the top of the stele names her, she is likely to be the woman represented on the stele. On the loutrophoros we see a second female figure, shaking hands with Theodoros, a young family relation of some kind. It is likely that we are seeing Hagnostrate attending to the tomb within a tomb; the scene on the loutrophoros shows her shaking hands with the young man in a gesture that is associated with farewell between the living and deceased in Attic funerary art, as Alan Shapiro has shown.[20] Perhaps we need to consider Hagnostrate as acting in an ideal manner, like Hegeso, but here her virtue is that before she herself died, she showed great devotion to the family's dead. The scene is illuminating in that it shows how the living would attend to the tomb, showing both respect for the dead and the virtue of the living. Because the ancient Greek underworld was a shady, unpleasant place, it was of the utmost importance that the deceased be remembered by his or her family. The investment of resources into art for tombs shows its importance for family and society, and creates a distinct need for the production of the same artists who could also provide works of art for votive offerings.

Domestic Spaces and Objects

Our knowledge of the domestic context of Greek art is less well preserved. In part, this is because houses were rebuilt and reused; there is not a Greek equivalent of Pompeii that preserves not only the walls of the houses, but also the artifacts that went in them. Excavations of cities that have been destroyed violently, such as Olynthos, do preserve some evidence, but much of the more valuable material at these sites would have been removed or looted, either at the time of destruction or from later scavenging.

As can be seen in a display of domestic artifacts from Priene during the Hellenistic period and now in the Berlin Antikensammlung, much of what survives is plainer and more utilitarian than what we have seen from sanctuaries and tombs (Figure 57). Pottery, including bowls and various containers, lamps, tools, and utensils in bronze, jewelry and fibulae (safety pins), and bells and weights make a random impression.

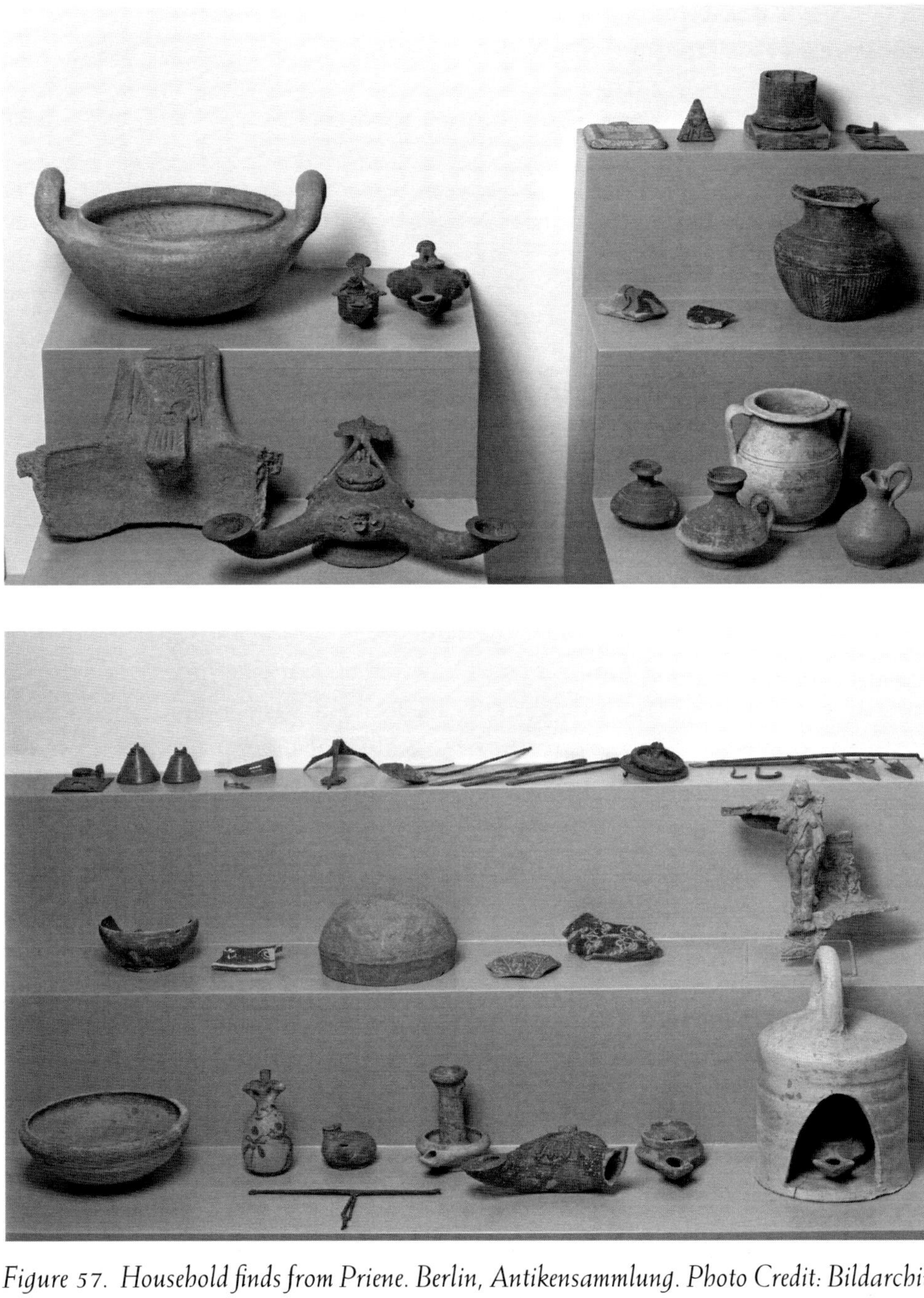

Figure 57. Household finds from Priene. Berlin, Antikensammlung. Photo Credit: Bildarchiv Preussischer Kulturbesitz/Art Resource, New York.

Based on the excavations at Olynthos, we can summarize some of the categories of artifacts and functions as follows:[21]

- Food preparation: grindstone, mortar, cooking vessel, brazier; mostly terracotta but some of stone and metal
- Food consumption: plate, bowl, serving vessel (*lekanis*), cup
- Storage: pithos, amphora, pelike, lekythos, askos
- Ritual and washing: small altar, louter
- Weaving: loomweight, spindle
- Jewelry and adornment: mirror, fibula, earrings, ring, necklace, comb
- Furniture: boss or joint
- Lamps, mostly terracotta but some metal
- Figurines, mostly terracotta but some metal
- Tools and utensils: tweezers, spit

Many times such objects are undecorated or carry simple patterns. Mold-made works, such as terracottas, bowls, and lamps, can carry more figural or ornate decoration, although in a more mass-produced style.

Jewelry is generally of metal or gemstones and could also have some figural decoration on a miniature scale. Much less of this survives, however, and it was probably absent from many households, as it would be more of a luxury good. A gold ring from southern Italy, for example, shows a seated woman in intaglio – that is, in negative relief, sunk below the smooth surface of the ring's bezel (Figure 58). Whether metal or gem, such intaglio reliefs could be impressed on a soft surface, such as clay or wax, to create a raised relief and might be used as a seal or signature. The choice of subject matter would be highly individualized as well as being luxurious, and we must keep that in mind in attempting to interpret it.

The seated woman on the gold ring bends her head forward and rests it on her hand; her elbow is placed on her thigh to support the head. The pose is very similar to representations of Penelope, the wife of Odysseus, who appears like this in front of her loom. The figure, whether Penelope or not, is a paradigm for the ideal wife – faithful to her husband and guarding the fortunes of her house against monumental challenges. As an article of personal adornment as well as a means for signifying personal identity, we should consider this subject in a different contextual light than if it had appeared on a drinking cup or in a monumental sculpture.

There is also a large category of pottery vessels surrounding the drinking party or *symposion*, a social event occurring within a domestic context. Held in a special room in the house called the *andron*, or men's room, it had not only specialized pottery but also wooden couches and tables. We can get

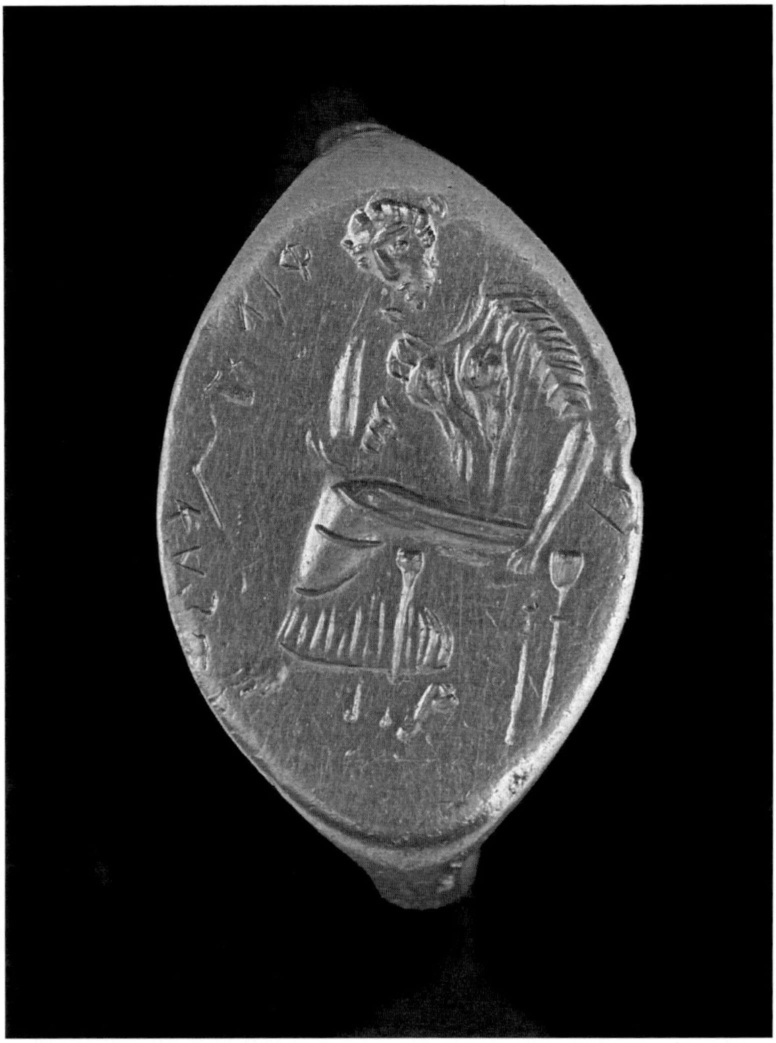

Figure 58. Gold ring from Southern Italy or Sicily with seated woman (Penelope?), fourth century BCE. *London, British Museum, 1867.7–28.402. Photo: © Trustees of the British Museum.*

a very generalized sense of the proceedings on the exterior of a kylix by Makron, itself a drinking cup used in the symposion, which has here moved into a more amorous phase of entertainment (Figure 59). The men recline on light wooden couches with cushions and pillows; one holds a skyphos in one hand. The couches line the sides of the room, leaving open the center space, and women are disrobing and joining the men on the couches. Under one handle is a large bowl or krater, placed on the floor of the room, in which wine (from an amphora) and water (from a hydria) would be mixed.

A pitcher (oinochoe or olpe) would be dipped into the krater and filled with the drink and then poured into the cups of the guests (kylix, skyphos, among others), sometimes through a strainer. At the opposite handle stands a small boy holding both strainer and oinochoe and ready to pour more wine. One of the women holds a kylix loosely by the handle; she and her companion look toward the servant or slave, perhaps wanting more wine.

Not all symposia included sex; we will return to this issue in discussing gender and sexual identity in the next chapter. Indeed, the subject matter of the cups and kraters that would be used in a symposion is vast and is usually found on nonsympotic vases as well. Some of the shapes that could appear in a symposion, such as the amphora and hydria, could also be used for storage of food, wine, and water elsewhere in the house. Still, the cup does give us an idea of the intersection of social activity and domestic life in the Greek city.

In conclusion, one of the difficulties in considering context is that a specific type of artifact may have several potential contexts in which it would be found. Even in the case in which we have an excavated findspot such as a tomb, all we know certainly is that the object ended its life there. Before that, it could have been used in several other contexts, perhaps in other locations too.

For example, an object such as the bronze caryatid mirror that we have seen in previous chapters (Figure 2) could certainly have been a domestic object, given to a girl or young woman as she neared puberty, a symbol of her upcoming status as a bride and eventually a mother. The mirror would have helped her to prepare for her roles in public festivals or for household rituals. The mirror could also have been a votive object dedicated in a sanctuary, such as one of Artemis, in recognition of a benefit from the goddess, such as marriage or a successful childbirth. A few mirrors have inscriptions that record such a dedication, but these may not have been purchased as votives, as there was both a material as well as personal value in an object like a bronze mirror. A mirror might also have been included as a grave good, although much more rarely than jewelry in Greece. So too, a mirror might have been made in a place like Corinth or Athens and exported to another area of Greece or to a non-Greek land. Each transaction could change the importance or meaning of the work, but this is a history that is lost to us. Understanding how the work creates an effect through the combination of maker, patron, subject, and viewer can at least be understood through its agency, an approach that we will discuss next.

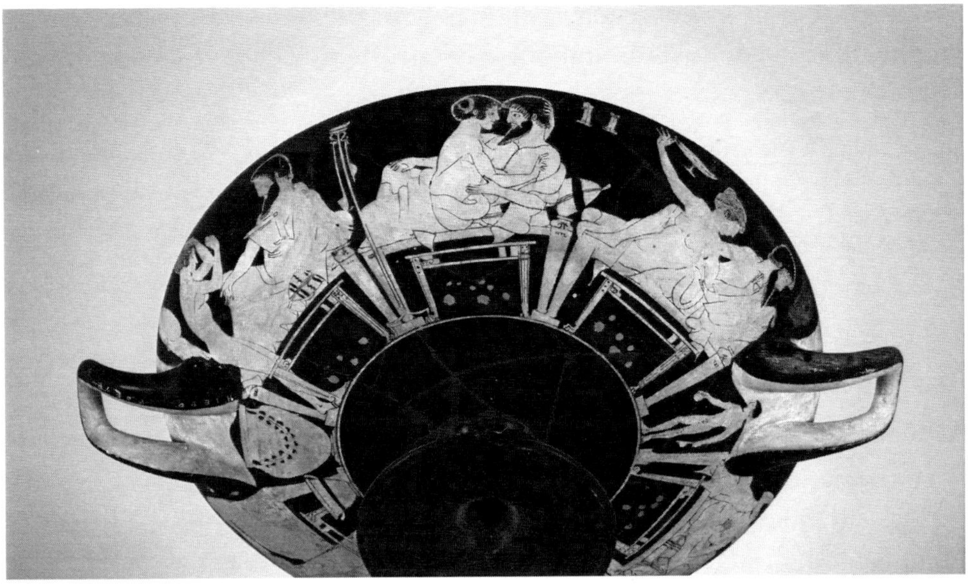

Figure 59. Attic red-figure kylix attributed to Makron, c. 490–480 BCE. *Symposion scene. New York, Metropolitan Museum of Art, 20.246. Image Copyright © The Metropolitan Museum of Art/Art Resource, New York.*

Agency

Agency is a more anthropological approach to art developed by Alfred Gell in the 1990s. He questioned the definition of a work of art as an object that primarily created an aesthetic response in a viewer, or that conveyed a symbolic meaning. Rather, as Gell explains,

> art is a system of action, intended to change the world rather than encode symbolic propositions about it. The "action"-centred approach to art is inherently more anthropological than the alternative semiotic approach because it is preoccupied with the practical mediatory role of art objects in the social process, rather than with the interpretation of objects "as if" they were texts.[22]

In other words, Gell is interested in what art objects do, rather than what they look like and what they mean, outside of how these features enable their acts to be effective. There are aspects of Marxism in this approach, as he considers how the object is manufactured and distributed, and the theory can be applied within a variety of contexts. As we shall see, it also encompasses elements of ritual analysis and object biography. The diagrammatic aspect of the theory, however, gives it a particular usefulness as a contextual approach.

To carry out this approach, Gell maps out the "art nexus" – the chain of interactions that funnel through the work of art. He defines four components of this nexus:

- *Index*: the physical, material object or thing, such as a bronze statue or drinking cup (This is not to be confused with the use of the term *index* in semiotics or structural analysis. The word is used by Gell to avoid the aesthetic criteria that frequently define a "work of art." To keep the terms distinct, we will use the term *index-artifact* when discussing agency.)
- *Artist*: the person who makes or manufactures the index-artifact or work of art
- *Prototype*: the entity or concept that an index-artifact represents, which could be quite lifelike in the case of a realistic portrait and its subject, or could be much more abstract or schematic, as in the representation of a god or hero by an attribute or form
- *Recipient*: the person who experiences the index-artifact and its agency (the viewer).

The relationship of these participants in the nexus is governed by their role as either *agent* or *patient*. Agency is essentially the ability to cause action, to make something happen, or to exert an effect, whereas the patient is the object of the agency. For something or someone to be an agent, there must be a patient that is acted on or receives the message. It is important to note that any of the four components of the nexus can be either an agent or a patient, depending on the context.

Gell developed a diagrammatic way of mapping out the relationship of the components by using directional arrows linking the terms to show the exertion of agency: agent→patient. So, for example, we can see in the creation of the kylix by Douris (Figure 3), discussed in previous chapters, as an act of agency in the artist's creation of the object (which is then the patient):

artist→index-artifact (cup)

The index-artifact, in turn, creates an effect on the viewer or recipient. In this role, it serves as an agent, as in the typical situation of a museum viewer (patient) looking passively at an object:

index-artifact (cup)→recipient (viewer)

As the agent-patient relationship is by definition a dyad, brackets help to sort out the cumulative effect:

[[artist (Douris)]→index-artifact (cup)]→recipient (viewer)

Because the cup includes a representation of Theseus, we can identify Theseus as a prototype in the art nexus. Here one must consider whether the prototype serves as an agent, or if it is a patient. In the case of a portrait or archetype, we would say that the prototype acts on the artist (prototype→artist), in that the artist needed to produce an image of Theseus:

[[[prototype (Theseus)]→artist (Douris)]→index-artifact (cup)]→recipient (viewer)

One can say that the idea or prototype of Theseus has exerted agency on the artist in the selection of the subject matter, perhaps because the artist was producing the work for a shrine of the hero. However, if Douris has selected the subject matter for the cup and determined the details of its representation, then we would describe the agency differently and insert it into the previous diagram as:

[[[artist (Douris)]→prototype (Theseus)]→index-artifact (cup)]→recipient (viewer)

The value of a diagram is that it can visually represent the chain of relationships for a work of art, which can get still more complicated and can involve multiple individuals in any one of the four roles. For example, a merchant who buys the cup for resale in another city serves first as a recipient-patient, but in selling the work the merchant becomes a recipient-agent in a transaction with a new recipient-patient – the owner of the work. A diagram can express this double role and sequence of actions clearly.

As Robin Osborne has pointed out, the theory on agency presumes a unidirectional flow, but it is possible that there is mutual agency at work. A buyer has been acted on by agreeing to give up something of value for a work, but this is a more active role as a viewer than that of the museum viewer looking at an object, or the owner looking at something already purchased. That action has the potential for making the recipient in turn an agent, as by declining to purchase a work, the recipient rejects the agency of the artist/work. If the artist must then adapt the wares or subjects to generate a sale, the recipient exerts agency over the artist. This is the role that a patron would play.

We can see this dynamic by looking at a votive dedication from the Acropolis: a small bronze statue of Athena Promachos (Figure 60). Inscribed on the base of the statue is the dedication:

Meleso anetheken dekaten tathenaiai
Meleso dedicated [this] tithe to Athena

The inscription is engraved onto the base of the bronze. As was the kore of Nearchos, this work was made for someone going to the Acropolis to make

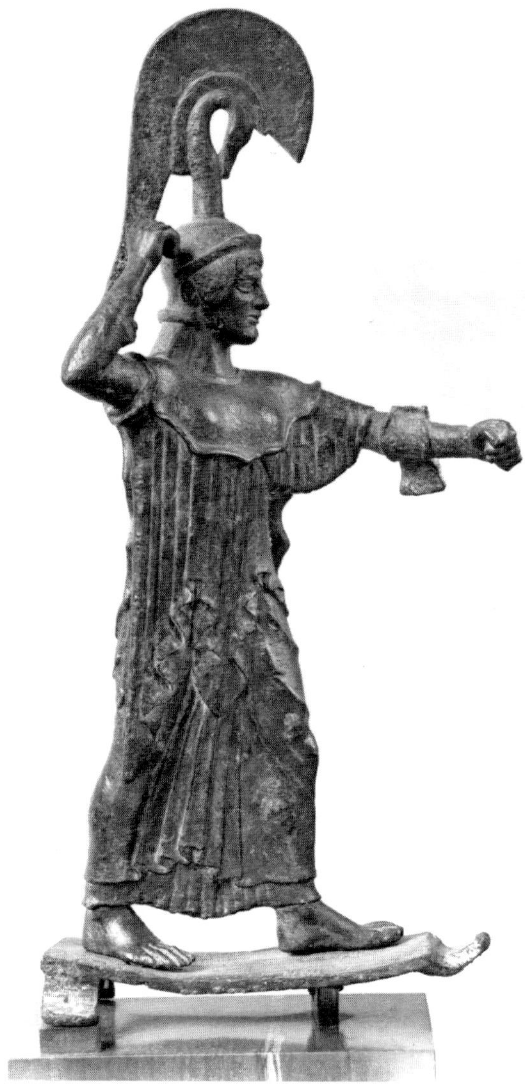

Figure 60. Bronze statue of Athena Promachos from the Acropolis and dedicated by Meleso, c. 500–470 BCE. Athens, National Archaeological Museum, 6447, now transferred to the Acropolis Museum. Photo Copyright Deutsches Archäologisches Institut Athen, Neg. Nr. D-DAI-ATH-Akropolis 4742. Photo: G. Eva-Maria Czakó.

offerings to Athena. Given its small scale and typological subject matter, it is perhaps more likely that the statue was made ahead of time by an artist for sale to those visiting the sanctuary. Its votive purpose as a work acknowledging the power of the goddess would have had an agency over the artist as a prototype, directing both the content and form of the work. Clearly, however, the inscription was added after the production of the work as a second action. By having her name inscribed on the work rather than simply purchasing and then giving it to the sanctuary, Meleso in turn becomes an agent by altering the work (either herself or by direction to the artist or a third party). Giving the now modified statue to Athena, the goddess becomes at once agent and patient, prototype and recipient. We might diagram the different phases of the interactions like this:

Manufacture and purchase:

> [[[Prototype (Athena)]→Artist]→Index-Artifact-1 (statue)]→Recipient-1 (Meleso)

Votive acquisition:

> [[Prototype (Athena)]→Recipient-1 (Meleso)]→Index-Artifact-1 (purchased statue)

Votive offering:

> [[[[Recipient-1 (Meleso)]→Index-Artifact-1 (purchased statue)]→Artist (to add inscription)]→Index-Artifact-1a (inscribed statue)]→Recipient-2/Prototype (Athena)

We can combine these series of actions into a diagram, or "Gellogram," as Osborne and Tanner have termed it (see Diagram 1).[23]

This diagram is helpful in explaining the effect of votive offerings. It is easy to say in the abstract that religious devotion acts as an agent, inducing action by others. The diagram of the nexus, however, shows that the dedicated

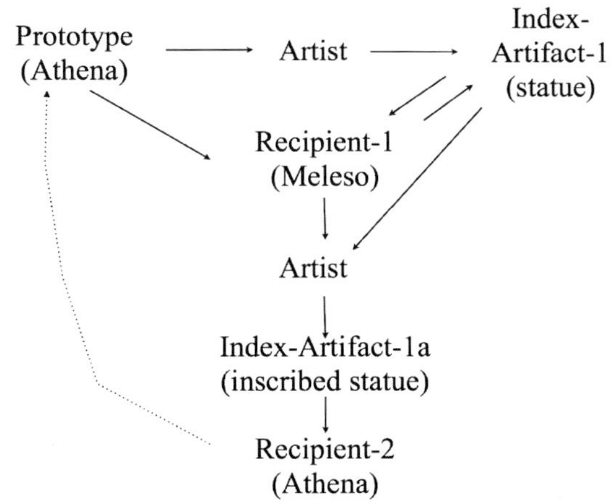

Diagram 1. "Gellogram" of Figure 60.

statue continues to exist in the sanctuary as the visible evidence of the act of devotion. Athena becomes an agent through these acts of devotion, which later visitors to the shrine can see for themselves. The cumulative effect of these acts as a sanctuary deposit makes the Prototype/Athena increasingly effective as an agent, initiating new acts of votive offerings.

One criticism of Gell's approach is that it treats each act of agency as the same, so two representations of Athena might have little to distinguish themselves in terms of agency. Indeed, the artistic quality of the index-artifact, whether material, subject matter, or style, would likely have an impact in its agency on the viewer/patient. Clearly, gold kraters weighing thirty talents attract more attention than miniature pottery kraters or cups dedicated at a neighborhood shrine. Building out of marble is potentially a more effective act than building out of limestone in exerting one's agency. Gell's diagrams simplify the complexities of an individual situation, but they provide a framework for pinpointing where such qualitative distinctions could create a maximum impact.

Ritual Analysis and Cultural Poetics

As both the review of the contexts earlier and the discussion of agency just now indicated, many of the potential settings for a work of art are connected with religion, whether as part of the sanctuary and its decoration or as votives left by devotees. In addition, graves can be considered as religious sites, cemeteries being spaces set aside from daily life and funerals being rituals with prescribed behaviors and supporting objects. Indeed, one could argue that most surviving art comes from a context that is ritualistic in character; this extends even to political/civic works such as the Tyrannicides, which would have been commissioned and installed as a public act, the result of a series of political actions that would have had their own forms to follow. It is important, then, to consider how the ritual actions and performances that were part of the social and religious fabric of the Greek city affect our understanding of the work of art.

The study of ritual and its relationship to art developed out of cultural anthropology and the recognition that rituals were dynamic social practices, systems of signs that worked collectively to create meaning. As Clifford Geertz stated, to analyze ritual is "to synthesize a people's ethos – the tone, character, and quality of their life, its moral and aesthetic style and mood – and their world view – the picture they have of the way things in sheer actuality are, their most comprehensive ideas of order."[24] *Ritual analysis* is one potential label for this approach, as is *cultural poetics*, a term developed by Stephen Greenblatt to describe the interdisciplinary study of text, object, and context; this term has appeared in some of the literature of Greek art history.[25]

Even though ritual usually involves prescribed actions and words that are consistently reproduced over time, it should not be seen as rigidly coded and artificial. Some rituals do gain character and authority because of their antiquity or difference from "normal" actions, but ritual can also be adaptable and creative. It can be public or secret, simple or complex, sacred or secular. Therefore, when undertaking a ritual analysis, one needs not only to consider the broad structural patterns that can describe ritual, but also to be aware of the individual qualities of a specific ritual and its transformation over the course of time.

As Catherine Bell has explained, for ritual to be effective it should be modeled on social behavior and should seem "instinctive" or "natural" to its participants.[26] At the same time, however, it is more formally organized and is something that is set aside from everyday experience. A ritual's forms and actions should be known in advance so participants can prepare for it, or be able to undertake the appropriate actions in a sudden situation, such as a funeral. The performance of ritual serves to construct social and religious relationships through the role played by each group or type of participant. Participation, however, does not necessarily entail full belief in the religion or ideology underlying the ritual. Rather, acquiescence indicates at least tacit acceptance of the social relationships and expectations in exchange for the advantages of meeting social or material needs. To the degree that individual belief and social or religious principles are aligned, one can say that a ritual is effective.

There are many levels of ritual to consider within Greek culture. Festivals such as the Panathenaia are perhaps obvious examples of large, full-scale rituals, but the religious calendar was full of events dedicated to both pan-Hellenic and local deities. These were major civic events that could include large processions, musical and dance performances, athletic competitions, sacrifice and the subsequent banqueting, and offerings to the gods. There were also smaller rituals that negotiated an individual's relationship to the gods, such as votive offerings. These are acts that would be repeated independently, but countless times throughout the year; large civic festivals could involve thousands acting at one time. Political events, including elections and assemblies and various forms of decision-making, were also ritualistic in their actions.

Other rituals helped to negotiate an individual's place within society. Initiation rituals marked the stages of the *ephebe* or young man's training for his civic role and helped to create the network of social relationships that would sustain him in public life. Marriage was the major transitional ritual for women, marking their move from their parents' houses to those of their new husbands. Funerals negotiated the departure of an individual from society, and began their commemoration for future generations. In many of these rituals there is what can be generally described as a *liminal state*, a transitional period in which the individual is removed from one set of circumstances – childhood, maidenhood, life – and is suspended in a transitory state before becoming fully vested in the new state – adulthood, marriage, ancestor.

Beyond transitional rituals, there were also more frequent events in domestic settings, such as symposia, which were more loosely structured and flexible but had some general expectations of actions and equipment. Libations were simple rituals but would require some equipment such as an oinochoe and phiale, and would be connected to events such as departures, arrivals, gatherings, beginnings and endings, invocations, and honoring the dead.

In exploring the impact that ritual has on our understanding of an object, one needs to consider the performance of the ritual as a stage production.

- Consider the *setting and staging* of the event: What kind of space is used? Are there special buildings or paths set out for the events, and how do these frame the events? How does the plan of the site allow for the organization of the people and permit them to see, hear, or otherwise participate?
- Next, consider the *cast* of the ritual, including their number and composition within subgroupings: Who are the "leaders" of the ritual, and what are their roles, groupings, and number? Who are the "witnesses" or "participants," and how does their number and organization reflect their roles within the ritual?
- What are the *actions* of the cast? Who does what and to whom? Are the actions unusual or do they require some special skill or knowledge? What is the order of the actions? Is there instrumental music, singing, or dancing? Is there a sacrifice, offerings, or the distribution of food or other material? Are there ancillary activities, such as games or drama performed as part of the complete set of actions?
- What are the *scripts* used by the cast? Are there set texts that are used repeatedly year after year, or are there new compositions that are performed? Is there a liturgical script that codifies the proceedings?
- What type of *movement* is required for the ritual? Are there processions leading into or out of the ritual, and how are they organized? Once the participants are in their initial place, is there internal movement within the ritual, or performances such as a dance? How are these coordinated with the architecture and space for the ritual? How do they engage the cast and negotiate the relationships between the sacred and the civic, between the leaders and the participants?

- What is the *dress and demeanor* of the cast? Is it recognizably different from everyday costume or behavior? Does it convey status or role within the ritual?
- Finally, what types of *equipment* are needed for the ritual? What types of objects or tools are needed to perform physically some of the actions? What objects are visual focal points for the ritual? Who uses or handles this equipment, and who sees it in use? What types of objects are made specifically for the ritual and used only in association with it? Does it have a special form only found within ritual settings? Who provides the objects, and what happens to them?

Certainly it is the last category in which artworks might figure prominently. Beyond just identifying its specific role, knowing how an artwork fits into the ritual and intersects with the other elements of the ritual provides an opportunity to consider its significance and impact. Further, if the artwork has figural subject matter, understanding the circumstances under which the images would be viewed provides us with a framework for considering how it might have been perceived differently than if the same subject were found in a different setting.

Putting ritual analysis into effect requires asking a great many questions, for which there are frequently only the most general answers. As studies of the Parthenon frieze in the framework of the Panathenaic festival have shown, the evolution of the festival and the late date of the documentary sources make correlating the frieze to the contemporary mid-fifth-century festival difficult. Many participants, actions, and equipment found in the sources are missing from the frieze, and there are elements in the frieze that are not found in the sources. Given the gaps of our evidence for much of Greek ritual and its development, we generally must limit ourselves to a consideration of the general significance, rather than the particular significance of a ritualized work of art.

We can consider both ritual and its representation on a loutrophoros by the Analatos Painter, now in the Louvre (Figure 61). The vase is an important example of the development of the Orientalizing style out of the Geometric in the first decades of the seventh century BCE, but contextually it is likely to have served a funerary purpose like much of the Late Geometric pottery with figural decoration that preceded it. Although the findspot is unknown, the size of the vase (80 cm) makes it large enough that it might have been a grave marker. The shape has sometimes been labeled as an amphora, but with its elongated profile and long, narrow neck, it is much closer to the shape we today call the loutrophoros, which was a tall container that carried water used for ritual washing, either of the dead or of a bride before her marriage. The shape is a ritualized form of the more normal amphora or storage container and continued to be used for funerary markers into the fourth century (see Figures 46 and 56).

Two of the friezes have figural subjects. On the body is a chariot procession, a theme used on funerary kraters since the mid-eighth century and signifying an honorific procession for the deceased. Greek art rarely shows the actual funeral cortege going to the cemetery, so the procession here should be regarded as emblematic of the use of chariots in honorific processions generally. For a funeral this might be connected with the laying out of the deceased, the *prothesis*, or with the procession from the home to the cemetery, or perhaps with funerary games, such as chariot races. The point is that the frieze does not represent one specific thing. Rather, it signifies the type of participants, action, and equipment that would be part of the funerary ritual of an elite person. The size, shape, and distinctive style of the vase would also signify its role as equipment within ritual connected to an elite figure at this time and place.

Rather than a prothesis, however, the frieze above shows two pairs of male and female figures holding branches; they flank a double-flute player in the center of the panel. These figures serve as a chorus, singing and/or dancing. Although the branches can be associated with purifying the corpse, they are more frequently associated with the dances of maidens, which were an important component of festivals featuring girls who were coming of marriageable age.[27] Two other components of the decoration also have symbolic elements that connect to ritual. The sphinxes on the top, here in a Levantine version (walking, winged, and female, based on hair style), were originally funeral symbols in Egypt, but in Greek art become more widely deployed as a symbol of transitions and crossing boundaries. The snakes that are modeled as relief appliqué on the shoulder of the vase also signifying movement across boundaries, whether death or the transition between maiden and bride.

It is possible that the loutrophoros was used as a grave marker, or in association with the washing of a corpse or bride. The decoration would suggest that it might have served the latter function, or perhaps have been the grave marker of a woman who died before she could marry. Thus, we should probably interpret the work within the context of the transition of a young woman to the next stage of her life, whether as a bride or as the honored dead. The scenes on the vase can signify both the types of actions that she performed in religious ritual and the rituals that would have been performed for her to mark her new place in the tomb or home. The special shape of the vase, combined with the subject matter, become a concrete,

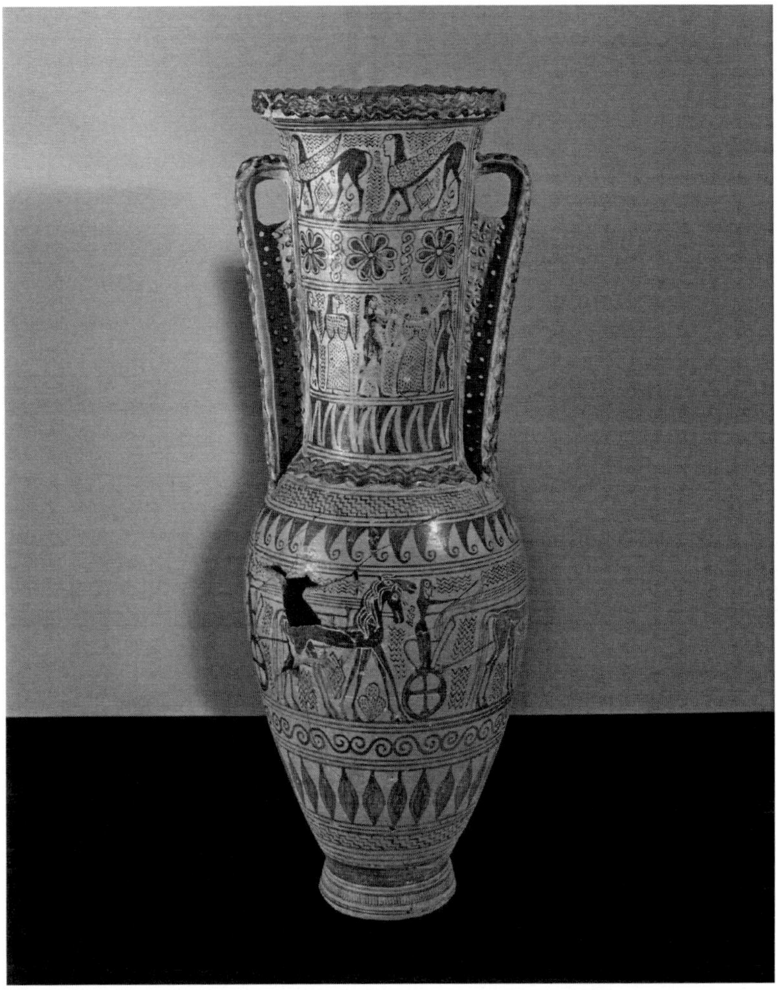

Figure 61. Proto-Attic loutrophoros amphora attributed to the Analatos Painter, c. 690 BCE. *Paris, Musée du Louvre, CA2985. Photo: Eric Lessing/Art Resource, New York.*

visible reminder of important social and ritual actions. Although the scenes are generic rather than specific in terms of the identity of the figures, the context of the viewing circumstances would have provided some specificity and association for the original viewers and reminders of rituals that would have been familiar to them.

The equipment for a ritual does not always need to have special decoration or form as long as it can carry out its function, but frequently we find decoration that transforms a common object type into a special work. For example, the so-called Queen's Vase in Figure 62 is a straightforward oinochoe with trefoil mouth. The vessel is coated with a faience glaze and has relief decoration on its front that serves to distinguish it from a normal

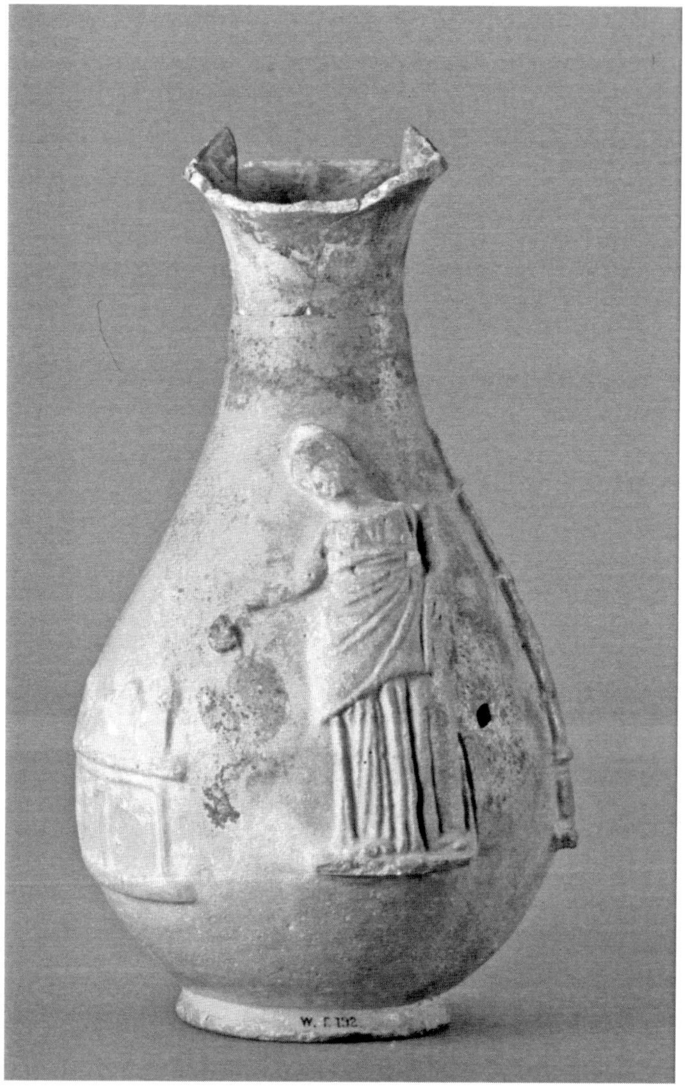

Figure 62. Egyptian faience Queen's Vase with Arsinoë III (221–203 BCE). c. 220–200 BCE. London, British Museum, 1856.12–36.192. Photo: © Trustees of the British Museum.

pouring vessel. The relief shows an elaborately dressed woman cradling a cornucopia in her left arm while pouring from a phiale in her right hand onto the ground. Next to her is an altar. These vessels were used in cults associated with the queens of Egypt, and it is likely that the figure on this vase is Arsinoë III (reigned 221–203 BCE). The Egyptian queens were objects of veneration themselves; the cornucopia that she holds is an attribute of a goddess and signifies the importance of the queen for attracting the benefits of the gods.

The oinochoe would have held the liquid that was poured into the phiale held by the queen, so the decoration of the vase shows the next stage of the ritual action. Although the vase shows the queen who was being venerated, in the actual ritual her role would have been performed by a priestess pouring the offering from a phiale. When used in a libation, then, the jug would remind the participants of their association with the priestess, who signified the queen, who in turn signified the gods who would bring prosperity to the members of the cult.

These jugs were made in Egypt, probably in Alexandria, where they were used in the ruler cult. The jugs themselves were widely distributed throughout the Mediterranean, from Turkey to Italy, and have been found in graves. From this, it would seem that the use of the vases in the ritual would have given them a commemorative value for their owners, who may have participated in these ceremonies. The distinctive glazing and decoration would have marked them as special in form and purpose, even when not in use. The production of the vases from the early third century BCE into the later second century shows not only how ritual can endure, but also how it responds to new needs at the beginning (the promotion of the Greek rulers of Egypt). It can eventually give way to other rituals or shift to other forms of equipment or action over time. For each vase, though, there is an individual participating in a ritual at a particular time and place that invests it with a specific significance that is encoded in its decoration.

An object such as the Queen's Vase might also be a votive offering in a sanctuary after its use, and we can see that many votive objects commemorate the ritual activity of their dedicators. For example, a votive relief of the second century BCE in Munich shows a ritual to honor a god and his consort, seen in large scale on the right (Figure 63). In the center is an altar, behind which are four figures of various size. To the left are four more figures. The smaller figures hold a vase and a sacrificial animal, while two women look on. Next to the altar the smallest figure holds up a basket covered by a cloth, while the man behind the altar is picking up material held in a basket, presumably an offering for the start of the ritual.

The scene is a pastiche of different moments, but encodes some of the key components of a ritual, including the procession to the sacred space; the bringing of equipment and offerings to be used; the differentiated roles of the participants in the ritual, including witnessing as well as action; the ordering of the participants in space to carry out the actions; their distinctive dress or lack thereof; as well as some of the actions themselves. From the man's

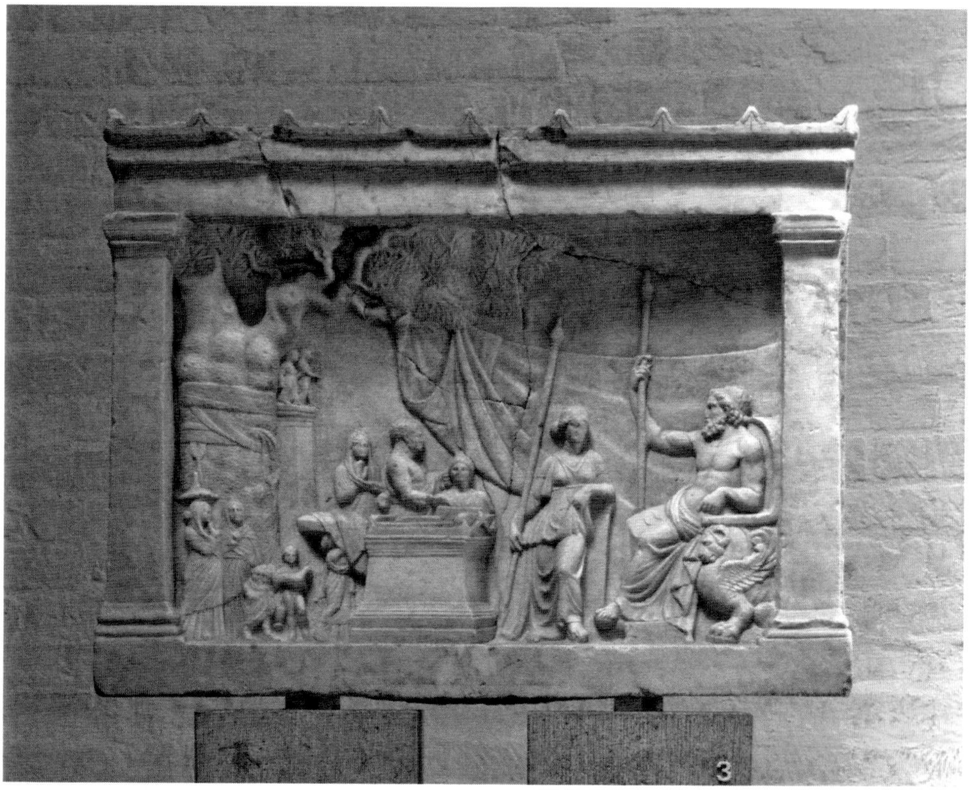

Figure 63. Votive relief with family making sacrifice to gods, c. 200 BCE. Munich, Glyptothek, GL 206. Photo: Renate Kühling. Staatliche Antikensammlungen und Glyptothek München.

posture and gaze toward the gods, one might also surmise that he is addressing them through an invocation or prayer. His action has prompted a response from the woman behind him, who raises her hand with palm outward.

The scene is set outdoors with a curtain tied to a tree, marking the enclosure. The scene itself is set in an architectural frame recalling a temple or treasury. As a votive relief dedicated in a sanctuary, this work would be significant not only as an offering to the gods, but also from the rituals that had been performed by its dedicators. The gift is meant to be not only an agalma pleasing to the gods, as was the kore of Nearchos discussed earlier, but a commemoration of the pious actions that were presumably pleasing to the gods as well.

The importance of ritual can also provide a means for interpreting scenes on objects that are not specifically intended for use in a ritual. For example, scenes of the apotheosis of Herakles on later sixth-century black-figure vases, such as the hydria in Madison that we saw in the last chapter (see Figure 43), have been interpreted politically. John Boardman suggests that scenes showing Athena and Herakles with a chariot in these apotheosis scenes refer to Peisistratos's second attempt to take power in Athens. Rather than regarding these scenes as specific propaganda, we could think of this as an example of the power of ritual to create a social relationship, in that Peisistratos used processional rituals already familiar to Athenians as a way of announcing his previously negotiated bid for power. Because simply showing up with a woman dressed in armor might not be very effective at signifying his installation, it was preceded by proclamations and coincided with calls for responses. People responded in the manner prescribed by learned ritual and, by doing so, they acquiesced in the installation, at least for a time.

In this light, as Rebecca Sinos has argued, we should regard the chariot scenes on vases as epitomizing this ritualistic use of chariots, such as in wedding processions or funerary processions.[28] The chariot serves as a sign of the temporary elevation of status of the participant. The hydria, as a vase that held water and would be positioned at the door of a house holding a prothesis, could signal this new status for the deceased, just as the apotheosis of Herakles marked his acceptance into Olympus after his death. If we consider that the hydria could also have held water for a symposion, the reward of Herakles would mark the triumph of the hero and his paradigmatic status as the virtuous male, a role model for the men in the symposion, who could also recall the deeds of Herakles in songs. Each ritualistic occasion would bring a different gloss to the subject matter of the apotheosis of Herakles, and shows how context should help shape interpretation.

Object Biography

In looking at ritual analysis, we noted that the repeated performance of the ritual served to invest it with continuing significance, and that familiarity was important in its effectiveness. Objects can be reused during these rituals, but frequently they are made for a specific performance and then stored or discarded, as with grave goods. Usually we have little concrete evidence from either the records of the rituals or the objects themselves about an actual, single performance. Objects associated with ritual must often be approached mostly in general terms, but with some consideration that they belong to a specific point of time and place. In many ways, each ritual act is unique, and artwork can demonstrate that specific circumstance if we turn our attention from the performance and action as a setting for the object, to the object itself.

We conclude this chapter by considering the approach of object biography, which seeks to focus on the social history of the object and significant moments in its existence or "life." As Igor Kopytoff has aptly summarized:

> In doing the biography of a thing, one would ask questions similar to those one asks about people: What, sociologically, are the biographical possibilities inherent in its "status" and in the period and culture, and how are these possibilities realized? Where does the thing come from and who made it? What has been its career so far, and what do people consider to be an ideal career for such things? What are the recognized "ages" or periods in the thing's "life," and what are the cultural markers for them? How does the thing's use change with its age, and what happens to it when it reaches the end of its usefulness?[29]

The core of the approach is to focus on objects as *commodities* – that is, things that are exchanged and that have social potential. This term does have a Marxist implication, as it denotes something that is made and distributed. However, it is important to distinguish *commodity* as a more focused term than words such as *product, object, good*, and *artifact*. Products or goods that are made or consumed for sustenance or some other utilitarian function do not necessarily have a *social life*; they can be consumed privately or passively. A commodity is a thing that is consumed socially and that has a value for both the person giving it and the person receiving it. A small statue purchased for decorating a private room is a product, whereas the same statue purchased to be dedicated as a votive offering in a sanctuary has a social life that makes it a commodity. Thus, it is not the type of object or artifact, as much as its intent or potential for social exchange, that can make it a commodity, rather than a product or good.

Arjun Appadurai distinguishes three aspects to the life cycle of a commodity.[30] First is its *commodity phase*, when it is something that is actively exchanged. Second is its *commodity candidacy*, or its availability for exchange. Third is the *commodity context*, the social arenas in which the commodity candidacy can be realized in the commodity phase. Thus, we might think of the commodity as something that can move into and out of the commodity phase, depending on its availability in an appropriate context and its suitability for exchange. The small vases from the Stele Shrine at Corinth (see Figure 54), for example, were candidates for being commodities once they were made; their small size made them impractical as ordinary vessels, so they had to await a proper context, such as the dedication of the shrine, before they could realize their value and enter fully into a commodity phase.

The manner in which objects become commodities can vary, as Appadurai has summarized. An artwork can become a commodity by *destination* – that is, it was intended for exchange, as in the case of the production of votive objects. Artwork could also become a commodity by *metamorphosis*, intended for a practical use but designated as a commodity through the action of its owner. A battle helmet is not a commodity while serving as armor, but it could become a commodity by being designated as a votive offering. Once dedicated, however, an object ceases to be a commodity because it is removed from circulation; it becomes an *ex-commodity*. This leads to a third means of becoming a commodity: by *diversion*, when something that is not intended for exchange is forced back into a commodity phase. Looted artwork from a sanctuary, for example, could become a commodity once again through this action of diversion.

In addition to the components of the commodity situation (commodity phase, candidacy, and context) and the means of making an object into a commodity (destination, metamorphosis, diversion, and its opposite, termination), we can also think about the means of exchange. First is the exchange of a commodity for money, which allows for some kind of comparison of the value of commodities and noncommodities. A second means of exchange is barter, in which goods of equal value are traded. Finally, gifts are a form of exchange, although one in which there is more of a social value rather than a material value set on one side of the exchange. Thus, for example, a gift to a guest can be seen as a commodity that realizes the value of the social relationship, and can embed within the commodity an expectation of future obligation on its recipient. Two more terms can also serve to distinguish the quality of the commodity within these exchanges – whether a commodity is common or singular. A commodity that is widely and readily exchanged, such as the small votive cups, is *common*. A work that has limited exchangeability, such as a custom-ordered work that has features making it appealing to a small number of people, would be *singular*.

To see how we might apply this approach, we can look at a spouted bowl in the British Museum from the Late Geometric period (Figure 64). The vase is of Attic manufacture but was said to be found near Thebes, and its decoration is highly unusual for its period. On one side is a procession of three riders, and on the other we can see a large ship with two rows of oarsmen. On the left is a large man stepping into the ship and grabbing the wrist of a woman, who holds a wreath in her other hand. Much commentary on the scene has focused on identifying the subject of this abduction, and the leading iconographic suggestions have been that it represents Theseus leaving with Ariadne, or Paris leaving with Helen.

Rather than taking an exclusively iconographic approach to the work, Susan Langdon has studied it as an example of how a Geometric object serves to express social identity and relationships. The object is not a krater, but a special type of spouted bowl classified as a *louterion*, a vessel used to transport heated water to pour into a bath. The size of the bowl would be more suited for two people to carry, and the elaborate decoration would suggest a purification ritual rather than an ordinary bath. Louteria have been found in graves associated with funerary rituals, but they are also used for other purification rituals associated with weddings, as we noted with the loutrophoros earlier (see Figure 61). The abduction imagery can be linked through the vessel shape with rites related to legitimate marriage.

In terms of object biography, the work is certainly singular in the combination of vessel type and subject matter, and we must consider not only how this work came into existence, but also how it got from Athens, where it was made, to Thebes, where it was found. Its singular commodity quality suggests that this would have been a commodity by destination or intention, and, if associated with a wedding, was potentially involved in a gift exchange. Langdon proposes the following scenario:

> A socially powerful father in Athens agrees to give his daughter to a man of equal status. The girl is betrothed with an endowment of fine goods including this krater as wedding present. It might be intended for his or her nuptial bath, literal and ritually purificatory cleansings that separated the bridal couple from their previous lives. The vessel might eventually be used for the bathing of male guests that in epic was a significant role of wellborn hostesses. Its decoration has specific relevance to the occasion and the couple. By recognizing his social status through imagery of horsemen, charioteers, and heroic adventurer, the vessel compliments the husband and his lineage.[31]

In this object biography, we can say that the object's commodity candidacy originates in the phase when it was ordered by the father from the potter/painter and then placed into the dowry. The commodity context would be the betrothal and marriage when the vessel, along with the bride, was given to the groom, who then took it to Thebes. The commodity phase would continue at least until the completion of the marriage in Thebes. If we consider that the work might have continued to be used for the washing of guests, it would continue to have a function, no longer as a commodity that was exchanged, but as a social object that derived its significance from the original exchange. This would distinguish its social life from its object biography, which focuses on exchange.

The vessel could become a commodity again. It might, for example, be given as a guest-gift to a visitor, or perhaps be regiven as an heirloom in part of a daughter's dowry. Although the findspot is unknown, it is also possible that it was placed in a grave, reentering a commodity phase. It would be "exchanged" upon the death of its owner to his or her heir; the new owner

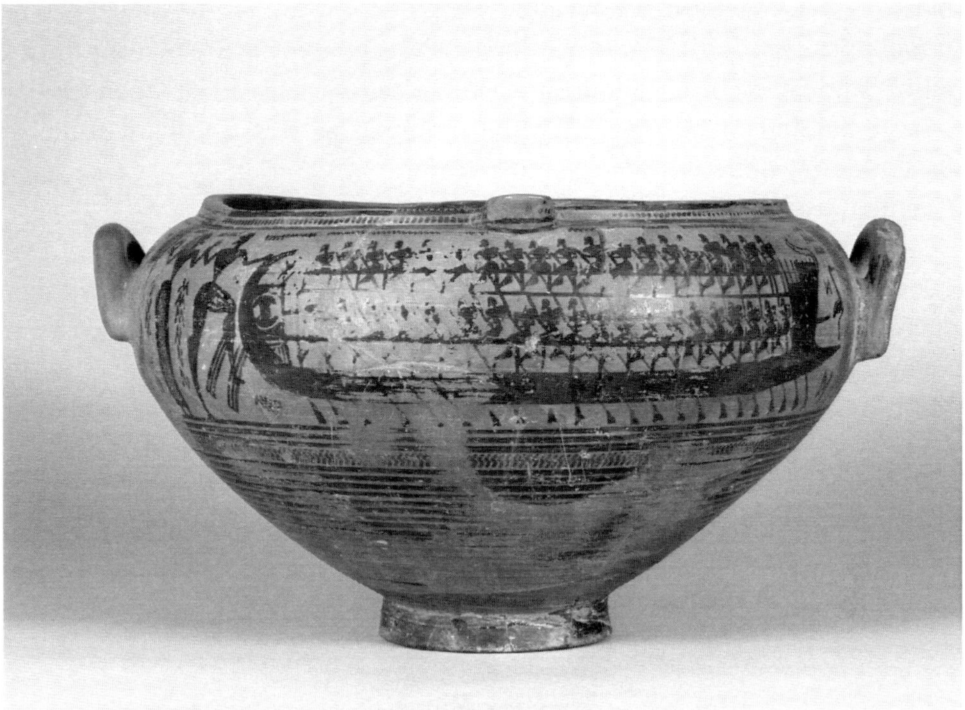

Figure 64. Late Geometric Attic spouted bowl from Thebes, c. 730–720 BCE. London, British Museum, 1899.2–19.1. Photo: © Trustees of the British Museum.

might give it to the deceased to be placed in the grave in recognition of the deceased's importance to the heir, the family, and the community. Once buried, the bowl would cease both its cultural biography, having been removed from the possibility of exchange, and its social life, having been removed from living society. Of course, once dug up, the vase reentered the world of exchange, but now as a cultural artifact, and with a new social life as an object of study and viewing in a museum.

Context Considered

The approaches outlined in this chapter look at the production, distribution, and function of artwork as an article of economic, political, social, religious, and/or cultural life. The style and subject matter of the artwork are not irrelevant in this context, but are seen as fulfilling the object's purpose or function rather than being ends in themselves. As we have seen, there are several ways of going about this, each with specific questions and pieces of information that we would want to address as part of a contextual analysis, but we run into the issue of the level of information about context. Although style and meaning can be considered by addressing the object directly, objects do not frequently encode their specific history and context as frequently in their fabric, and archaeological information is often missing. Even when we have a large amount of information about context, as with the Parthenon and its sculpture, there is still some uncertainty and ambiguity because of the fragmentary documentation and date of the sources.

The challenge of a contextual approach, then, is that we must frequently consider the general features of economic, ritual, or transactional circumstances. Even at this level, however, the consideration of context for an artwork, based on what information we do possess, can enhance our understanding of the impact of style and meaning in the work, derived from more object-focused approaches. Most of these contextual approaches have been developed more recently and have not been applied systematically across the history of Greek art. As they are, and as more information from excavation and study emerges, we can hope to sketch a clearer picture of context to apply to the study of objects.

Further Reading

Marxism, Socioeconomic Context

Generally, see Eagleton 1996, 190–9 and D'Alleva 2005, 48–60. Foundational is Baxandall 1972.

On the processes for various media, see the suggested readings in Chapter Two.

On socioeconomic aspects of vase painting, see Johnston 1979 and 2006, Vickers 1985a, Hannestad 1988 and 1989, Scheffer 1988, Arafat and Morgan 1989, Boardman 1991b, Johnston 1991, Rasmussen 1991, Williams 1991, Gill 1991, Vickers and Gill 1994, Whitley 1991, Sparkes 1996, 140–67, Tsingarida 2009, and Langridge-Noti forthcoming.

On sculpture, see Mattusch 1988; Stewart 1990, 33–72; Spivey 1996, 54–77; Palagia 2006; and Younger and Rehak 2009.

Political Context

In addition to the sources mentioned (Boardman 1978a, Watrous 1982, Morris 2000, Neer 2001), see also Pollitt 1997 and the essays in Buitron-Oliver 1997, Boedeker and Raaflaub 1998, Kurke 1999. See also Scott 2007 on the Siphnian Treasury.

General Context

For a broad overview that also ties to the interpretation of meaning, see Bérard et al. 1989.

On more public contexts, see Kurtz and Boardman 1971, Simon 1983, Garland 1985, Morris 1987 and 1992, Day 1994, Polignac 1995, Neils 1996, Derderian 2001, Keesling 2003, Barringer 2008. On portraiture, see Dillon 2006. On Athens, see Camp 1986, 2001; Camp and Mauzy 2009.

On more domestic contexts, see Lissarrague 1990 and 2001, Oakley and Sinos 1993, Nevett 1999, Cahill 2002. For Athens and the Acropolis as sites, see Hurwit 1999, Camp 1986 and 2001. For Delphi and Olympia, see Barringer 2008; Scott 2010.

Agenda and Agency

Generally, see Gell 1998. For the application to art history broadly, see the introduction and essays in Osborne and Tanner 2007, particularly the essays by Tanner and Osborne in that volume.

Ritual Theory and Cultural Poetics

On the background of this approach, see von Gennep 1960, Geertz 1973, and Bell 1992 and 1997. For application to Greek art, see the essays in Dougherty and Kurke 1998 and 2003, as well as Dodd and Faraone 2003 and Yatromanolakis and Roilos 2004. In addition to some of the sources for ritualistic contexts, see Thompson 1975; Vidal-Naquet 1986; Hedreen 1992, 125–78; Houby-Nielsen 1995 and 1996; Stansbury-O'Donnell 2006, 89–127; Marconi 2007; and Barringer 2008.

Object Biography

Generally, see Appadurai 1986b, especially the essays of Appadurai and Kopytoff, and Gosden and Marshall 1999. On the relationship to agency and ritual analysis, see Gosden and Marshall 1999, 169–78. On the use in Greek art, see Papadopoulos and Smithson 2002 and especially Langdon 2001, 2006, and 2008.

FIVE

IDENTITY

In the previous chapter, we considered approaches to an artwork that focused on its production and function. As the discussion of the Thebes krater suggested (see Figure 64), the bowl had significance as an object exchanged between individuals as part of a social compact (marriage). It may also have had a social life between or after these exchanges as an implement for rituals that were part of social life. For its users, we can also consider that this object reflected the social positions and roles of its viewers and their relationships to one another. The man leading the woman is heroic in scale and in his action; he is elite in status, as he has access to a ship; he must be from a different place than the woman, as he is taking her away by ship. The woman, by her dress and attributes, must also be elite, but she is submitting to the will of the man and is leaving her home, both domestically and geographically. Although a simple scene in its style, it displays markers about gender, class, and nationality or ethnicity that define these two figures as similar in some ways and different in others.

In this final chapter, we consider how art can serve to define identity for the people who would be associated with it, as viewers, patrons, owners, and creators. More particularly, we look at gender and sexuality, class and polis, ethnicity and foreignness as categories for which art can provide evidence of social definition. These are not approaches that have a defined and specific procedure, such as formal analysis, iconography, or Marxism. Rather, they are perspectives or points of view that use a broad range of the methodologies that we have already discussed to focus on specific issues of identity and social relationships. This discussion is supplemented by two approaches that focus on the processes of individual and social identification. Diffusion theory and postcolonialism look at the processes of interaction and the migration of ideas and forms as examples of dominance or interaction across cultures. First, though, we begin the chapter with a discussion of psychoanalysis and the gaze, which focuses on the interaction of the viewer and object and the construction of identity.

Questions of identity are not simple. Individuals do not always conform to social expectations; departure from "normal" is not necessarily transgressive. We must remember that any social system is complex, with a range of variables that define its members and a range of values within each variable that can fit within the normative. Furthermore, the pictures that we see in art are constructions and are *not* snapshots of reality. They, too, are individual creations that may represent "normal," but a normal that can be, on one hand, artificially simplified to represent an ideal that rarely exists in fact, or, on the other hand, artificially complicated by combining actions or things that would not be done together. In either case, the picture is a synthesis of ideas rather than a reality. We need to allow for a greater social complexity than the pictures present, and to consider using a more complicated approach by combining different methodologies when considering questions about identity.

Psychoanalysis, Gaze, Vision, and Identity

The term *psychoanalysis* probably conjures ideas about therapy with a couch or about repressed sexuality, which would seem to have little immediate relevance to Greek art. However, if we consider briefly the development of psychoanalysis under Sigmund Freud and its revisions under Jacques Lacan, we can see that it can provide a useful tool for art historical analysis.

One of Freud's fundamental insights was that the human mind is the place in which an individual balances the innate desire for pleasure and gratification with the need to work within the structure of human society to survive. Desire must be repressed to accommodate the behavior expected by society. In Freud's theory, the part of the mind that is driven by desires is the *id*, and the conscience or expectations of society form in the *superego*. The *ego*, or Latin for "I," is the place where these two forces are balanced.

Although this is a great oversimplification, Freud saw this development of the psyche, starting from the unrepressed desire of the infant, as a process of social development. The small child, in learning to use a toilet, learns to repress the immediate gratification of defecation to meet the demands of his or her parents. In the development of sexual behavior, Freud understood that humans have an inherent range of behaviors, and that society, through the child's relationship with the mother and father, channels these behaviors into a form that is socially acceptable. In the Oedipus complex, a young boy desires to sleep with his mother, but realizes the danger posed by his father and sees the potential risk of castration, as he becomes aware of the genital differences between male and female. The boy represses the desire for his mother and begins to identify with his father, taking on a more "normal" heterosexual identity, one that is "unified" with his biological sex. Although the specific details of this process have more to do with Freud and Viennese society at that time than with a universal human condition, the important point is that gender and sexual identity are constructed by an individual and are not inherently biological.

Jacques Lacan shared with Freud an emphasis on desire and the development of socially acceptable behavior. Rather than sexual desire, he based behavioral development on language. Analogous to the id, Lacan used the term the *Real*, which is the raw state of existence as seen in a newborn. As the infant develops, he or she moves into the *Imaginary*, in which the child becomes aware that the world is made of distinct images, such as the mother, and sees himself or herself, as when looking in a mirror, as belonging to and controlling these images and the environment. In the *Symbolic* phase, the child learns to speak. By learning words and their meaning, the child not only learns to name what is present, but also recognizes what is absent and what he or she may not be able to possess. With language also come the social codes that serve to regulate behavior and identity.

For both Freud and Lacan, the idea is that the individual develops a unified self, aligning biological sex, gender identification, and sexual orientation, that is socially acceptable. This model, however, tends to favor the behavior and status of white, upper-class males. Whereas their analyses give a great deal of attention to sexual behavior and gender identity formation, identity is also social, national, civic, ethnic, linguistic, religious, and so forth.

Of particular interest for art history, Lacan devoted a great deal of thought to the role of vision in this process of socialization by focusing on the gaze. Not only does an individual subject realize in the Symbolic phase that something unseen can be named and desired, but the subject also becomes aware that he or she can be seen by others. To distinguish these intersecting viewing points, what an individual sees is called the *gaze* (small g), whereas the collective sight that encompasses the individual is the *Gaze* (capital G).

Thus the subject becomes concerned with how others view him or her. This can even extend to images such as portraits or statues that stand in for authorities, such as rulers or gods, whose Gaze is still present through their representation. Thus the subject, aware of the Gaze, acts in accordance with its presence.

The question to ask first is: How can one apply psychoanalysis to Greek art? Following Terry Eagleton's synopsis of the applicability of psychoanalytic theory to literature, there are several choices for adapting this theory to the visual arts: we can look at the artist, we can look at the work's contents, we can look at its formal construction, or we can look at the viewer.[1] We do not have enough personal information to focus on the Greek artist, nor do we have enough information about the psychological symbolism and motivation of the content. However, we do have some understanding about the way Greeks understood vision for us to examine the gaze/Gaze and its role in constructing identity for the viewer through art.

Basically, Greek visual theory understood vision to be akin to touch, although the actual processes described by different theorists could vary greatly.[2] For example, the Atomists believed that seeing was the result of a tiny *simulacrum*, or replica of the object entering into the eye, and through the optic nerve into the mind or *psyche*. In justification of this, one can see a reflection of the objects in the visual field when looking into someone's eye; these images are tiny replicas of the real objects, streaming from the object into the eye.

A second school of thought, connected with Plato, was of the *visual fire*, a ray of light that emanated from the eye. When it hit an object, that sensation was transmitted back to the body, like reaching out and touching the object. Like touch, sight can thus stimulate a physiological as well as a psychological reaction in the viewer.

A third school of thought, deriving from Aristotle, speculated that there was a visual medium, or *pneuma*, like the air. Motion in the pneuma created waves that reached the eye. The moistness of both the pneuma and the eye allowed the transfer of the wave into the eye, creating a vision of the object. This is not unlike two objects striking one another in the air, which creates a percussive sound wave that reaches the eardrum, and then transmits the sound to the mind.

Fundamental to all three theories, none of which corresponds to our scientific explanation for sight, is that what one sees physically enters into the body and mind and can have a physiological as well as a psychological impact on the viewer. For example, Aristotle explained that a painting of a corpse can be pleasurable because it is a learning experience, whereas seeing the corpse directly can make one ill.[3] The difference is that in looking at a corpse, the corpse itself is touching the psyche, and its pestilence enters into the body. In the case of a painting, it is only an image of a corpse. With an image, one can contemplate without the same physical connection to the real thing and the consequent reaction, so one can learn from the experience. One could contemplate the heroism of the deceased, and learn to emulate it and incorporate it as part of one's own identity. For Plato, however, this posed a danger. He argued that mimetic drama and art showing bad behavior would corrupt the viewer, as these bad examples would touch the psyche negatively – an argument that continues into the present over video games.

This summary drastically oversimplifies both psychoanalysis and Greek theories of vision. However, the point is that we can develop the idea of the gaze/Gaze and the viewer's experience of art as a model for how a work of art can construct identity, whether gender, sexual, ethnic, civic, or other. This can then give us a framework for using additional approaches, such as object biography or ritual analysis, to understand more completely how art can help to construct identity.

What we want to consider is the relationship of the artwork and its subject matter with the viewer: What does it suggest about the self-image of the viewer (gaze)? What does the viewing context suggest about what others think about the viewer (Gaze)? Does the viewer live up to the image set up by the artwork and social expectations? How does the artwork reinforce the status and self-image of the viewer? Does this self-image position the viewer in a lower or higher status based on their identity, whether gender, sexual, civic, class, or ethnic?

In this light, we can consider once again the bronze caryatid mirror seen in previous chapters (Figure 2), as vision and gaze are intimately bound together in the mirror's function.

When the viewer gazes (small g) at the mirror, there are actually two objects on which she can fasten her line of sight: the reflection of her face and the female figure that is the handle. The female figure is a sign of something that is desired – the idealized form of a woman in Greek society. Whether iconographically it represents a goddess such as Aphrodite or a mortal making an offering, the bronze figure's actions show piety as well as *aidos*, or modesty. Her body is covered by her peplos and her gaze is steady and slightly down turned, as indicated by the tilt of the head and the lowered line of the eyelids, yet she has both beauty and stature, as well as poise and control, thus conforming to the ideal woman.[4]

The modesty of her gaze, which avoids direct confrontation with her surroundings, contrasts with the direct stare of the two erotes who are crowning her. Their gaze could be considered as representing the Gaze of the culture, evaluating the behavior and form of its members. In this case, by their gestures they recognize the excellence of the caryatid as an ideal figure. Curiously, the gaze of the viewer becomes part of this collective Gaze, and by joining her gaze with the action of the erotes in looking at the caryatid figure, the viewer acknowledges the validity of the ideal. Thus the viewer becomes part of the community ethos by participating as one of the multiple viewers of the figure.

The reflection in the mirror's disk above the caryatid sets up a comparison between the ideal figure and the viewer. To the degree that the reflected image duplicates the features of the ideal, the viewer can see herself as reflecting that ideal image and assuming the social identity that it represents. Interestingly, to see the caryatid to compare it with her reflection, the viewer must lower her gaze, thereby duplicating the gaze of the caryatid, who looks at something in her hand. The mirror thereby encodes form, action, and symbols that not only provide a model to emulate for individual identity, but also make the viewer part of the social collective that upholds that idea through the Gaze. It can be useful to diagram these relationships to see them more clearly, using arrows to indicate both the gaze and Gaze (see Diagram 2).

The mirror is divided into three parts: the reflection in the disk, the *ideal* (caryatid), and the collective *group*, represented by the erotes. Indeed, as the discussion of aidos suggested, the social group is the origin of the Gaze, and it can be epitomized by elements within the artwork, such as participants and spectators, but is also represented by the setting. Because an object would usually be viewed within the context of a social setting, one must remember that other people are present as part of the viewing experience and constitute a collective group.

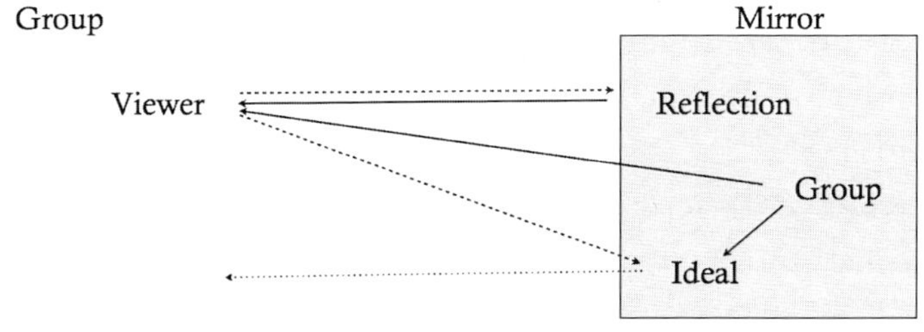

Diagram 2

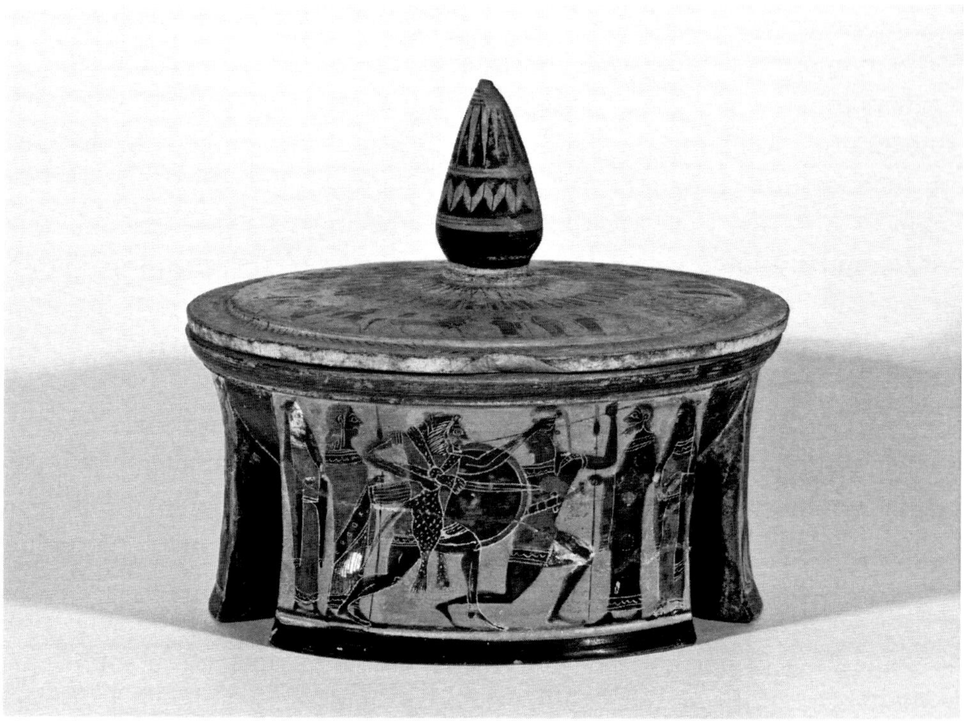

Figure 65. Attic black-figure pyxis, c. 560–550 BCE. Herakles and Amazon fighting. Berlin, Antikensammlung, F3988. Photo Credit: Bildarchiv Preussischer Kulturbesitz/Art Resource, New York.

The gaze (small g) of the viewer, indicated by the dashed line, has two main focal points: the viewer's reflection and the ideal of the caryatid figure. This second focal point also receives the attention of the erotes, and their acknowledgment of her ideal qualities is encompassed within their Gaze, indicated by the solid line. The convergence of the viewer's gaze and the collective Gaze on the caryatid allow the viewer to affirm the ideal and unite the viewer and the group. The Gaze of the erotes also looks out toward the viewer, making her directly aware of the Gaze. So, too, her own reflection looks back at her; the quality of that image would become a self-judgment of the viewer as to whether she conformed to the social ideal of the caryatid below. The ideal figure on the handle, however, turns her gaze away from all (dotted line). She becomes a complete object in the process, and in some sense an objective standard by this detachment.

A curious twist on the dynamics of vision can be seen on a pyxis showing Herakles fighting an Amazon (Figure 65). To either side are spectators who watch the scene, but given their formal dress and poses, they are not part

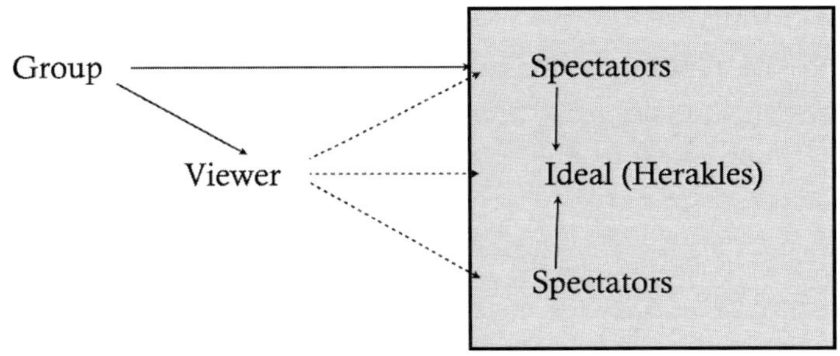

Diagram 3

of the narrative action. Instead, they are spectators watching the story, not unlike the actual viewer of the container. To the left are a woman pulling her mantle forward and a mantled youth holding a spear; to the right a bearded man holds a spear, with a second woman pulling her mantle behind him. These figures respond to the deed of Herakles: the men by formally standing at attention and observing him statuelike and thoughtfully, the women by opening their mantles from their faces as the gesture of a bride when she meets her bridegroom, the *anakalypsis*. Herakles is a model for both – one as the epitome of heroic behavior by which their actions would be measured, the other as a model of the ideal husband. Not only is the narrative action a model for the viewer of the pyxis, but the spectators in the picture also model the behavior expected of a viewer looking at the scene (see Diagram 3).

The viewer can model his or her behavior to be similar to that of the spectators, and thereby can look like an ideal member in the eyes of society and its collective Gaze. This Gaze encompasses both the viewer and the work of art, the pyxis. As a commodity that has been purchased, the pyxis has already been acknowledged as an acceptable social artifact. If we think of the viewer as a woman, who would have been the most likely user of a pyxis, we can also note that the Amazon being attacked by Herakles would be a negative role model, an anti-ideal, according to the social "norm." Thus there is a choice for identification presented to the viewer's gaze, one "normal" and the other not, with the attendant consequences.

As an approach, the consideration of the gaze/Gaze and the construction of identity will vary according to the nature of the artwork, its subject matter, and the viewing circumstances. Indeed, identity is constructed through many different experiences and the effects will vary depending on the situation. For example, we would have to analyze a large-scale sculpture differently from a work held in the hands of the viewer, whether a vase or a mirror. A statue such as the Getty Youth would have been seen in a public context and by a potentially more varied audience (Figure 66). Looking at this work, we can think about how desire is also captured in what the viewer sees.

The bronze statue shows an Olympic victor, as defined by the olive wreath on his head. The statue was found off the coast of Italy; it is dated by most scholars to the second half of the fourth century BCE and is associated with the workshop of Lysippos, although radiocarbon dates of organic material in its core indicate that the date for casting might be third century.[5] Although the original context and specific dedication are unknown, we can analyze the appeal of the statue as commemorating an athletic victor. As Deborah Steiner has discussed, ancient accounts about athletes point to the moment when the victor is crowned as being the height of his glory, as he is recognized for his achievement by the assembled viewers.[6] Victor statues were generally life-size in scale and stood in for the original athlete. As one inscription states:

> Come to know Theognetos looking upon him, the boy Olympic victor, skilled charioteer of the wrestling, most beautiful to see, but in competing no worse than his form, who crowned the city of good fathers.[7]

As Steiner has pointed out, the viewer of the statue stands in for the original audience that witnessed the crowning of the original athlete. The bronze surface is sleek and lustrous and recaptures the sensual pleasure of looking at the athlete's smooth, oiled skin. When the viewer would read the inscription, he or she would recreate the original accolade and acknowledge the sentiments accorded to the figure. As the inscription on Theognetos points out, the viewer would know him and his beauty; the statue would become an object of desire that the viewer would want to possess. As with language for Lacan, the image becomes a sign for that which is absent but also desired.

If we think about this from the point of the portrayed, we can also understand the particular power of a portrait. In commissioning a portrait that stands in place of himself, the subject can continue to command the desire and attention of society. He becomes the ideal, and is no longer mortal. This is implied in another epigram for an Olympic victor from the fifth century BCE:

> Euthymos of Lokris, son of Astykles, I won the Olympic games three times. And he set up this image for mortals to look upon.[8]

In the first line, the statue speaks as if it were the living person, but the second line moves into the third person. This shift places increasing distance

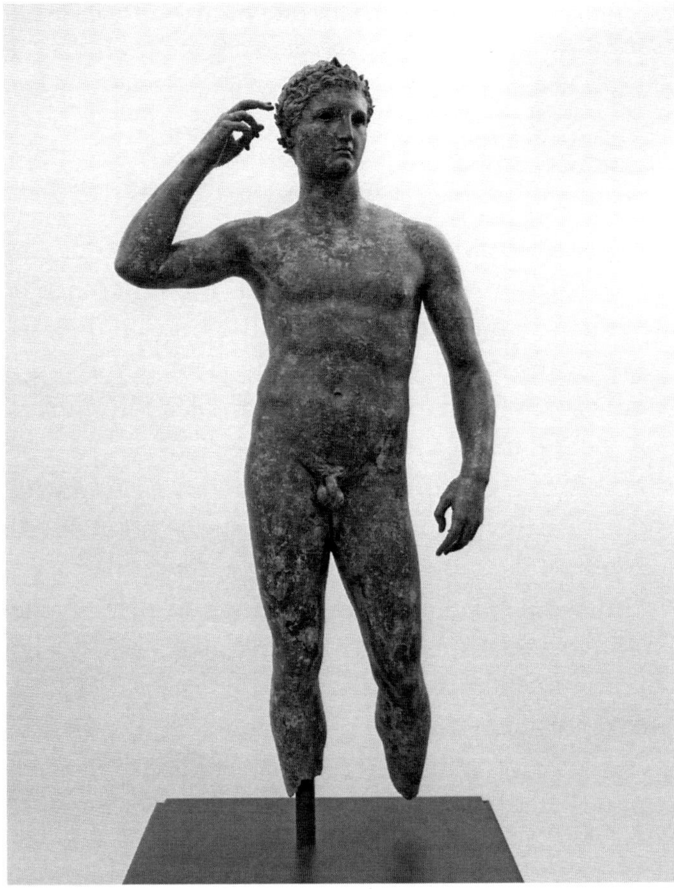

Figure 66. Getty Youth, later fourth century BCE. *Malibu, Getty Villa, 77.AB.30. Photo: The J. Paul Getty Museum. Villa Collection. Malibu, California.*

between the viewer and the subject of the portrait, and by referring to the viewers as mortals, Euthymos suggests a sharp contrast with his own immortality via the *eikon* or image and its inscription. This is quite a departure from the idea of *aidos*, which in the early fifth century dictated that even a triumphant athlete should cast down his eyes, avoiding direct engagement with the Gaze. For a later statue such as the Getty Youth, the figure looks off beyond the viewer, as if to another realm.

To summarize, we might consider the following questions as suitable to a psychoanalytic analysis:

- How is the gaze in all its components constructed? What is the relationship between the gaze of or within the work, the gaze/Gaze of the viewer, and the Gaze of the group or social setting?
- What are the models of form and behavior (ideals) that are encoded within the work?

- How do ancient sources inform us about the process of seeing and the way it affects the viewer? How are we meant to react to a specific work or type?
- What are the categories of identity, and how are these referenced in the work?

Feminism, Gender, and Sexuality

There is an obvious contrast between the male Getty Youth and the female caryatid figure of the mirror. Most obvious is the difference in dress (nude versus heavily clothed), but there is also a difference in their gaze, outward-looking and downward-looking, respectively. This difference in the display of the body and its action is hardly unusual, and leads us into considerations of gender identity and its construction in Greek art.

A **feminist** art history, as with other approaches dealing with sexual identity, ethnicity, nationality, and postcolonialism, is not a specific procedure such as iconography or agency, but might be better termed a *perspective*. These are approaches that focus on a particular group of people, their art or representation, and their relationship with other groups with whom they have contact. To do this, a feminist art history employs a range of methodologies to analyze the representation of women and the way in which ideology filters those representations to construct a specific idea of women and men. Further, it explores how these images serve to promote the individual or cultural agendas that shape women's lives.

Because ancient Greek women have left us very little direct testimony, either as writers or artists, being attentive to the strengths and weaknesses of different approaches for a feminist or gender analysis is important. Women can be associated with some objects as users, but they may not have made them or even purchased them. Many objects with representations of women were not meant to be used by women, and so we have to consider how to account for a complex range of imagery that connects to a variety of agendas or ideas, some of which are contradictory or depart from the social norm.

We began Chapter Three with an *iconographic* analysis of the caryatid mirror in Figure 2. As we noted there, this involved a detailed visual analysis of the work, identification, classification, and interpretation of the significant forms, and the use of texts to corroborate the iconographic conclusions. In turning to the poem by Alkman, we noted the emphasis on modesty in the choral performers, who praised their leaders extravagantly. The downturned gaze, formal clothing, and quiet poise of the caryatid figure resonate with this idea of the modest woman performing a ritual function before the city. As a method, iconography has been the foundation for much of the feminist analysis of images of women.

Other ancient sources speak about the modesty expected of women and their need to acquiesce in their roles as wives and mothers.[9] Indeed, the picture painted by the written sources speaks of a decidedly second-class status for women in ancient Greece, and particularly in Athens, whence many of the surviving texts come. Proper women were expected to stay in the home and to interact only with the men of their immediate family. Women were excluded from the symposion, unless they were there as paid entertainers, or *hetairai*, who could include sexual favors or prostitution as part of their services. Proper women were expected to be industrious, productive in weaving cloth and managing the household stores efficiently. They were not considered to be as rational or in control of their emotions as men, and were thought to be more highly sexed than men and in need of control by them. Their legal and citizenship rights were restricted. Women who violated the expectations of society were the subject of ridicule and blame, whereas those who conformed were praised. If we listen to the advice of Perikles, even to be named as a virtuous woman in public was too much notoriety; the ideal woman should not be seen or heard of at all.

Recent studies on gender and women in Greece have begun to build a more complex understanding of the representation of women and their social, religious, and economic context. The gender segregation within the household that literary sources describe was not practiced closely in less elite households or on an everyday level, as studies of the Greek household suggest. The roles of some women, such as priestesses, were highly visible and potentially powerful and praiseworthy. The use of multiple sources and approaches has helped to create this more complex and nuanced understanding.

A *poststructuralist* approach to meaning, for example, emphasizes the importance of context for understanding the work. In this light, one might well question the validity of using a seventh-century BCE poem by the Spartan poet Alkman to analyze the fifth-century, Argive mirror in Figure 2. Indeed, if we look at a different mirror from Lakonia (the region controlled by Sparta), we see a very different image of an ideal woman (Figure 67).[10] The basic structure of the mirror is the same, but the caryatid here is nude, with a necklace and a baldric across her chest, from which dangles a sickle associated with athletic victors. Her hair is braided and bound, and she holds a vase or pomegranate in her left hand.

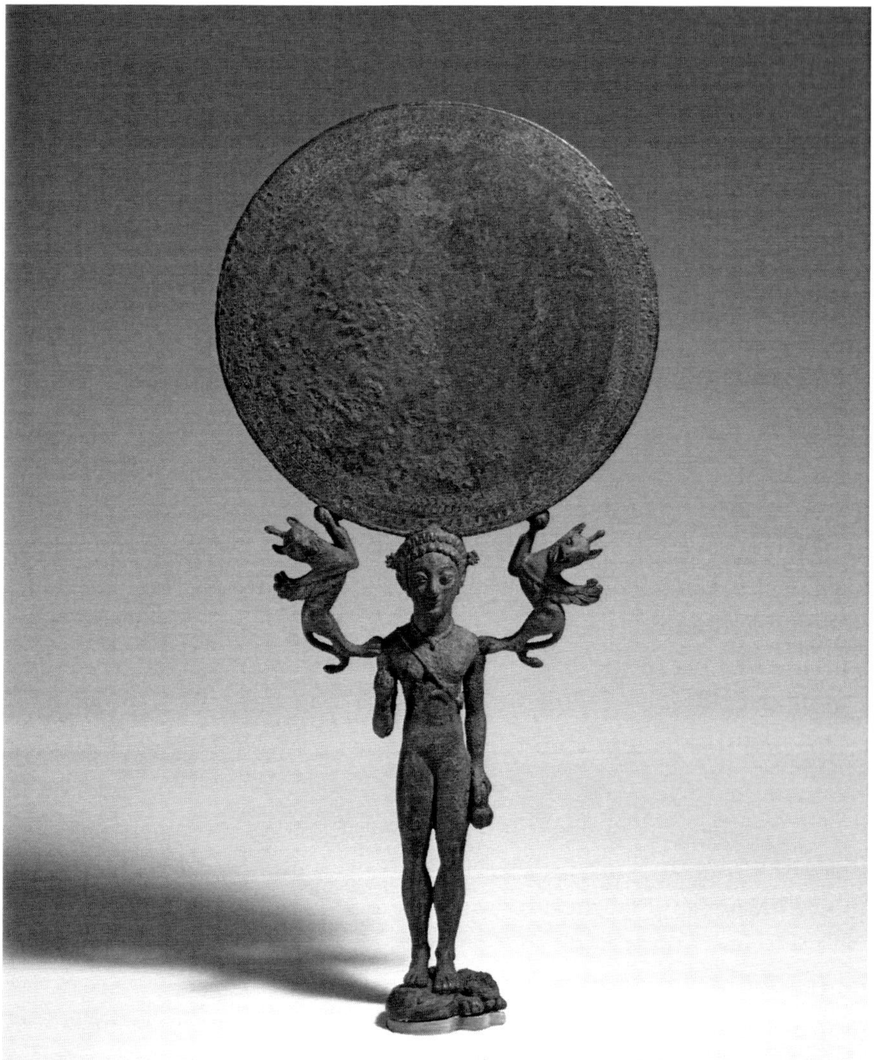

Figure 67. Bronze Lakonian caryatid mirror, c. 520 BCE. New York, Metropolitan Museum of Art, 38.11.3. Image Copyright © The Metropolitan Museum of Art/Art Resource, NY.

This work is one of a group of sixth-century bronzes, coming from the region around Sparta, that feature nude or mostly nude women. Some are athletes, whereas others are musical performers. There is very little that is "modest" about their representation when compared with that of the first mirror handle. The ideal that is being constructed by this object is quite different. Some sources indicate that there were athletic competitions for Spartan women as part of their initiation rituals, and that at some performances women could appear naked before an audience, as men did in some

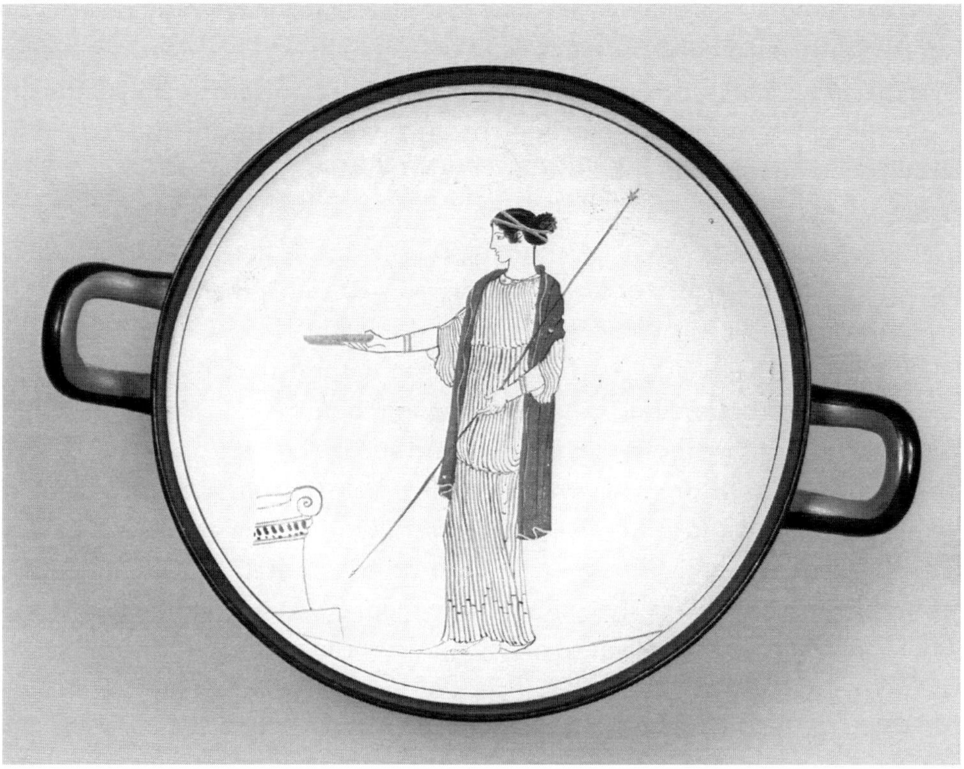

Figure 68. Attic white-ground cup attributed to the Villa Giulia Painter, c. 470 BCE. Priestess pouring a libation. New York, Metropolitan Museum of Art 1979.11.15. Image Copyright © The Metropolitan Museum of Art/Art Resource, New York.

of their performances. These sources are frequently critical of the Spartan practices and may exaggerate to make a point. Even so, this suggests that gender identity was a construction that could vary considerably by context and place. Therefore, we need to think about who purchased, owned, and used works and how the image was fabricated to meet their interests and agendas.

Thinking *psychoanalytically*, a woman using the Spartan mirror would have had a different model for identity and behavior than an Argive or Athenian woman using a clothed-caryatid mirror. The Lakonian caryatid stares back at the viewer and encodes a more assertive behavior as an ideal within the functioning of the gaze/Gaze and identity outlined earlier in Diagram 2. The fact that some of these mirrors have been found outside Lakonia hints that this alternative model of the female ideal might well have been appealing to non-Lakonians too.

In the previous chapter we also saw that *ritual* was a means for constructing social bonds and creating acquiescence in a set of beliefs and civic or religious systems. The lead performers of ritual have an important social status that is confirmed by the acknowledgment and participation of the assembled group who witness or follow their lead. Costumes, objects, and settings serve to enhance the status of ritual leaders, which in Greece included priestesses as well as priests. Although political rights may have been limited for women, ritual codes or laws gave priestesses status that transcended the everyday situation of women, as recent studies by Joan Connelly and the exhibition *Worshipping Women* have sought to demonstrate by using a variety of approaches that include both meaning and context.[11]

For example, if we look at a white-ground cup in the Metropolitan Museum of Art, we see a well-dressed woman standing before an altar, holding a phiale in her right hand and cradling a scepter with her left arm and shoulder (Figure 68). Iconographically, the woman has been tentatively identified as a goddess, possibly Hera, because of the scepter. As Connelly points out, however, identifying the figure on the basis of one attribute is problematic, as there are a number of similar images of women making an offering at an altar that cannot be identified as goddesses.[12] One needs to consider whether the image represents Hera acting as herself, or is rather a representation of a ritual honoring a goddess such as Hera, with perhaps the priestess dressing in a manner similar to the goddess and serving as her embodiment as part of the ceremony. We saw in the last chapter that Peisistratos dressed up a woman named Phye for his ritual entrance into Athens as its new leader, and Rebecca Sinos has argued that ritual impersonation or epiphany was part of the process of giving honor to a god. Thus, we might consider the figure on the cup as a priestess who becomes like the goddess for the participants of the ritual.

Through ritual analysis, one can see another dimension of women's roles and status within Greek society that differ from some of the textual sources. Of course, an elite religious role with its social and economic benefits would not be representative of all women or of everyday practice, but it does show a complexity that would accord some women important status. This, then, finds expression in the representation of their role in ritual or in the representation of the women as individuals through statues and other portraits, such as the Queen's Vase discussed in the previous chapter (see Figure 62).

A contextual approach can also help to distinguish the representation of more everyday women, as can be seen by two works in Berlin that have been displayed together, a cup by Douris whose interior shows two women

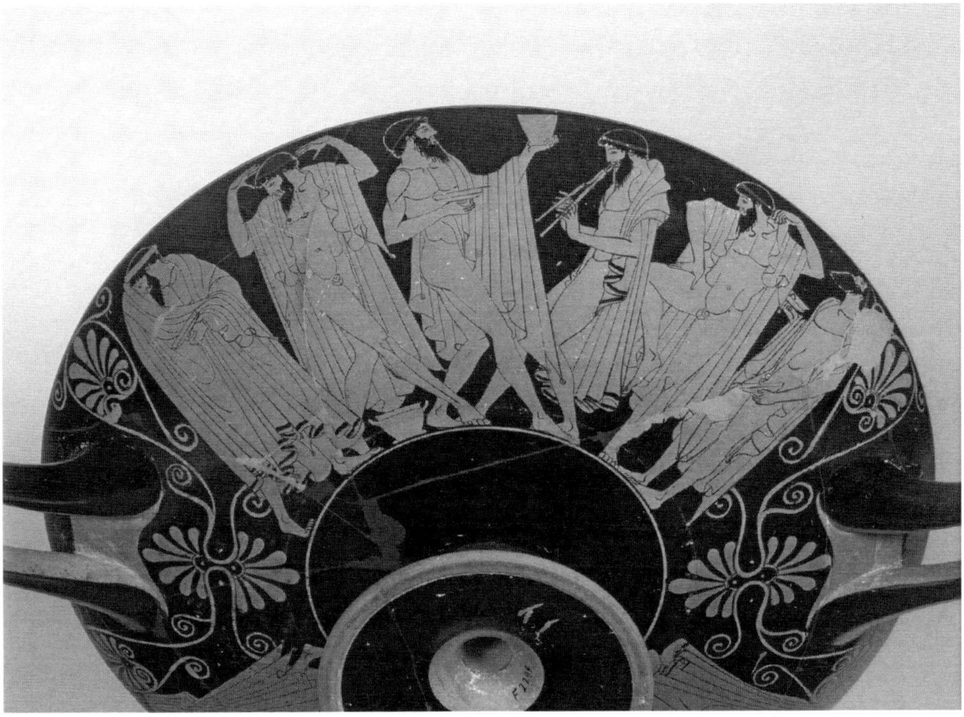

Figure 69. Attic red-figure kylix attributed to Douris, c. 480–470 BCE. Exterior: Komasts. Berlin, Antikensammlung, F2289. Photo Credit: Bildarchiv Preussischer Kulturbesitz/Art Resource, New York.

working with wool (Figures 69 and 70) and an object called an *epinetron* that fits over the knee of a woman to protect the leg while spinning wool (Figure 71).

The exterior of the Douris cup shows a line of men with mantles participating in a *komos*, a celebration associated with the symposion in which men dance and participate in a procession, probably through the neighborhood (Figure 69). On each side of the cup there is one man holding or playing an aulos, while the others either dance, hold a cup, or both. About half of the men have mantles that have fallen open, making them essentially nude. Their behavior seems natural, given their drinking, but is it realistic to consider that this behavior was normative or acceptable? Male nudity was a feature of Greek life, but its time and place were constrained to athletics and the gymnasium and to the symposion, as we saw in Figure 59. The andron would have been too small to accommodate the komos on this cup. The action seems more likely to be taking place outside of the house, since the literary sources suggest that this behavior would cross the boundaries between the men's and women's spaces if it were to occur within the house

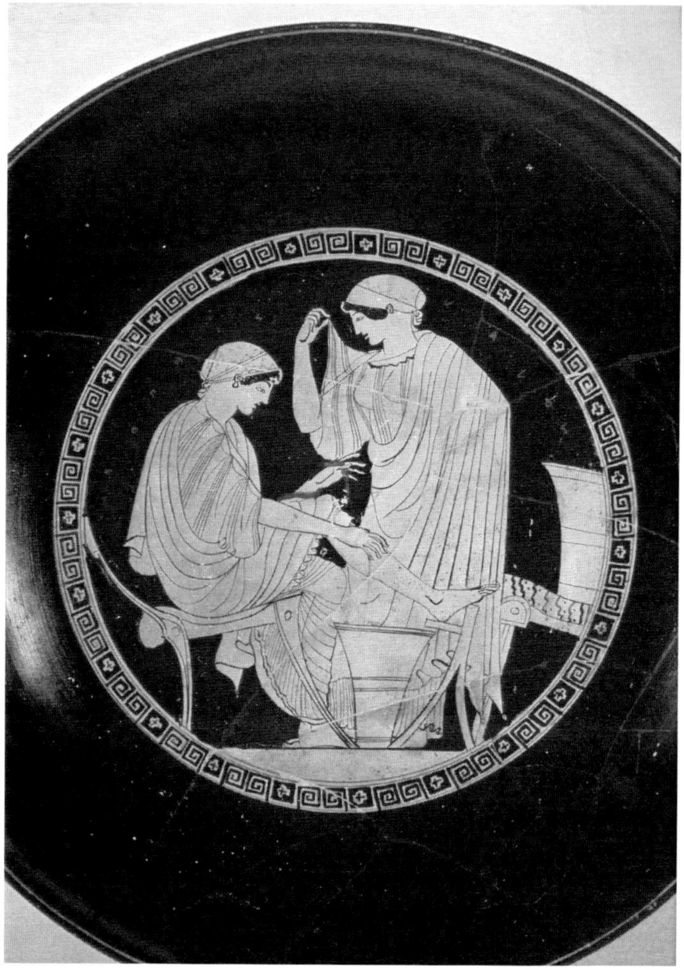

Figure 70. Attic red-figure kylix attributed to Douris, c. 480–470 BCE. Interior: Women. Berlin, Antikensammlung, F2289. Photo Credit: Bildarchiv Preussischer Kulturbesitz/Art Resource, New York.

and its courtyard. Rigid gender segregation, however, would be hard to accomplish within the size and plan of the average household. In the end, it is hard to see this picture of male behavior as realistic, even if it epitomizes the festive nature of the komos and symposion.

The inside of the cup shows an interior scene with two women (Figure 70). One woman sits on a chair while pulling a strand of wool above a *kalathos*, or wool basket. A second woman pulls at her mantle, recalling the anakalypsis gesture of the bride but without any referent to a bridegroom in the picture. The furnishings signify that we are in an interior space, but are we in the women's quarters, or *gynaikonitis*, of the house that the literary sources describe? Should we interpret the picture as two women who are virtuous by being industrious, while the men carouse on the outside of the cup? The women wear double garments and headdresses and are respectable in their appearance, except for the bit of leg shown by the seated woman. Given how formally dressed and industrious the women are, should we consider this as a bit of titillation for the viewer of the cup? Because a kylix such as this is associated with the symposion, and likely a male viewer, should the picture then represent the male view about women expressed in the literary sources? Thus we would have a contrast between the space and activity of women inside the house, and the behavior of the men on the outside of the cup, which frames, symbolically, the public realm of men's lives.

As with the outside pictures, is the interior picture real and accurately reflective of the lives of Athenian women in the early fifth century BCE? If we consider a man drinking from the cup during a symposion, he would see only a flash of the picture while drinking, because wine would cover the picture while the cup was being held. This would make the incongruity of the formal attire of the women and the bit of exposed leg more likely to be a fantasy, a picture for the drinker to enjoy while in the world of men, confirming the stereotypes that society constructed for gender roles. However, the cup comes from the cemetery at Vulci in Etruria, so that we have to consider whether the assumption of a male, Athenian symposion for context is the only possible point of view. Etruscan social values and gender relations were different, and we must consider that the vase painter, Douris, knowing that many of his wares would be exported, composed his pictures to be appealing to a different audience with a different ideology. Further, can we assume that the only viewer would be male, even if the cup had been sold locally in Athens? A cup in a household might be used by any of its inhabitants, and a female viewer might have viewed the lack of verism of the women's actions with irony or humor, rather than titillation. Indeed, the humor would likely have been apparent to men as well, who had seen women actually working wool.

To understand the picture's context more fully, we could turn to a Marxist approach that would look at the socioeconomic factors surrounding the production and distribution of the artist's works and similar subject matter. As Sian Lewis demonstrated with some cups showing degrading and exploitative sexual acts, one must explore the contextual data behind such scenes.[13] She points out that there are only five such scenes, many fewer than their frequent reproduction in scholarship would suggest. Based on the

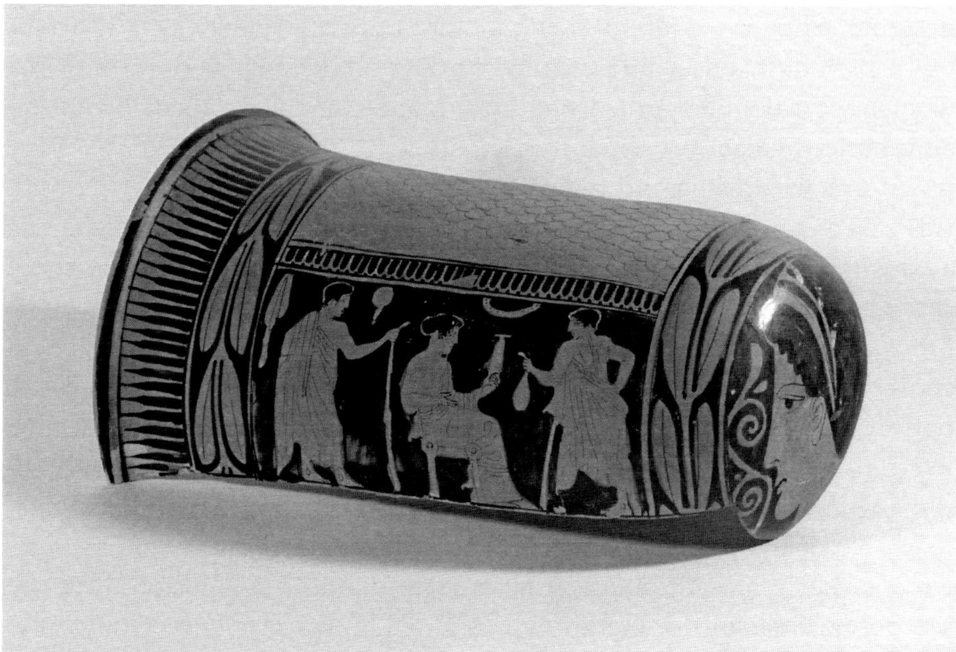

Figure 71. Attic red-figure epinetron attributed to the Painter of Berlin 2624, c. 450 BCE. Berlin, Antikensammlung, F2624. Photo Credit: Bildarchiv Preussischer Kulturbesitz/Art Resource, New York.

provenances of some of the cups, it is probable that they were all exported. Furthermore, the violent scene is often matched with a nonviolent scene on the same cup, so there is a question about which is the normative representation and which is not. Context, then, does not seem to indicate a systemic pattern that would reflect an Athenian attitude advocating violence toward women as acceptable. The situation is more complex and needs to be approached with that in mind.

The picture on the epinetron is also a domestic scene, but one in which two young men interact with a seated woman (Figure 71). A mirror and cloth hang from the wall, signaling an interior space associated with the woman. The men wear mantles and hold walking sticks, signaling their men-about-town status. The woman holds up a large alabastron (perfume container), and one young man holds up a pouch. We cannot see what is in the pouch; this has caused some controversy for interpretation.[14] One possibility that has been suggested is that it contains knucklebones for gaming; the other is that it contains coins and is a money purse. In such scenes, where a man is holding up a purse to a woman, the interpretation has frequently been that these are men negotiating the services of a hetaira for an upcoming symposion such as the one in Figure 59, and that we are in her household.

It would seem that the young man is not offering to play a game, so money would be a more likely signification for the purse. However, money purchases many things and we should consider, semiotically, that its meaning will vary within the picture's field of signs. Here we should consider that a sign such as the purse could signify the purchase of oil, making this a commercial transaction and the woman a merchant selling to a client. The woman, being seated and centered in the picture, becomes the focal point of the scene – but is this because of her erotic appeal? The epinetron itself is an object unlikely to have been purchased or used by a man, so we must consider that this is an object purchased by a woman that could represent her point of view. Therefore the central position and seated pose of the woman could be signs of respectability and status. If so, this suggests that women's position in Athenian society as shopkeepers and patrons of art is more complex that the literary sources would suggest.

Turning to agency, for example, we might consider further the relationship of the components of the nexus for the epinetron and the cup. It is probable that neither object was a commission, so we should probably think of the artist as initiating the process of manufacture. The artist chooses the prototype (subject matter) for the index (artwork), and then sells it to a recipient. In making two different types of objects, however, an artist does not arbitrarily choose the prototype/subject matter, but would choose subjects that would be effective for the eventual recipient. In comparing a sympotic drinking cup with a wool-working device, there would be a potential difference in the gender of the recipient for each work. An artist would choose a prototype/subject that might appeal to the identity and status of a male drinker on one hand, and to a woman working wool in a household on the other hand. After the purchase, the recipient/purchaser can use the index/object within a social setting, creating a second chain of agency, as can be seen using Gell's scheme. In this second chain, the purchaser, Recipient1 or Recipient2, moves from being a patient (P) when purchasing the work of art to an agent (A) when using it:

[[[Artist (A)]→Prototype1]→Index-Artifact1 (**cup**)]→Recipient1 (P)

[[Recipient1 (A)]→Index-Artifact1]→Recipient1.1 (P)

[[[Artist (A)]→Prototype2]→Index-Artifact2 (**epinetron**)]→Recipient2 (P)

[[Recipient2 (A)]→Index-Artifact2]→Recipient2.1 (P)

Each recipient, then, exercises some agency in choosing a work that expresses that recipient's identity and status to his or her associates. This second level of agency is the one that constrains the initial choice of the artist in making the work, as without a sale to the recipient, no act of agency would take place at all.

We can think about a Marxist and market approach to develop a further nuance of the comparison. The kylix discussed earlier (Figures 69 and 70) was found in a tomb of the Etruscan cemetery at Vulci. It may well have been made for export, along with many other works by Douris, including the cup in Figure 3, so the selection of the scene may reflect the artist's speculation about what would sell in the Etruscan market. Indeed, some subjects on Attic pottery have been shown to be almost exclusively found in exported pottery. We must question, then, whether the scenes that represent gender issues and relationships reflect Athenian values, or Athenian perceptions of external market desires, or some combination of both.

In contrast, the epinetron (Figure 71) comes from Athens, and was produced and consumed within a local market. It, too, reflects what the producer speculated would be desirable within the Athenian market. Given the restricted clientele for an epinetron, though, its subject matter reflects what the artist thought an Athenian woman might purchase. This does not make the epinetron true to life and the cup not; rather, it demonstrates the complexity behind the construction of gender representations in both.

In summary, a feminist approach to Greek art will likely draw on a number of different approaches. Art presents an image to the viewer that can serve as a positive or negative model for appearance and action; understanding how the gaze/Gaze helps to shape identity shows how these models might encode identity and behavior. The meanings of these images and symbols will vary according to the context, so we have to look not only at a generalized meaning, but also at its specific interpretation based on maker, patron, and the function or role of the object, when these are known in some degree. This creates a more complex challenge for a feminist art history, as is also the case for other forms of identity.

Sexual Identity

Another layer of identity to consider here is **sexual identity**. The previous discussion has implicitly focused on heterosexuality as the primary form of sexual identity or orientation for men and women, but we also must consider that sexual identity includes other forms, such as homosexuality and bisexuality.

We have already noted that there was little age distinction between women as they are represented in art, but that artists did signal adult status in men by depicting a beard and youthful status with a beardless figure. This distinction is most likely an artificial convention, but it is important as part of the construction of male sexual identity within the institution of Greek pederasty. As Andrew Lear and Eva Cantarella have recently explained,

> [this consisted] of erotic relations between adult men and adolescent boys. The limits on this practice – how widespread it was in terms of geography and social class, precisely what was approved and what was disapproved, when and how it began to be practiced, when and why it stopped – are the subjects of much debate among modern scholars.[15]

As a social practice, pederasty is complicated by being more than sexual orientation, as it would not be a substitute for the social practice of heterosexual relationships that provided citizens and heirs for property. An adult male would, in certain periods and places, be expected to have both types of relationships, as both were important to the enculturation of men and women and the creation of social identity. Indeed, as Gloria Ferrari has argued, we might well consider that Greek culture created three genders, one female and two male (youth and adult).[16] Pederastic practice created a relationship that developed the adult identity of the young male in a way that was more transformational than the change of status for a young woman from kore to bride. Visually, the beard, or its lack, becomes a signifier of this status.

How to approach pederastic imagery and the questions of sexual identity, then, is as complicated as a feminist analysis. The written sources are mostly later than the visual representations of pederastic courtship and relations, and both bodies of evidence are beset by the usual problems of accidents of survival, contradictions, or bias. As with a feminist analysis, approaching the issue requires using a variety of means.

Lear and Cantarella have produced the most thorough iconographic approach to the problem to date. They review the written sources on pederasty and then follow a clear iconographic approach to the imagery, beginning with visual description and moving into iconographic and iconological analysis. A demonstration of the analysis can be followed in the discussion of another cup by Douris in the Metropolitan Museum of Art (Figure 72).

The scene shows a youth seated on a chair and a man standing. Both wear robes that bare one or both shoulders and hold or lean on walking sticks. The scene is set in the gymnasium, as indicated by the sponge, net-bag, and aryballos on the wall. The older man is usually called the *erastes*, or lover, and the youth the *eromenos*, or beloved. The erastes is holding a bag up before the youth as a gift. Other, similar scenes show a hare, flower, or cock as a courtship gift. According to the literary sources, the eromenos should be modest and reluctant to accept the attention of a potential erastes. According to Lear and Cantarella, the scene epitomizes the pedagogical aspect of pederasty:

> [V]ase-painting associates pederasty with activities which the Greeks considered admirable in men and educative for boys. It portrays *erastai* as serving as role models for these activities and as praising and/or fostering these activities in their *eromenoi*. It therefore portrays pederasty as an integral part of the mode by which men of the elite pass on admired activities and attitudes to boys of the elite.[17]

The difficulty in the interpretation of the Douris cup is the sack held by the erastes. As we noted with the epinetron, such a sack could hold astragaloi (for gaming) or coins. By all accounts, the purchase of sexual favors was counter to the code governing pederasty, which would be contrary to the positive image that is reinforced by the inscription, *ho pais kalos*, or "the boy is beautiful." As Lear and Cantarella stress, the emphasis in courtship is on the gift and the relationship that it establishes between the erastes and eromenos.[18]

As in a feminist critique, we must allow semiotically that the purse, even if it contains money, may have different meanings than the purchase of sexual favors. Money is more than a means to purchase something; it can be a gift, reward, or prize, or perhaps a sign of wealth and eligibility. If pederastic imagery addresses the relationship of erastes and eromenos and their sexual and gender identity, then money may serve a variety of paradigmatic functions that do not indicate prostitution. Perhaps the youth is an orphan, needing a patron to provide necessities for training; perhaps the money is a prize for winning a competition. Within the context of the drinking cup, one also has to consider that the drinker might be either an erastes or an eromenos, so the image reflects the situation of the symposion and models the relationship and identity for the drinker, who would interpret the picture according to his own situation.

Other approaches put pederasty within its sociopolitical context. For example, in the last chapter we looked at the statues of the Tyrannicides

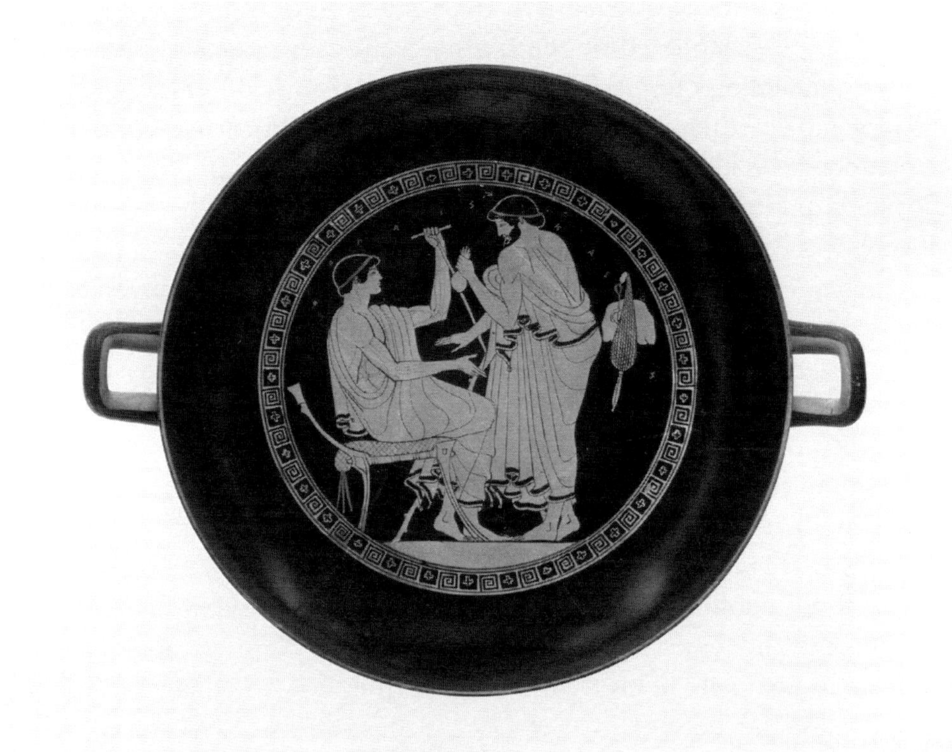

Figure 72. Attic red-figure kylix attributed to Douris, c. 480 BCE. Man and youth. New York, Metropolitan Museum of Art, 52.11.4. Image Copyright © The Metropolitan Museum of Art/Art Resource, New York.

(Figure 50) as an example of a civic and political context for a work, but this Marxist analysis can be extended to consider sexual identity. To summarize the context, the original group was commissioned by the city of Athens and made by Antenor around 509 BCE. This sculpture group was taken by the Persians in 480 and was replaced by a second commission from the city in 477/476. As a public commission by the democratic government that had replaced the tyranny of Hippias in 510, one can, from a Marxist approach, see how the control of production and placement and the use of civic ceremonies would make the work effective ideological propaganda.

Beyond politics, the statues encompass issues of identity and pederastic practice, as the two figures, Aristogeiton and Harmodios, were erastes and eromenos, respectively.[19] Both Thucydides and Aristotle describe the events leading to the killing of Hipparchos by the two, and although they diverge in their details, both agree that Hipparchos or his brother Thessalus had desired Harmodios but was rebuffed by the young man in favor of Aristogeiton. In fear of being forced to submit to their attentions, and after the sister of Harmodios was slandered by the spurned suitor, the pair plotted to kill the brothers, including Hippias. Thucydides and Aristotle differ on the target of the plot and whether it was personal revenge or a political act, but in the end Hipparchos was killed, followed immediately by the death of Harmodios at the hands of Hipparchos's bodyguards and later by the death of Aristogeiton after he was tortured.

A look at the political context of this sculpture, then, provides an example of understanding how the ideals promoted iconographically and semiotically by the imagery on drinking cups gain resonance as a means of social identity. The events were both political and personal. The sculptural group becomes a visualization of the ideal of the pederastic relationship, both personal and civic, in the reaction to the threats to the social order by the actions of the sons of Peisistratos.

As the discussion of psychoanalysis and the gaze suggested, these visual models, both public (Tyrannicides) and private (Douris cup), are seen both individually and collectively at the same time. Approaching pederastic imagery contextually helps to illuminate further how the images shape both sexual and social identity.

Other Forms of Identity: Class, Civic, Ethnic

Identity is multilayered; other forms of identity can be explored using a multilayered art historical analysis such as we have considered with a feminist art history. Pederastic courtship and practice were not only related to gender and sexual identity, but also associated with the elite classes of Greek society. As the Greek city or polis developed, there emerged a tension between the aristocratic elite and the newly enfranchised classes. The story of the Tyrannicides is one that involved the aristocratic elite in Athens, but the commissioning of the statue group was made by the democratic government that had replaced the tyranny led by one aristocratic group. Whether the killing of Hipparchos was personal or political, the commissioning of the statue was political, as was the transformation of the elite killers of a member of the elite ruling family into democratic agents.

This is not the only example of how art can frame and make visible the tensions between classes and the role of class in **civic and class identity**. In looking at the Siphnian Treasury (Figure 1) in the last chapter, we noted that it could be analyzed in terms of a Marxist-political approach. Building the Treasury was an assertion by the polis of its authority in settling disputes and establishing a well-ordered community. As Richard Neer explains more

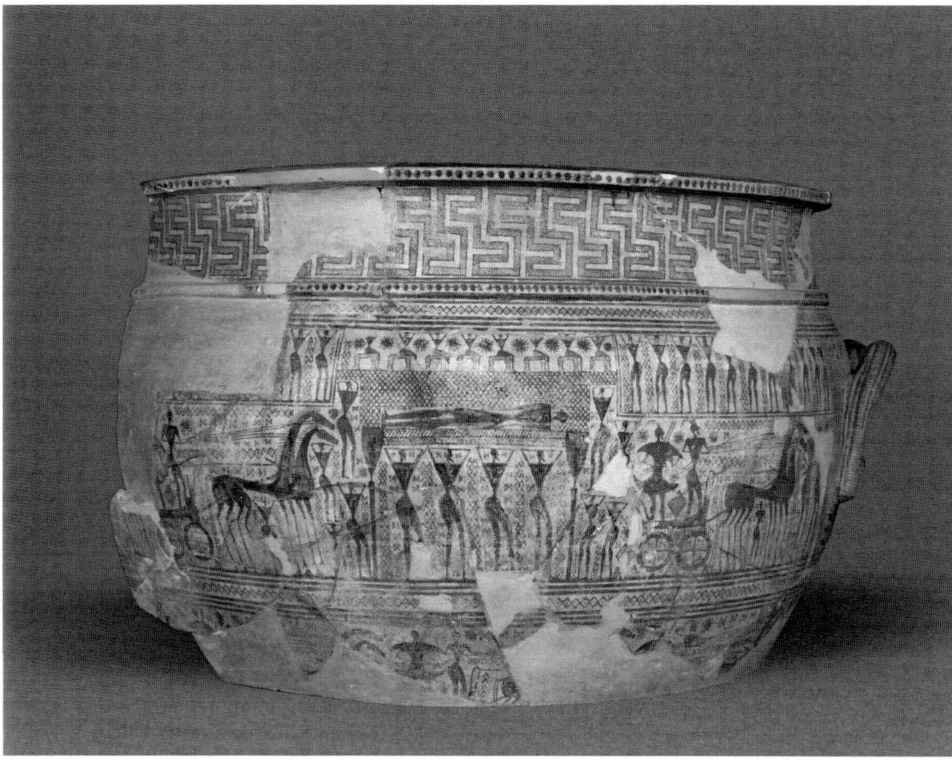

Figure 73. Attic Geometric krater attributed to the Dipylon Master, c. 760–750 BCE. Paris, Musée du Louvre A517. Photo: Réunion des Musées Nationaux/Art Resource, New York.

specifically with regard to the dispute over the tripod, this analysis also touches on class identity and the resolution of tension between classes.[20] The tripod is an elite sign of victory, especially in contests such as the Delphic or Olympic games; these athletes were usually from the elite classes and able to afford the time and expense of training and competition. Although it was an individual honor, it was also a civic honor, important to the prestige of the city. As a metonym of elite victory, the appearance of a tripod in the struggle between Apollo and Herakles in the Treasury's pediment is a reflection of the tension between the elite class and the "middling" culture responsible for building the structure.

Issues about class can be explored even earlier in Geometric art. The huge fragmentary krater in Figure 73 originally stood about 1.5 m tall when intact (compare Figure 35). The top figural frieze shows a funerary prothesis, with the deceased laid out on a couch and covered by a checked cloth, while seated and standing mourners flank the couch on either side and above and below it. On either side of the funerary bier and in the register underneath are chariots and horses carrying warriors whose bodies are shaped like shields with two large indentations; these are usually called Dipylon warriors, after the name of the cemetery in Athens where many of these vessels and their curious warriors were found. Under the handle, unseen in the photo, is a large ship being rowed. The krater belongs to the Dipylon Workshop, which created these huge funerary vessels with complex figural scenes around 760–750 BCE.

The depiction of action on a grand scale, an innovation of this time, has raised the question of the source for the development of this imagery. Inspiration from the Homeric epics has often been cited as one possible source. Most of these debates focus on the artistic motivation for the scenes, but we can also look at this in terms of patronage and class. James Whitley studied the use of stylistic motifs and funerary contexts during the so-called dark ages, the eleventh through the eighth centuries, and determined that innovations in figural imagery in Athenian pottery could be linked to elite burial practices, which also included the use of gold, metal, and other precious objects as grave goods.[21] Large vases, at first simply decorated, marked the graves of the elite, but as time went on, the vases became more elaborate in their decoration.

The Louvre krater belongs to about two dozen large funerary markers that featured a mixture of funerary scenes and scenes of warriors marching and fighting. The decoration would have clearly distinguished the graves, in an age before large stone monuments and inscriptions, as elite burial sites. Whitley's hypothesis is that elite patronage provided the means and motive for the artists, through their stylistic and formal choices, to innovate. As stylistic innovations tended to diffuse to lower classes over time, artists had to create ever more distinctive scenes for their elite patrons. The analysis of style and context, then, provides a means for thinking not only about the production of the vases, but also about how the objects could be created as a means for expressing the class identity of the patron, even when the makers were not elite themselves. This would mean that the artists were "inspired" not by epic poetry, but by the needs of their clients to distinguish themselves through their actions while living and the splendor of their funerals when deceased.

In thinking about questions of civic and class identity, then, we must consider not only the meaning of a scene, but also its context and how its placement sets up a viewing situation that fosters identification of or with the particular group. A semiotic approach can illuminate how a specific sign can trigger associations with external concepts or ideologies, whereas a poststructural approach can explore how meaning is generated through the context for the viewer. Marxist approaches illuminate the economic means for conveying a political or ideological message, and object biography or agency can explore this on a more specific level. Depending on the circumstances, cultural poetics is helpful in showing how the actions of the viewers in relationship to the artwork can articulate or affirm the identity expressed in the work, and thinking about the gaze/Gaze and individual/group can show how this is internalized in terms of identity.

Ethnicity

This variety of approaches can also be brought to bear on one other area of identity that we will consider briefly: **ethnicity**. Gender, sexuality, and class describe divisions of identity within a group of people living within the city, but by ethnicity we are considering how a group defines itself relative to external groups. How to define ethnicity has been the subject of deliberation in recent years, as it incorporates aspects of geography, language, and genealogy. Herodotos mentions ties of blood (kinship), language, religion, and customs that distinguish the Greeks as a people, to which we can also add geography and external relations as factors defining a social and cultural group of people.[22] As Catherine Morgan has described it, ethnicity is "a statement of consciousness and a strategy of self-perception." This is a fluid definition of an *ethne* or people, in which the identity of a group is defined in relation to other groups. Thus, we can call the Greeks a people when compared with non-Greeks, but we can also distinguish regional variations among the Greeks, such as the Lakedaemonians and Euboeans.

As we noted in Chapter Two on stylistic analysis, the formal elements and qualities of a region's artwork can be quite distinctive from that of others, allowing us, for example, to readily identify Attic, Corinthian, and Kabiran pottery and distinguish them from one another. Stylistic analysis can be an important tool for recognizing a visual articulation of ethnic identity, but we have to question whether this is an external, or *etic*, distinction imposed by contemporary art historians, or an internal, or *emic*, distinction that contemporary members of the group would recognize as part of their self-perception.[23] Herodotos, for example, in discussing the sole Athenian survivor of a battle with the Argives and Aeginetans, tells us that the Athenian women were furious that the single soldier had escaped and stabbed him to death with their dress pins.

> So he too died; and to the Athenians this deed of the women seemed even worse than the defeat itself. They could think of no way to punish the women but to

> change their dress to the Ionian mode; for before this the Athenian women wore clothes of the Dorian fashion, which is very like that of Corinth. The Athenians now changed this into a linen tunic, that the women might use no pins. In truth, this women's clothing was not originally Ionian but Carian, for in Greece all the older sort of women's dress was what we now call Dorian. As a result of this, the Argives and Aeginetans have laid down a law for each of their peoples that their brooch-pins should be longer again by half than the usual measure and that, in especial, the women should dedicate the pins in the shrine of these goddesses and to it should be brought nothing Attic, not even earthenware, but that it be the rule henceforth to drink there from pots made in their own country.[24]

From this passage, we can see that dress fashion was an emic distinction for Herodotos and his readers, and that it distinguished ethnic identity. Indeed, the Argives and Aeginetans even exaggerated the length of their pins to make them even more distinctive from the typical Dorian look. Such recognition of visual markers of ethnic and cultural identity also extends to pottery, as the Argives and Aeginetans prohibited drinking from Attic cups in their sanctuaries. The implication is that Attic pottery was sufficiently distinctive visually from local pottery that it could be recognized and banned.

Ethnic distinctions, however, are not always observed in Greek art. The battle between Memnon and Achilles, for example, involves two levels of struggle between Greeks and non-Greeks. Memnon was fighting as an ally of the Trojans, but there is no distinction of his armor or body type from that of Achilles (see Figure 1), nor is there a distinction made between Trojans and Greeks in other examples of Greek art. Memnon, however, was the son of the goddess Eos and king of Ethiopia. Memnon, then, was doubly foreign compared with the Greeks, and yet is undistinguished in appearance from his main Greek opponent.

We can see this in an Attic vase painting showing Memnon with two of his followers on an amphora attributed to Exekias (Figure 74). The central warrior is Memnon, who wears the armor of the Greek hoplite. His two companions, however, bear different kinds of weapons – a light crescent shield (*pelta*) and club – and are distinguished by differences in the shape of the nose, lips, and eyebrow from the standard Exekian figure. The hair is noticeably tightly curled, which is emphasized by the use of clay dots to give it texture. This contrasts with the hanging and slightly curled locks of hair falling below Memnon's helmet. In the squire, the artist is clearly making a stylized rendering of an African physiognomy, but not necessarily one that reflects the reality of Ethiopia as a specific area within Africa. Memnon receives no such distinction.

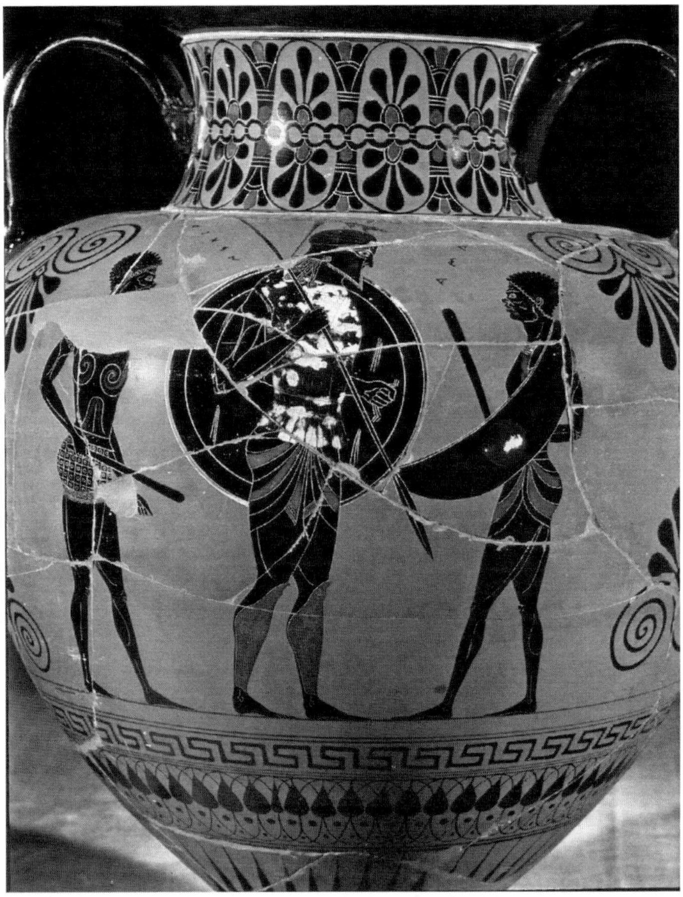

Figure 74. Attic black-figure amphora signed by Exekias, c. 540 BCE. Memnon and attendants. London, British Museum, B209. Photo: © Trustees of the British Museum.

What is the meaning or symbolism of this representation of a non-Greek on an Attic vase of the third quarter of the sixth century BCE?[25] Why is Memnon shown in a "normative" form, whereas his subjects are differentiated? Perhaps, as the son of a goddess, Memnon was imagined as similar to other heroes, such as Achilles, who were also the sons of gods or goddesses, and thus godlike in their appearance. If that is so, why then do normal Greek warriors look like Achilles, whereas normal Ethiopians do not look like Memnon? Might we consider this simply as an effort at ethnographic portrayal that can serve as a sign or attribute for Memnon, or is it symptomatic of a more ethnocentric view of non-Athenians and non-Greeks, and to some degree racist?

Answering these questions requires thinking not only about the attitudes of Athenian potters and painters, but also about the intended audience to whom the image was addressed, as with a poststructural approach. The vase is unprovenanced, but many of Exekias' works ended up in Italy, especially in Etruria. Perhaps the painter was intending a kind of encyclopedia of foreign peoples to appeal to the foreign purchaser, for the other side of the vase shows Achilles killing Penthesilea, the queen of the Amazons and another foreign ally of the Trojans, coming from somewhere in the steppes beyond the Black Sea. Penthesilea, however, is dressed as a male Greek warrior with full hoplite armor, so there is no effort at ethnographic representation except that only a non-Greek nation would arm its women. Is the ethnographic representation meant to appeal to the non-Greek clientele, if this vase were painted for export?

To complicate the matter further, the name Amasis is written above the head of the Ethiopian figure. This name is Egyptian and the name of the Pharaoh in the middle of the sixth century when this vase was made. It is also the name of a potter in Athens who was a contemporary of Exekias; this has led to the speculation that perhaps the potter Amasis was a metic, an immigrant working in Athens.

Is Exekias poking fun at the foreign origin of the potter Amasis, one of his competitors? If Amasis the potter were indeed Egyptian, the use of an Ethiopian figure as a representation would seem puzzling. Surely, Greek viewers were sufficiently aware of the standardized representations of figures in Egyptian art; would not the wigs and kilts that Egyptian men wore in their art have been sufficiently recognizable as "foreign" to the dress and hairstyle of the contemporary Greek audience, making a physiognomic distinction unnecessary? Is this distortion, then, a caricature? Is it meant in jest or with hostility?

Answering these questions about ethnic identity requires considering both the individual circumstances of the object's creation and its creator, the context of its acquisition and use, and how these fit with or deviate from the broader patterns of the culture as a whole. Is the representation of Memnon's attendants as African a typical iconographic convention that is consistent for a given period and place? Does the artist consistently make such ethnic distinctions when representing figures of different groups, either separately or in groups of other figures? Are there signs in the composition that connect paradigmatically to other forms or stories that allow us to consider if the sign is pejorative or not (the club, for example, would certainly evoke the idea of Herakles paradigmatically, which would be a positive association)? Does the context indicate that the viewers are in the same ethnic group as the artist, or members of a different group? Does the context indicate which

Amasis – pharaoh or potter – is meant, if either? If we knew the findspot of the vase, could we say whether the wares of Amasis and Exekias were in competition with one another economically, making the image both an example of personal identity for the artist as well as a standard expression of ethnic identity? These questions call for a complex approach involving multiple lines of inquiry.

Postcolonialism and Cultural Diffusion

These questions about ethnic identity draw on some of the approaches that we have covered earlier, but issues of identity are also wrapped up in an area of art history that usually comes under the heading of **postcolonialism**. As D'Alleva explains, "the term postcolonial refers not only to the shaping of new identities, and political and cultural practices in former colonies, but also to a body of theory that supports the study of the distinctive cultural, social, and political dynamics of both colonial and postcolonial societies."[26] The theoretical approach developed in the later twentieth century as many colonies of European nations gained independence, and has focused on the relationships between the colonizers and colonized and the continuing imbalance in terms of economic, political, and cultural control and relationships.

Postcolonial analysis, like feminism, can take a number of different forms, but there are some key terms, such as mimicry and hybridity, that have emerged, as well as the definition of forms of cultural diffusion that are useful in the study of Greek art, both in terms of identity and more generally for framing the relationship of Greek art to contemporaneous cultures.

We can begin by defining two terms, mimicry and hybridity. *Mimicry* refers to the adoption or imitation of a form, object, or idea of one culture, without much alteration, into the art and culture of a second. To simplify, we can call this form, object, or idea more generally an *artistic feature*. In postcolonialism, this would usually mean the forced use of an artistic feature of the colonizer's culture, such as a church in a European style, in place of a traditional or indigenous building and its typical style. The Greeks did establish colonies in the Mediterranean that sometimes replicated the culture of the mother city, but we need to remember that this type of colony had some differences from the modern form of colonialism, both in its relationship to the mother city and to the local, non-Greek population. Under a strongly asymmetric relationship between two cultures, mimicry can be a means of enforcing or expressing cultural control by one group over another. However, two groups may be more symmetrical or equal in their relationship, so mimicry can also be an expression of cultural influence rather than coercion.

Carla Antonaccio has offered a good working definition of *hybridity* for the study of Greek art: hybridity refers "to how material culture was manipulated, combined, and deployed in practice to express identities – and how (material) cultural encounters in turn shaped identity, in colonial contexts but also in the metropoleis of Old Greece."[27] In hybridity, the artistic feature(s) of one culture is blended with the feature(s) of the adopting culture, so one can see elements of both in the resulting work. As an example, Antonaccio points to the grave assemblages in fifth-century BCE Corinth and Athens, noting the strong predominance of locally produced vases as grave gifts in these two cities, both of which were also heavy exporters of vases to Greek cities in Sicily and southern Italy. In Syracuse, on the other hand, a Sicilian city founded as a colony of Corinth, graves more often contained a mixture of goods from both Corinth and Athens, as well as from other areas of Greece. The choice of grave goods in Syracuse, then, might be seen as an expression of its status as a Greek foundation in a non-Greek land and the resulting negotiation of a new identity through different choices in artistic features.

Hybridity extends to the blending of motifs within a work of art, such as the adoption of the sphinx in Greek art during the seventh century and its blending with preexisting motifs, as well as the adaptation of new types of objects, materials, or techniques to existing art. The result is a blending, but we need to consider both the relationship of the original model to the new work or "copy," and the sociopolitical strategy behind it.

Margaret Miller's study of the relationship between Athenian and Persian art and culture in the fifth century draws on the models of cultural receptivity and **diffusion** studies.[28] As she notes, most of the models developed from anthropology assume that there is an asymmetric power relationship, donor and recipient, between the two cultures involved, but in fact the receptivity of one culture to another is independent of power or social complexity. *Diffusion*, narrowly defined, is the spread of artistic features from one place to others. *Acculturation* examines the impact of the diffusion on the recipient, and, in particular, how the recipient conformed to the donor in a hierarchical relationship. Thus we get the model of *center-periphery* diffusion, with the idea that the periphery is somehow "backward" when compared with the center and needs to "raise" its cultural level. This correlates with the idea that a center also exploits a peripheral area as a net consumer of its resources.

As Miller notes, it is more productive to think of cultural receptivity and diffusion in terms of social texture and need. By *social texture*, we refer to the divisions and standing of different groups, particularly within the recipient culture. Who adopts the new artistic feature, and where do they fit within the social structure? Is it the elite, the working class, or slaves who are linked to the artistic feature in question? Does the artistic feature create status by its strangeness or rarity? By *social need*, we must think about what advantage is gained by the adoption of a new visual idea. Does the need to find a new market necessitate the adoption of an artistic feature that would be appealing to that market? Is it the need to express political power and control that motivates the adoption?

These questions about social texture and social need point out that there are no universal rules for receptivity and borrowing. In essence, we need to consider two factors. First is the nature of the borrowing: What is done with or to the original model in the new work? Is it a situation of imitation or mimicry, in which the original model is reproduced, given differences in medium or technique, such as copying a bronze vessel in terracotta? Or is it a situation of adaptation or hybridization, in which elements of the original are merged with indigenous elements to create a new work? Does this adaptation involve straightforward incorporation of the original, or does it get distorted in the process? Finally, is it a more general question of "influence" – that is, the adjustment of an artistic feature over time that can be clearly linked to a foreign model? This is a much more gradualist type of situation, and less tied to the political relationship of the two cultures than mimicry or hybridity would be.

Second, we need to think about the motivation for the transfer of an artistic feature. We think of three broad possibilities: domestication, symbolic domination, and symbolic subjugation. In *domestication*, the strangeness of the foreign artistic feature is removed or reduced by making it part of the familiar and everyday of the recipient culture. In this case, there would seem to be a symmetry or equivalence between the two cultures and a minimal political agenda. In *symbolic domination*, the foreign artistic feature is deployed in some way to show the power or control of the recipient culture. In *symbolic subjugation*, the foreign artistic features becomes a means for showing the control of the donor culture, as is more typically the case of European colonization in the nineteenth and twentieth centuries CE.

Following Miller, we can combine the nature of the borrowing and the motivation together in a chart (Table 5) that defines the results of each situation.[29]

Table 5. Patterns of cultural diffusion

	Mimicry/Imitation	Hybridity/Adaptation
Domestication	*Familiarization*: artistic feature becomes common and incorporated into the recipient culture, making it familiar	*Neutralization*: artistic feature is modified or adapted to become new but common within the recipient culture
Symbolic domination (increase power of recipient)	*Marginalization*: artistic feature is imitated but restricted in its deployment to lower strata of society, making it less prestigious or powerful	*Perversion*: artistic feature is modified in a manner that inverts its meaning or status and shows control by the recipient culture
Symbolic subjugation (increase power of donor)	*Emulation*: artistic feature is imitated or adopted by the recipient culture at the compulsion of the donor culture or an effort to associate with the donor culture	*Assimilation*: artistic feature is modified and blended with that of recipient culture to show acceptance by recipient culture

We can explore these ideas by turning to some examples. Around the year 500 BCE, Athenian potters began to produce cups made in the shape of animal heads, and these continued to be produced during the first half of the fifth century. In Figure 75, the body of the cup is in the shape of a donkey's head, on which a flaring cylinder with the rim of the cup is set. The ears frame a picture of a woman playing the double flute and a dancer with krotalae. A handle was attached at the back of the cup/donkey's head and a foot attached to the base.

This type of cup derives from Near Eastern containers such as Figure 76, a *situla*, or ritual bucket, made of bronze and found in a tomb at Gordion along with a ram's-head version.[30] This type of object is carried by servants or courtiers represented on Assyrian palace reliefs and could include heads of lions, rams, or bulls; the vessel was used to measure wine for elite guests, to then be poured into a drinking cup. Two other versions of the animal head vessel were developed, a bent version usually called a *protome* that became popular in Achaemenid Persia (Figure 77), and a longer, horn-shaped version with an animal's head called a *rhyton*. The latter had a hole at the base, and

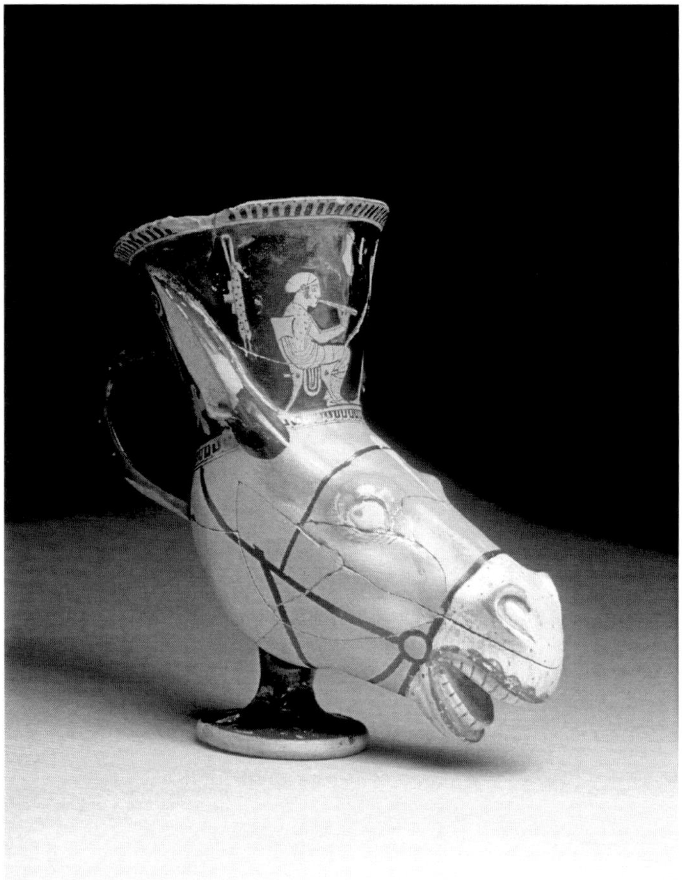

Figure 75. Donkey-head rhyton by Painter of Brussels R330, 470–460 BCE. Musician and dancer. Paris, Musée du Louvre, Cp3561. Photo: Réunion des Musées Nationaux/Art Resource, New York.

reliefs show servants using it as a funnel to pour wine into a cup. The animal-head container, then, is closely associated with elite drinking in the Assyrian and, later, Persian empires and circulated quite widely; the example from Gordion, in central Turkey, is from the region of Phrygia, which borders on the Greek settlements on the Aegean coast.

As Miller points out, Attic potters began creating their own versions of the animal-head vessel at the end of the sixth century BCE, but altered it by attaching a handle on the side to hold as a cup and placing a foot under it similar to those of Attic drinking cups. The Attic examples do not have a spout, and would have been used only as drinking cups. Figural scenes are sometimes shown on the conical upper section of the cup; their scenes generally draw on the repertory of Attic vase painting and are not

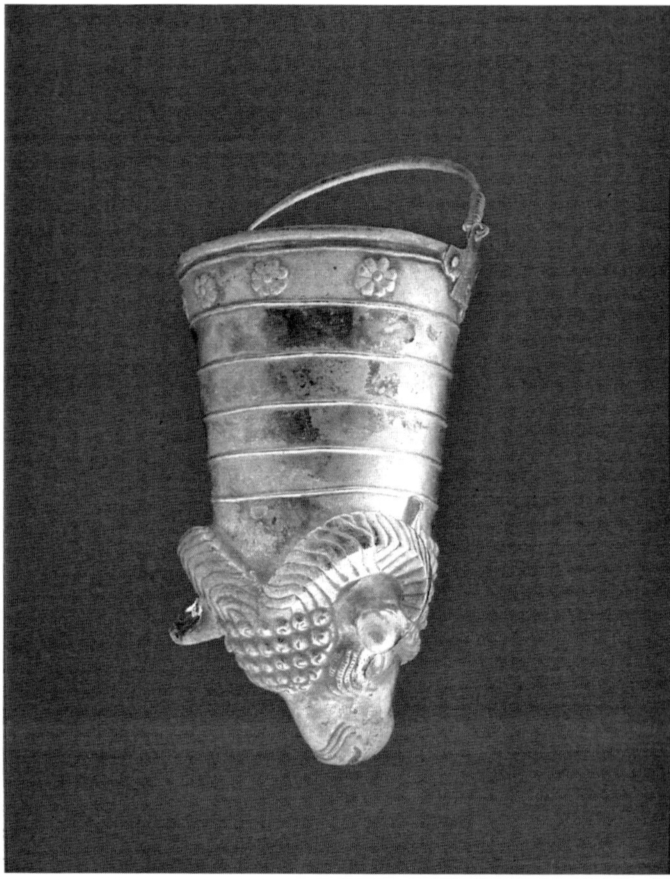

Figure 76. Animal-head situla from Gordion, c. 750 BCE. Ankara, Museum of Anatolian Civilizations 12508. Photo: Courtesy of the Penn Museum, #103009.

imitations of the ornament of the Near Eastern examples. Thus, we have a case of a work being hybridized, combining native Attic medium, painting techniques, function, and subject matter with the shape and object type derived, most likely, from Persian examples.

The question, then, is: What is the motivation for this hybridization? The series starts at a time when Athens was only beginning to be involved directly with the Persian empire politically, but the protome became much more popular after the victories over the Persians in 480–479.[31] Is this an example of domestication, which would indicate that the original article, as a prestige good, was adapted to Athenian usage to elevate the status of its user, or was it a way of expressing Athenian success in the struggle with the Persian empire, which continued to ebb and flow throughout the first half of the fifth century? In the latter case, we would have a process of perversion, distortion of the model that is intended to deemphasize its elite status.

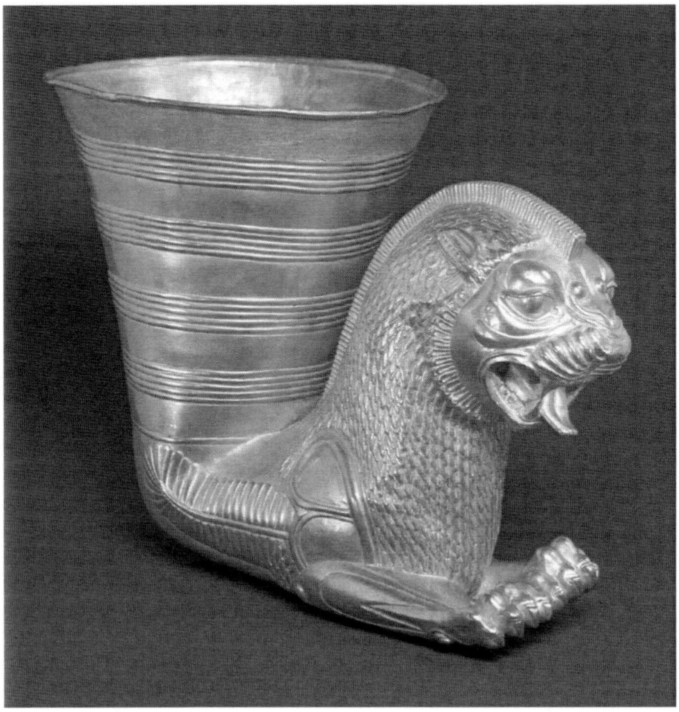

Figure 77. Achaemenid Persian gold protome, fifth century BCE. *New York, Metropolitan Museum of Art, 54.3.3. Image Copyright © The Metropolitan Museum of Art/Art Resource, New York.*

The use of a donkey's head would suggest this latter strategy, in that the donkey is neither a fearsome animal like a lion or a sacrificial animal like a ram, but is associated with Dionysos. Further, rather than having an elite or heroic scene decorating its top, the cup shows two women rehearsing. Whether we regard this scene as women rehearsing for a festival or hetairai practicing for a symposion is a question for a feminist analysis, but in either case it is decidedly not the world of the elite male banquet for which the original model was used. The medium is also much less valuable than its metal models, so the elite shape has been further changed to fit within the ethos of Attic culture.

Other examples of animal-head cups do have heroic scenes and more noble types of animals, so we should be careful not to draw too general a conclusion from a single example, and should rather look at the overall patterns of production and distribution. Certainly the examples from before 490 would have been less motivated by feelings of Attic dominance over Persia, and we should consider that the object would likely have been intended to enhance the prestige of its owner because of its unusual qualities

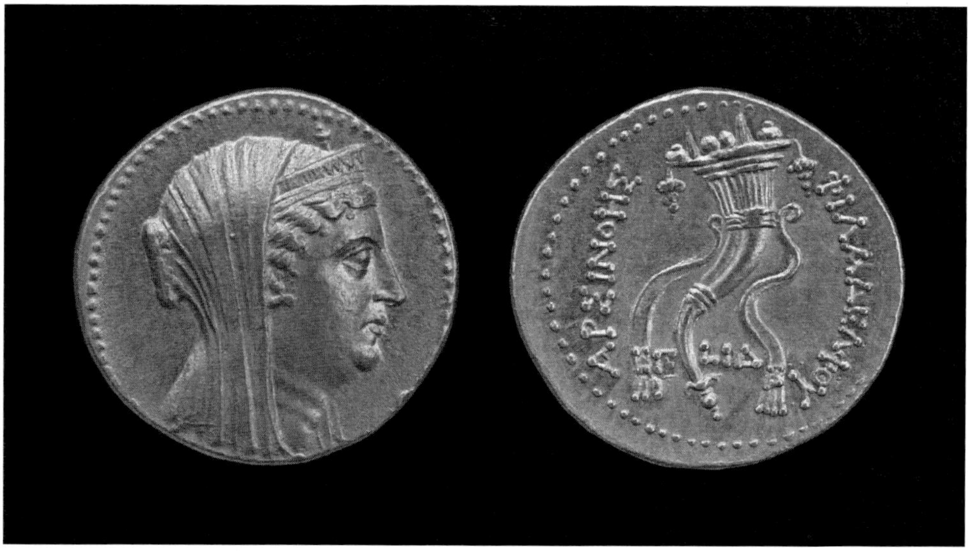

Figure 78. Coin of Arsinoë II minted in Paphos, third century BCE. *London, British Museum 1987.06–49.141. Photo: © Trustees of the British Museum.*

compared with a typical drinking cup, regardless of whether domestication or domination was the motivation.

Another example of artistic reception can be found in Hellenistic Egypt. The Ptolemaic dynasty was established by Ptolemy, one of the Macedonian generals of Alexander the Great. The dynasty ruled Egypt for three centuries and, although later kings and queens were born in Egypt, ethnically they remained Macedonians and did not intermarry with the native population. The Ptolemies ruled from Alexandria, a Greek foundation in Egypt, and much of the art produced there is decidedly Hellenistic Greek in its style and subject matter, as we saw before with the Queen's Vase (Figure 62) and the statue of the old woman (Figure 39).

The dynasty issued coins carrying images of its rulers, and these too featured an individualized, Hellenistic portrait of the ruler, such as that on the coin of Arsinoë II minted in Cyprus (Figure 78). Circulated among the population, its acceptance, through its function as money, would convey the dominance of the Macedonian rulers over their native subjects. From the point of view of the recipient in agency theory, whether Greek, Cypriot, or Egyptian, its use demonstrates the agency of the prototype (Arsinoë II) and the acquiescence of the recipient/viewer. If the recipient were Egyptian, its use might also be seen as an example of emulation.

The Ptolemies could, however, be much more subtle about projecting an image of power, and we have an alternate portrait of Arsinoë II that was

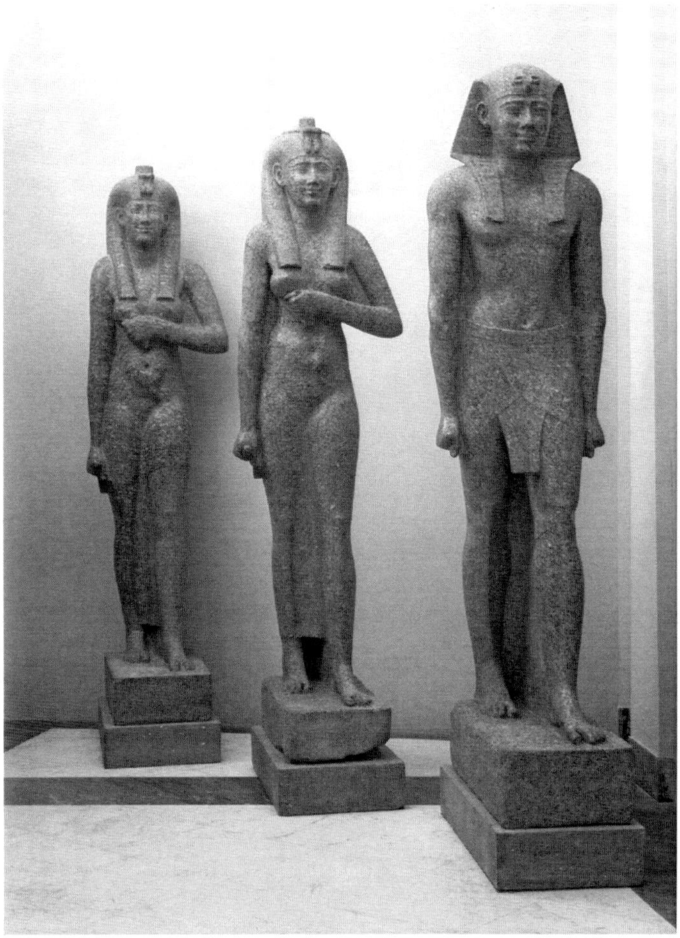

Figure 79. Statues of Arsinoë II from Alexandria (center), with unknown princess (left) and Ptolemy II (right), third century BCE. *Vatican Museums, Museo Gregoriano Egizio. Photo: Scala/Art Resource, New York.*

more likely produced for a native Egyptian audience because its inscription is in Egyptian. The statue (Figure 79), now in the Vatican Museum, is done in a very traditional Egyptian style and material, red granite. Its iconography is also decidedly Egyptian in the long sheath dress, striding pose, wig and crown, and implements. The back slab of the statue is intact, as is traditional for Egyptian statues placed near or against a wall. If there were no inscription, we would be uncertain as to the identity of the individual, but we would be certain that we were dealing with the ruling elite of Egypt, given the signs, form, and cost of the work. As a commission by the ruling Greek elite, this work uses the Egyptian style and symbols to express domination, but by directing such works at an Egyptian audience, it is *marginalizing* the

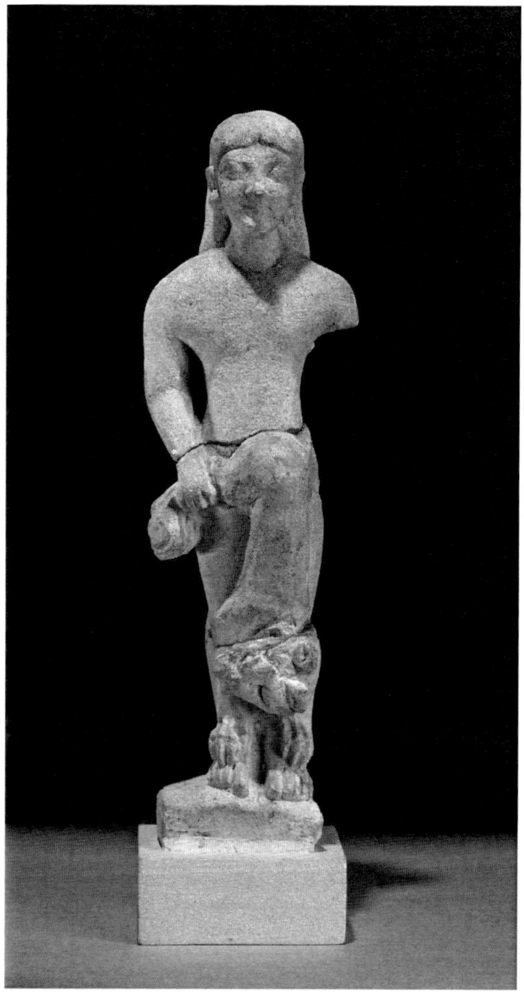

Figure 80. Stone statue of man holding lion from Naukratis, c. 550 BCE. London, British Museum, 1886.6–1.27. Photo: © Trustees of the British Museum.

traditional Egyptian style, asserting the Greeks' control over the art and the culture from which it is derived. Unlike the animal-head cup in Figure 75, however, the ultimate viewer is likely not Greek, but Egyptian.

Sorting out the influences and agendas behind works of art at the intersection of cultures however, is complicated by uncertainty, in many cases, over the cultural identity of the artist and the patron, the place of production, the availability of sources, and more. For example, a small limestone figure from the Greek colony of Naukratis in Egypt, follows the archaic kouros schemata for the treatment of the male body (Figure 80). It was dedicated in a sanctuary of Aphrodite and may represent a hero or god, as the figure also

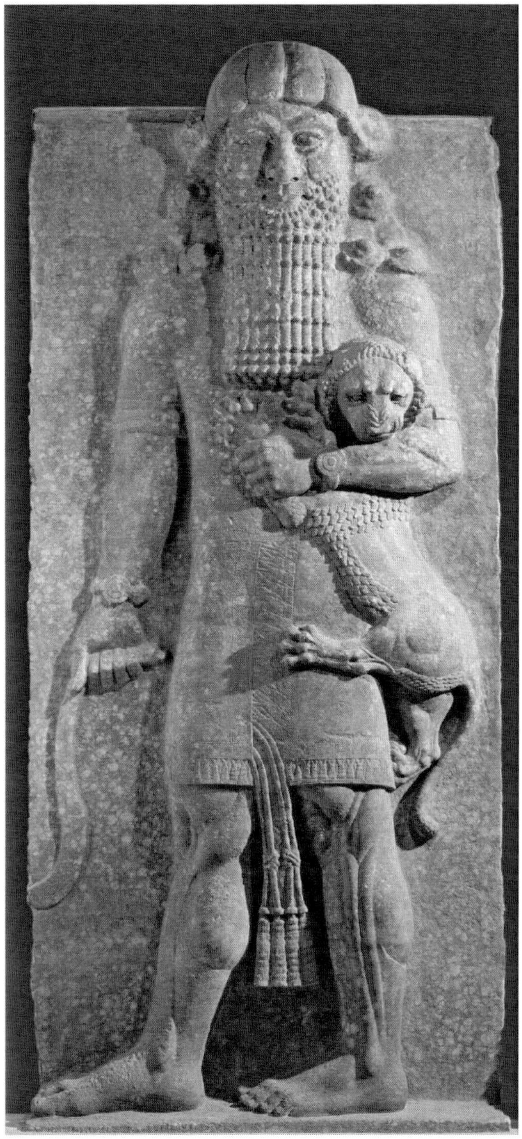

Figure 81. Neo-Assyrian relief from palace at Khorsabad, c. 720 BCE. Paris, Musée du Louvre. Photo: Réunion des Musées Nationaux/Art Resource, New York.

holds a lion in one hand. This motif is not Egyptian, but derives from Levantine art, where a heroic figure holding a small lion flanked the doorways of Assyrian palaces (Figure 81), or figures showing a mistress of animals, who would hold two small animals symmetrically to either side. Clearly the motif has been adapted to a Greek style and conception of the male figure, but the presence of this figure with Levantine motifs in Egypt creates a series of questions about the "orientalism" of the work, and we are not certain if the work was made locally or perhaps in Cyprus.

Ann Gunter has framed some of the problems faced in analyzing such works and determining what stylistic traits should be considered Greek and which Near Eastern (or, by extension, those of another culture):

> Are we confident that these divisions reflect the artisan's region of origin or ethnic identity? Should minor differences be considered intentional indicators of separate ethnicities or assertions of well-established artistic traditions – cultural statements, so to speak? Could some variations reflect the individual voice of a patron, or do they perhaps result unintentionally from the imprecise technology of copies? What about stone sculpture, whose authorship – or cultural/stylistic label – cannot be so rigorously defined on technical grounds? When copies (or "adaptations") so resemble foreign models that they present complex problems of attribution for modern scholars, it seems legitimate to ask in what sense they were understood in antiquity as "Greek." Artisans could obviously distinguish their own products from imports, but did those who commissioned bronze cauldrons with sculpted attachments, for example, intend for others to be aware of this distinction?[32]

Answering these questions requires thinking about style, signs/symbols and meaning, and the analysis of context; the results, when available, could vary considerably from object to object or across periods and places.

We also must be careful to be aware of assumptions that creep into the analysis of art that can be seen as "derivative." Red-figure pottery from south Italy, for example, flourished beginning in the later fifth century BCE.[33] At the beginning, it shows signs of Attic influence in terms of style, technique, forms, and subject matter. Indeed Attic vases were imported there in significant quantities during the fifth and into the fourth century. By the fourth century, though, regional styles developed that were recognizably distinct from those of contemporary Attic pottery. As we can see in Figure 82, an elaborate loutrophoros from Apulia, the red-figure style has been modified to include substantial amounts of added yellow and white, producing a rich four-color effect. The picture composition is very complex and spread out on multiple levels, creating a space in which the figures move at several levels.

The presumption in the scholarly literature has been that these Apulian vessels were created by artists in the Greek city of Taranto, which was the major Greek center in the region of Apulia. Attic vases would have been imported to that city for distribution into the Italic, non-Greek areas of Apulia, and the trade in Apulian ware would have followed the same distribution pattern. The representation of scenes drawn from Greek plays

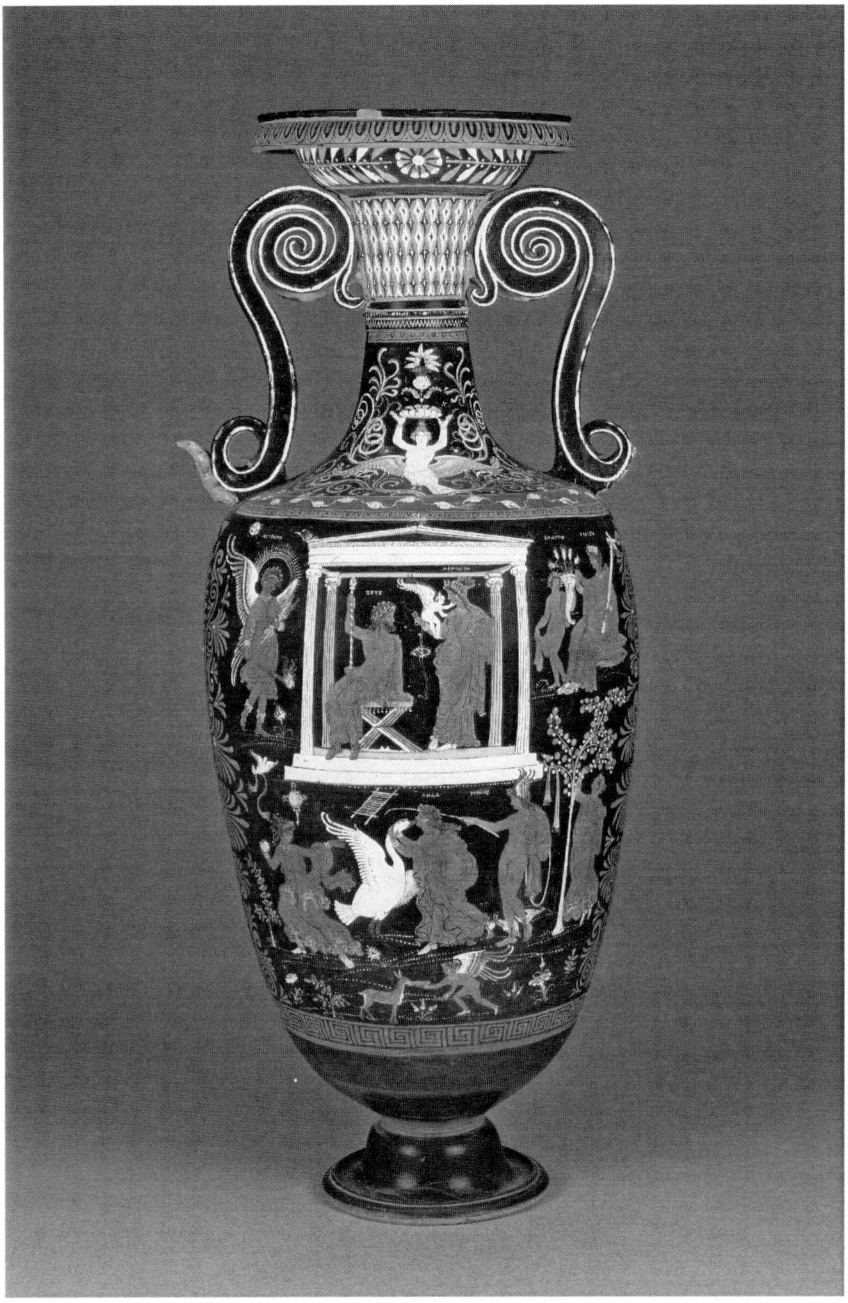

Figure 82. Apulian red-figure loutrophoros attributed to the Painter of Louvre MNB1148, c. 330 BCE. Malibu, Getty Villa, 86.AE.680. Photo: The J. Paul Getty Museum. Villa Collection. Malibu, California.

also has suggested that the vases were, in some sense, conspicuous works of Greek culture.

As Thomas Carpenter has recently argued, however, this model is not supported by the contextual evidence. Very few of the elaborate vases such as the loutrophoros have been found in Taranto; almost all are found much further north in the Italic areas of Apulia, as in the city of Ruvo. There is evidence that these areas were also in direct contact and trade with Athens, so Taranto was not essential as either a production or distribution center for the pottery. Most of the vases with tragic scenes come from Italic tombs and not Greek tombs, so their selection and production needs to be addressed in terms of Apulian and not Greek cultural practices. Indeed, Apulian vases are rarely found outside of Apulia, so the vases must have met local needs and ideas.

In light of this, one must question whether Apulian vases are the work of western Greek artists, or are the work of Italic artists producing for the Italic peoples of Apulia. One method of analysis alone is unable to answer this question definitively, and one must consider that scholarly presumptions about the relative status of Greek and Italic art and culture may influence the analysis. In a center-periphery model of cultural diffusion, this would lead toward a more hierarchical model of artistic ideas and objects flowing from Athens to Taranto to the rest of Apulia. A model that looks at a more complex and variable flow of ideas can lead to a different conclusion about the relationship of cultures and their art, and how they express social identity.

Further Reading

On the background of psychoanalysis and its development as a literary and art historical theory, see Eagleton 1996, 131–68, and D'Alleva 2005, 88–121. On vision and gaze generally, see Jay 1993. There are other psychoanalytical theorists, such as Klein, Kristeva, and Winnicott, who could not be included in this all-too-brief discussion but who may be more appropriate models for some problems or works.

For the adaptation of various forms of psychoanalytic theory to Greek art, including considerations of vision and gaze, see Frontisi-Ducroux 1996, Stewart 1997, 13–23 et passim; D. Steiner 2001, esp. 185–250; Stansbury-O'Donnell 2006, 52–88. For portraits, see Dillon 2006.

On Greek theories of vision, see Lindberg 1977 and Laks 1999.

On feminist analysis of Greek art and literary sources, see Fantham et al. 1994, Blundell 1995, Reeder 1995, Kolokowski-Ostrow and Lyons 1997, and Lefkowitz and Fant 2005. For new critiques, see Lewis 2002, Ferrari 2002, Connelly 2007, Bundrick 2008, and Kaltsas and Shapiro 2008. On women and the household, see Nevett 1999.

On approaches to sexuality, see Shapiro 1992; Stewart 1997, 63–85 et passim; Parker 2001; Ferrari 2002, 87–111 et passim; Hubbard 2002; and Lear and Cantarella 2008 with earlier bibliography.

On class, see Morris 2000, esp. 109–91, and Whitley 1991, Neer 2001 and 2002, and Hall 2007.

On ethnicity, see Morgan 1991, 2001, and 2003; Hall 1997, 2003, 2007; and Antonaccio 2009 as well as the essays in Cohen 2000, Malkin 2001, Dougherty and Kurke 2003, and Hales and Hodos 2009. See also Snowden 1970 and 1983.

See also Vidal-Naquet 1986 for a range of identity issues addressed in this chapter. For general discussion of identity within a specific material context, see Osborne 2007b; Hales and Hodos 2009.

On mimicry and hybridity, see generally Bhabha 1994, and for Greek art, Antonaccio 2003.

On cultural relations and overviews of the center-periphery model, see Rowlands 1987 and Champion 1995. For discussions of the relationship of Greek art to other cultures, see especially Miller 1997, as well as S. Morris 1992 and 2007, and Gunter 2009. For an overview of the relationship of Greek art and its neighbors, see Boardman 1999.

On the assessment of Greek vases and their Italian and Etruscan markets, there has been a substantial amount of reconsideration in recent years. For South Italian pottery, see Carpenter 2009 on the potential for non-Greek artists for Apulian ware. For Etruscan markets, see Small 1994; more broadly, see Arafat and Morgan 1989. On aspects of the trade, see Hannestad 1988, 1989, 1999; Scheffer 1988, Osborne 1996b, Crielaard et al. 1999, Stissi 1999, and Langridge-Noti forthcoming.

There has been much debate over the bias of scholars concerning Greek art, generated by Martin Bernal's volumes titled *Black Athena* (see Bernal 1987, 1991, and 2006). For critiques of Bernal's hypothesis, see Lefkowitz and Rogers 1996; for Bernal's response, see Bernal 2001.

Conclusion

It has often been noted that the Greek word for art, *techne*, also included what we would consider crafts, such as shoemaking or shipmaking. The philosophical and aesthetic distinction that we make between fine arts on one hand and crafts or decorative arts on the other is not one that the Greeks would have made. As J. J. Pollitt defined it, techne was "organized knowledge and procedure applied for the purpose of producing a specific, preconceived result."[1] Pottery, painting, bronze sculpture, or terracotta all required skill, thought, and convention to be successful – and useful to society.

I would like to suggest that this definition of techne be applied to art history as a discipline of organized knowledge and procedures to synthesize a history of Greek art. When approaching an object, we need to think about it broadly and ask questions on different levels. A complex approach to art history that draws on multiple lines of inquiry offers an opportunity for filling in some of the missing pieces of our knowledge. Furthermore, reaching a similar conclusion via multiple approaches provides a stronger argument that our interpretation has some validity and some chance for bridging the gap between the ancient experience of art and our own.

Such a multidimensional approach – looking at style, meaning, context, and identity – is not without ancient precedent either. For example, when Pausanias saw the Chest of Kypselos in the Temple of Hera at Olympia, he devoted hundreds of lines to its discussion – about eight pages in modern editions. Although much of the text concerns the subject matter of the many miniature scenes, we can see from the following excerpts that he was also concerned broadly with its visual qualities, date, context, and issues of identity:

> There [in the temple of Hera at Olympia] is also a chest made of cedar-wood and on it are figures, some made of ivory, some of gold, and some carved out of the cedar-wood itself. It was in this chest that the mother of Kypselos, the tyrant of Corinth, hid him when the Bacchiadai were eager to find him just after his birth. In gratitude for the saving of Kypselos, his descendants, who were called "Kypselids," set up the chest as an offering at Olympia. The Corinthians of that time called chests *kypselai*, and it is from this that the name "Kypselos" was given to the child. Near most of the figures on the chest there are inscriptions, written in the archaic characters. . . .
>
> Beginning our inspection of the chest from the lower section, we find that the content of the first space is as follows. Oinomaos is shown pursuing Pelops, who holds Hippodameia. Each of them has two horses, but those of Pelops are endowed with wings. Next is shown the house of Amphiaraos and some old woman, who carries the infant Amphilochos. Before the house stand Eriphyle holding the necklace, and by her are her daughters Eurydike and Demonassa, as well as the boy Alkmaion, who is naked. Asios, in his epic, makes out Alkmena to be the daughter of Amphiaraos and Eriphyle. Baton, who is the charioteer for Amphiaraos, holds the reins in one hand and a spear in the other. Amphiaraos has already placed one foot up on the chariot, but he holds an unsheathed sword and, having turned around toward Eriphyle, is so beside himself with anger, that he just barely restrains himself from striking her. . . . [Pausanias continues with a scene-by-scene description of the five levels of decoration on the chest.]
>
> As to who the person was who made the chest, I have been able to form no idea at all; the inscriptions on it, although some other person might conceivably have composed them, are most probably, by any conjecture, to be ascribed to Eumelos of Corinth.[2]

Pausanias first gives some attention to the appearance of the chest, specifically to its materials of cedar, ivory, and gold. A little further on he notes that it is divided into registers with scenes. He does not describe the style of the figural decoration directly, but he does indicate that it has an archaic style of lettering, and his reader could presume that the carving style was similarly old. Although the chest can be dated approximately by association with the ruler Kypselos, who ruled Corinth c. 655–625 BCE, Pausanias's description of the style of lettering as archaic would appear to be based on its formal qualities and organization. Elsewhere in his guidebook he speaks of art as archaic in style, so he had some frame of reference for classifying works by style. At the end of the passage he states that he cannot attribute the chest to a specific artist, but conjectures as to the poet who wrote the inscriptions on the basis of comparison to an attributed processional hymn of Eumelos.

Although this is not a textbook model for a stylistic or formal analysis, the elements of these approaches are here.

The largest amount of attention is given to the subject matter carved on the chest. Here we can see that Pausanias would be comfortable with an iconographic approach, relying on texts as needed or inspired. However, he also interprets the signs that he sees directly in a way that is reminiscent of semiotics. He describes Amphiaraos as angry, but the archaic date of the chest would preclude a mimetic representation of anger. Rather, he decodes the signs present in the picture – the unsheathed sword and backward glance – as signifiers of Amphiaraos's anger toward Eriphyle. He notes that she is holding "the necklace," the bribe she received to decide in favor of her brother that her husband would join the battle against Thebes. Interestingly, this confirms Sourvinou-Inwood's semiotic interpretation of the sword in pursuits as having a nonsexual meaning.

Some items on the chest defy interpretation, such as his description of Artemis in the fourth register: "I do not know the reason why Artemis has wings on her shoulders; she also holds a leopard in her right hand and a lion in her left."[3] We can speculate that she was shown in a Near Eastern manner as the mistress of animals, an imitation or adaptation that is found in various media of that period and is an example of cultural diffusion. Still, Pausanias is willing to confess his ignorance, and present-day art historians should also be mindful of the limitations of our knowledge.

About the context, Pausanias notes the history of the object within the ruling family of Corinth and the particular circumstances of it being a hiding place for the baby Kypselos. We can go further and turn to object biography to note that this functional object became a commodity through metamorphosis when it became a dedication at Olympia. It can be seen ritualistically as an offering of thanks, but it also expresses a political agenda, as it confirmed the legitimacy of the ruler Kypselos, not only before the people of Corinth, but also before the eyes of all of Greece at the Panhellenic sanctuary of Olympia. Indeed, the descendents of Kypselos became known as the Kypselids, so we can also begin to think of this in terms of elite identity. As Pausanias notes, the word *kypselai* is specifically Corinthian, so that we can also consider that the chest and its dedication represented civic identity to a viewer.

Even though Pausanias was not an art historian himself, the issues that he engages in his discussion do touch on the different levels of art history that we have discussed in this book, and he brings out some points relevant to specific methods as well. He focuses mostly on the content, which would seem appropriate given the vast number of scenes within a confined area, but his approach is more complex than simply listing scenes. He is fascinated by what he sees and seeks to explain it fully for the reader. In our contemporary effort to understand Greek art, this is a good model to follow. The techne of art history, I hope, will help us along the way.

Further Reading

On Pausanias as an art historian, see Elsner 2007, 51–8. On the development of art history in ancient Greece, see now Tanner 2006, 205–76.

GLOSSARY

Absolute chronology (chronology) A specific calendrical date for a work, usually based on external documentation.

Abstract (formal analysis) A rendering of a natural figure that is schematic and reduced and does not appear lifelike. It is the opposite of naturalism.

Acculuration (postcolonialism/diffusion) The impact of cultural diffusion on the recipient, and, in particular, how the recipient conformed to the donor in a hierarchical relationship.

Actions (ritual) The gestures and actions undertaken by individuals in the performance of a ritual, such as pouring a liquid offering or sacrificing an animal.

Adaptation (postcolonialism/diffusion) In cultural diffusion, the merger of elements of the original model or source with indigenous elements to create a new work. See also *hybridity*.

Agalma (context) A work of art that is a pleasing gift to the god or recipient, often used as a votive offering.

Agenda (poststructuralism) The motivation, purpose, or goal, often ideological, behind the production or interpretation of a work.

Agent (agency) Within the theory of agency, the individual or entity that is causing an action or creating an effect, as in the production of an index-artifact (work of art) or in giving it to a recipient (patient).

Aidos (feminism and sexuality) Modesty in demeanor or bearing, frequently through a lowered gaze.

Anathema (context) The act of setting something up for the gods.

Antonymy (repetition theory) Reiteration of a composition with the substitution of an opposite term.

Aparche or first-fruit offering (context) An offering or votive to a god derived from the first proceeds, or the benefits of a trade.

Artist (agency) Within the theory of agency, the producer of the index-artifact or the work of art.

Assimilation (postcolonialism/diffusion) An artistic feature is modified and blended with that of recipient culture to show acceptance by recipient culture within the pattern of symbolic subjugation.

Cast (ritual) The participants of a ritual according to their roles within it, such as priestesses, choir, initiates.

Catalyst (structural analysis) A syntagmatic narrative function that is a pictorial action or figure that elaborates on the nucleus, but is not essential to the main action.

Center-periphery (postcolonialism/diffusion) Model for the study of cultural diffusion that compares centers as net consumers of the resources of peripheral areas, and as exporters of more "advanced" culture.

Commission (Marxism) A form of patronage in which the patron contracts with the artist to produce a specific work of art. The patron may control many aspects of the form and content of the work.

Commodity (object biography) Objects that are exchanged and have a social potential or meaning for the people giving and receiving it.

Commodity candidacy (object biography) The period of an object's social life in which it is available for exchange.

Commodity context (object biography) The social arenas in which the commodity candidacy of an object can be realized in its commodity phase.

Commodity phase (object biography) The period of an object's social life in which it is actively exchanged.

Common commodity (object biography) A commodity that is widely and readily exchanged, such as mass-produced votive offerings. The opposite of a singular commodity.

Continuous narrative (narrative) Multiscene narrative without borders or frames between individual pictures.

Cyclical narrative (narrative) Multiscene narrative with borders or frames between individual pictures.

Dekate or tithe offering (context) An offering or votive to a god derived from a portion of income or benefit realized from a god.

Destination (object biography) The manner in which an object can be a commodity by being made for exchange, such as the production of votive objects.

Diversion (object biography) The manner in which an object that is not intended to be a commodity becomes a commodity by being forced into exchange, as when an object dedicated in a sanctuary is taken and exchanged.

Domestication (postcolonialism/diffusion) Within cultural diffusion, a motivation for imitation or adaptation in which the strangeness of the foreign artistic feature is removed or reduced by making it part of the familiar and everyday of the recipient culture, but without a direct expression of political dominance or control.

Dress and demeanor (ritual) The costume and attitude required for the participants in a ritual and its setting.

Duplication (repetition theory) A repeated element that is intentionally identical to the original.

Emic (ethnicity) An internal distinction or recognition of ethnicity, such as differences recognized or expressed by people of the time.

Emulation (postcolonialism/diffusion) In cultural diffusion, imitation or adoption of the artistic feature by the recipient culture at the compulsion of the donor culture or as an effort to associate with the donor culture in the mode of symbolic subjugation.

Equipment (ritual) The physical objects needed for the performance of a ritual, such as an altar, baskets for carrying objects, sacrificial implements, vessels.

Ethos (history of style) The character expressed by a figure, particularly through its action (rhythmos) and emotion (pathos).

Etic (ethnicity) An external distinction or recognition of ethnicity, as by modern scholars of ancient society.

Exchange (object biography) The means by which an object changes hands during its commodity phase. This can include payment, barter, or gift.

Facilities (Marxism) The space or building needed for carrying out the production of art, such as a kiln or studio.

Familiarization (postcolonialism/diffusion) In cultural diffusion, an artistic feature's becoming common and incorporated into the recipient culture, making it familiar, within a mode of domestication.

Form elements (formal analysis) The basic visual forms or motifs of a work, including line, shape, color, and texture.

Form qualities or expression (formal analysis) The distinctive visual expression created by the work through its form elements and their combinations in form relationships.

Form relationships (formal analysis) The overall interaction or combination of the form elements that create patterns or composition.

gaze (lower-case g) (psychoanalysis) What an individual sees when viewing.

Gaze (upper-case G) (psychoanalysis) The collective or social sight – that is, the idea that an individual is observed collectively by other members of the group.

Gift (object biography) The exchange of an object during its commodity phase, when an object, such as a sanctuary dedication or wedding present, changes hands without return payment of money or goods.

Grave goods (context) Offerings, including jewelry, textiles, and pottery, that are placed in a grave with the remains of the deceased.

Grave offerings (context) Offerings, often pottery, that are left on top of the grave after burials or later commemorations.

Group (psychoanalysis) The social collective in which an individual operates.

Guarantor (Marxism) A third party who undertakes to insure the completion of a work of art by an artist for a patron.

Hybridity (postcolonialism/diffusion) A blending of the art of two cultures, in which the artistic feature(s) of one culture is blended with the feature(s) of the adopting culture, so one can see elements of both in the resulting work.

Iconographical analysis (iconography) Second stage of iconography that identifies the figures or stories and the basic meaning of the symbols.

Iconological interpretation or Iconology (iconography) Third stage of iconography that synthesizes the intrinsic meaning of a work.

Ideal (psychoanalysis) The standard of perfect appearance and behavior by which members of a social group could be measured, a form of presentation or action to be emulated.

Idealism or idealization (formal analysis) A rendering of a natural figure that represents the perfect form of beauty and proportions according to the period. It is the opposite of realism.

Imitation (postcolonialism/diffusion) In cultural diffusion, reproduction of the original model in a second culture, given differences in medium or technique.

Index (structural analysis) Paradigmatic pictorial function or element that refers to an action, event, idea, or person outside the immediate setting.

Index or index-artifact (agency) Within the theory of agency, the physical, material object or thing (the work of art) that forms part of the nexus or relationships among the artist, patron, and recipient.

Informant (structural analysis) Paradigmatic pictorial function or element that identifies participants or locates the narrative in time or place.

Itinerant distribution (Marxism) A form of dissemination in which works of art purchased by a merchant or wholesaler are then offered for sale at many points along a trade route.

Labor (Marxism) The human effort needed for the processes involved in making a work of art.

Liminal state (ritual analysis) A transitional period in which the individual is removed from one set of circumstances and is suspended in a transitory state before becoming fully vested in the new state.

Macro-propositions (viewer response) Ideas about content and narrative formed by the viewer, first upon encountering a work and modified during extended contact with the work.

Manufacturing and technical process (Marxism) The processes and steps needed to transform refined material such as bronze or clay into the finished product, such as casting, carving, and firing.

Marginalization (postcolonialism/diffusion) In cultural diffusion, imitation of an artistic feature of one culture that is restricted in its deployment to lower strata of a second society, making it less prestigious or powerful, in the mode of symbolic domination.

Materials (Marxism) The raw material needed to make a work, such as clay, metal ores, or stone.

Metamorphosis (object biography) The manner in which an object that was intended for practical consumption can become a commodity by a change in its purpose, as the dedication of a personal or household object in a sanctuary.

Metaphor (semiotics) A sign that refers to a figure, category, or idea to which it is not directly related.

Metic (Marxism) A foreign resident working in a city, usually in a skilled occupation, such as a sculptor or vase painter.

Metonym (semiotics) A sign that refers to a figure, category, or idea and is a part of that whole (a helmet as symbol of a warrior).

Mimetic (stylistic analysis) The idea that an image should replicate the appearance of a natural thing or person, "lifelike."

Mimicry (postcolonialism/diffusion) The adoption or imitation of a form, object, or idea of one culture, without much alteration, into the art and culture of a second.

Monoscenic narrative (narrative) Narrative picture with a single time and place.

Movement (ritual) The physical movement of participants in a ritual, including processions and dances.

Naturalism or naturalistic (formal analysis) A rendering of a natural figure that appears to the viewer as it would in nature. It mimics the natural form and is the opposite of abstraction.

Neutralization (postcolonialism/diffusion) In cultural diffusion, modification or adaptation of an artistic feature of one culture to become new but common within the recipient culture, the mode of domestication.

Nucleus (structural analysis) A syntagmatic narrative function that is the essential action and its participants on which a narrative hinges (subject–action–object).

Over-the-counter (Marxism) A form of patronage in which the artist makes works without a specific patron beforehand, and sells the works either directly to the public or indirectly through a merchant or wholesaler.

Panoramic narrative (narrative) Multiscene narrative with scenes taking place at the same time set next to each other.

Paradigmatic functions (structural analysis) Pictorial elements that connect the action of a narrative to time, place, or the identity of characters (informants) or to other stories and ideas (indexes).

Paradigmatic level (semiotics) Associative or homological relationship of signs within a picture to the cultural reservoir of signs outside the picture.

Parody (repetition theory) Imitation of a serious subject for comic effect.

Pathos (history of style) The expression of emotion in a figure through attitude and facial features.

Patient (agency) Within the theory of agency, the individual or entity that is being acted on by the agent or is the recipient of the message.

Patron (Marxism) The person paying for the work of art. The form of payment can include over-the-counter purchase, commission, or retainer.

Perversion (postcolonialism/diffusion) In cultural diffusion, modification of an artistic feature of one culture in a manner that inverts its meaning or status and shows control by the recipient culture, in the mode of symbolic domination.

Point-to-point distribution (Marxism) Dissemination of work in which the work, either individually or in batches, is purchased by a merchant or wholesaler directly from the artist and then sold at a specific location elsewhere.

Preiconographic description (iconography) First step of iconography that makes detailed descriptions of the significant forms or motifs found in an image.

Production (Marxism) The materials and processes used to make a work of art, including materials, refinement, manufacturing and technical processes, facilities, labor, and skill.

Progressive narrative (narrative) Multiscene narrative with scenes taking place in sequence set one after the other, but without repetition of characters.

Prototype (agency) Within the theory of agency, the entity or concept represented by the index-artifact (the subject matter or content).

Realism (formal analysis) A rendering of a natural figure that reproduces the entire appearance without embellishment or improvement – the opposite of idealism.

Recipients (agency) Within the theory of agency, the person or entity receiving or experiencing the index-artifact (work of art), which can include the person acquiring the work from the artist.

Redundancy (repetition theory) Repetition of all parts of an image to ensure alternative paths for the message.

Reduplication (repetition theory) Repetition of a visual element with a variation or inflection on the original.

Refinement (Marxism) The processes used in transforming raw materials into a workable artistic medium, such as the smelting of ore to produce metal.

Relative chronology (chronology) The place within a sequence of a specific work, before some and after others, often determined through excavation stratigraphy.

Retainer (Marxism) A form of patronage in which the artist is paid a salary and makes works as needed or requested by the patron.

Rhythmos (history of style) The representation of the pattern of movement necessary for the representation of an action.

Scripts (ritual) The prescribed texts and instructions for use in a ritual.

Setting/staging (ritual) Space, building, or structures needed for the performance of a ritual.

Sign (semiotics) Unit of meaning consisting of the signifier and signified.

Signifier (semiotics) The form that represents an object or concept in a sign.

Signified (semiotics) The object or concept that is represented in a sign by the signifier.

Singular commodity (object biography) A commodity that has limited exchange potential, such as a commissioned work for a dedication; the opposite of a common commodity.

Skill (Marxism) The specialized knowledge of processes, materials, and ideas that are combined with labor to produce a work of art.

Social life (object biography) Objects that play a role in social relationships or actions, as opposed to a work that is consumed or used as a tool.

Social need (postcolonialism/diffusion) The advantages for adopting an artistic feature in a recipient culture.

Social texture (postcolonialism/diffusion) The divisions and standing of different groups within a culture, particularly within the recipient culture.

Stele (context) A large slab set up as a commemorative marker, usually above a grave or in a sanctuary or civic setting.

Symbolic domination (postcolonialism/diffusion) Within cultural diffusion, a motivation for imitation or adaptation in which a foreign artistic feature becomes a means for showing the control of the recipient culture over the donor.

Symbolic level (semiotics) Internal relationship of a sign to what it signifies.

Symbolic subjugation (postcolonialism/diffusion) In cultural diffusion, a motivation for imitation or adaptation in which a foreign artistic feature becomes a means for showing the control of the donor culture over the recipient.

Synonymy (repetition theory) Reiteration or substitution of a thing or form with a related item of equivalent meaning.

Synoptic narrative (narrative) Narrative picture that combines multiple moments, places, or participants within the single picture.

Syntagmatic functions (structural analysis) Pictorial elements that combine to describe the core action of a narrative (nucleus) or elaborate on its qualities (catalyst).

Syntagmatic level (semiotics) Relationship of signs to each other within a semantic field.

Terminus ad quem (chronology) Point at which something was made (a specific date).

Terminus ante quem (chronology) Point before which something was made (a specific date).

Terminus post quem (chronology) Point after which something was made (a specific date).

Universal narrative (narrative) Narrative image that has no specific identification of the participants, but that could become specific by the interpretation of the viewer.

Verbatim repetition (repetition theory) Exact repetition of a visual element, allowing for differences of style.

Votive (context) An offering to a god in fulfillment of a vow or in recognition of a benefit.

NOTES

One: The Study and Presentation of Greek Art

1. Pausanias 10.11.2; Pausanias, *Description of Greece*, tr. W. H. S. Jones (London, 1989) 4, 427.
2. Herodotos 3.57; tr. Pollitt 1990, 184.
3. On the pedagogical nature of museums, see Hooper-Greenhill 2000, 1–22. In the early days of museums, it was felt that simply seeing a succession of works would infuse a knowledge of the history of art.
4. See http://www.britishmuseum.org/explore/galleries/themes/room_1_enlightenment.aspx (accessed September 1, 2009). The refurbished gallery opened in 2003.
5. On the epistemological strategies of premodern and modern museums, see Hooper-Greenhill 1992, 9–10. One could call the refurbished gallery in the British Museum a postmodern presentation, rather than a recreation. Experiencing the contrast between this room and the modern galleries on the other side of the Great Court is instructive.
6. See Preziosi 1993, 225.

Two: Description and Visual Analysis

1. Schapiro 1953, 145.
2. See, for example, the mini-histories of Quintilian and Cicero in Pollitt 1990, 221–3, as well as Pliny's *Natural History* (books 34–36), which is excerpted extensively in Pollitt. On these sources, see Pollitt 1990, 1–6.
3. Pollitt 1985.
4. See Panzanelli 2008, 120–5, nos. 12–13.
5. See De Grummond and Ridgway 2000.
6. See Marvin 1989.
7. See Pollitt 1974, 63–66.
8. Ridgway 2000, 86.
9. See Ridgway 1990, 219–21, for a discussion of the effect and the relationship to terracottas and dating issues.

10. London E38: EPIKTETOS EGRAPHSEN and PYTHON EPOIESEN. Orvieto 2581: EPIKTETOS EGRAPHSEN and HISCHYLOS EPO[IESE]N. Vienna 3695: DOURIS EGRAPHSEN and PYTHON (no verb). Berlin F1720: EXSEKIAS EGRAPHSE KAPOESEME, in Iambic trimeter.
11. For a selection of literary sources, see Pollitt 1990, 75–79. See the discussion of Tanner 2006, 164–9, who advocates the artist's agency in his discussion. On agency, see Chapter Four. On Pythagoras and Polykleitos, see Pollitt 1972, 105–10, and Stewart 1990, 160–3.

Three: Meaning

1. In Orthodox Christianity, iconography can also mean the writing of an icon, or religious picture, which is a different sense of the word.
2. *Greek Lyrics*, 2nd ed., tr. R. Lattimore (Chicago, 1960) 35. Second quote from p. 34.
3. Pollitt 1986, 16.
4. Watrous 1982, 171–2; Hurwit 1985, 295–6.
5. Brinkmann 1985, 110–21.
6. For the use of the term *pastiche* (or conflation) in iconography, see Oakley 2004, 85, 145, et passim.
7. Woodford 1982, 178–9.
8. For an iconographic study of the Parthenon, see Neils 2001. See also Connelly 1996 for a different iconographic argument. More generally, on the Parthenon program, see Hurwit 2004 and Neils 2005.
9. See the review by Neils 2001, 169–71.
10. Sourvinou-Inwood 1991, 29–98.
11. Snodgrass 1980b, 52.
12. Steiner 2007, 15–16, 22.
13. Steiner 2007, 129.
14. Steiner 2007, 194–95.
15. Keuls 1985, 47–64; Stewart 1995; Osborne 1996a; Lewis 2002, 199–205 and quote from 205; Lefkowitz 2002.
16. Williams 1992.
17. Boardman 1972.

Four: Context

1. Stewart 1990, 66.
2. Herodotos 1.14, tr. Pollitt 1990, 207. The second quote is from Herodotos 1.52, tr. Pollitt 1990, 208.
3. Baxandall 1972, 1–3.
4. See Small 1994.
5. See Langridge-Noti (forthcoming).
6. Pollitt 1990, 192–3.
7. See Stewart 1990, 66, and Neils 2001, 87–88.
8. Pollitt 1990, 192.
9. See Stewart 1997, 124–9.
10. Vickers and Gill 1994, 34–35.
11. Rasmussen 1991, 66.
12. D'Alleva 2005, 50.
13. Neer 2001.
14. Herodotos 3.57; tr. Pollitt 1990, 184.
15. See Morris 2000, 109–91.

16. See Boardman 1978a, 1978b; Watrous 1982.
17. On reading inscriptions aloud, see Svenbro 1993 and Steiner 2007, 68–73.
18. Keesling 2003, 3–10.
19. Stillwell 1948, 22–23, 72, and pl. 5 and 23; Stillwell et al. 1984, 186.
20. Shapiro 1990.
21. See Cahill 2002, 74–147.
22. Gell 1998, 6.
23. Osborne and Tanner 2007, 20.
24. Geertz 1973, 89.
25. Greenblatt 1980, 1–9. See also Dougherty and Kurke 1998 and 2003.
26. See Bell 1992.
27. Langdon 2008, 152–6 and 166–74.
28. Sinos 1998. One might think today of a hearse as a vehicle whose form and the context in which one sees it evokes associations with funerals, although the same shape was once used for ambulances, which were painted white rather than black.
29. Kopytoff 1986, 66–67.
30. Appadurai 1986a.
31. Langdon 2008, 31–32.

Five: Identity

1. Eagleton 1996, 155.
2. See Stansbury-O'Donnell 2006, 61–67.
3. Aristotle, *Poetics* 4.
4. See Ferrari 2002, 54–60 on aidos and its qualities.
5. Mattusch 2006, 234–5.
6. Steiner 2001, 222–34.
7. Kurke 1999, 144.
8. Kurke 1999, 147.
9. See, for example, Fantham et al. 1994, 74–83 and 101–13.
10. See Stewart 1997, 108–18 and 231–4; Pomeroy 2002, 164–7.
11. See Connelly 2007, Kaltsas and Shapiro 2008.
12. Connelly 2007, 111–5; Sinos 1998, 83–84.
13. Lewis 2002, 123.
14. On the controversy see Lewis 2002, 194–9; Lear and Cantarella 2008, 78–86.
15. Lear and Cantarella 2008, xv.
16. Ferrari 2002, 96.
17. Lear and Cantarella 2008, 72.
18. Lear and Cantarella 2008, 86.
19. See Stewart 1997, 70–75 and Ferrari 2002, 155–61.
20. Neer 2001, 295–297.
21. See summary in Whitley 1991, 181–3. See also Snodgrass 1998, 12–66.
22. Herodotos 8.144.2. See Hall 2003, 30–33; Morgan 2001, 76.
23. On emic and etic, see Hall 2003, 23–27.
24. See the discussion of Antonaccio 2003, 61–65.
25. See Bérard 2000, 395–402; also Snowden 1970 and 1983.
26. D'Alleva 2005.
27. Antonaccio 2003, 60.
28. Miller 1997, esp. 243–58 on cultural receptivity and diffusion.
29. Miller 1997, 248, with addition of the category of symbolic subjugation.
30. On the shapes, see Gunter 2009, 119–22.

31. See discussion of Miller 1997, 141–7.
32. Gunter 2009, 86.
33. See Carpenter 2009 for the following discussion.

Conclusion

1. Pollitt 1974, 32.
2. Pausanias 5.17.5–5.19.10, tr. Pollitt 1990, 210–5, with quotes from 210 and 215. For reconstructions based on Pausanias, see Pollitt 1990, fig. 9, and Splitter 2000.
3. Pausanias 10.19.5, tr. Pollitt 1990, 214.

BIBLIOGRAPHY

Alcock, S. E. and R. Osborne, eds. 2007. *Classical Archaeology*. Malden, MA and Oxford.

Amyx, D. 1988. *Corinthian Vase-Painting of the Archaic Period*. Berkeley.

Antonaccio, C. M. 2003. "Hybridity and the Cultures within Greek Culture." In Dougherty and Kurke 2003, 57–76.

______. 2009. "(Re)Defining Ethnicity. Culture, Material Culture, and Identity." In Hales and Hodos 2009, 32–53.

Appadurai, A. 1986a. "Introduction: Commodities and the Politics of Value." In Appadurai 1986b, 3–63.

______, ed. 1986b. *The Social Life of Things. Commodities in Cultural Perspective*. Cambridge.

Arafat, K. and C. Morgan. 1989. "Pots and Potters in Athens and Corinth: A Review." *Oxford Journal of Archaeology* 8, 311–46.

Arens, W. "An Anthropological Approach to Ritual: Evidence, Context and Interpretation." In R. Hägg, N. Marinatos, and G. C. Nordquist, eds., *Early Greek Cult Practice. Proceedings of the Fifth International Symposium at the Swedish Institute at Athens*, 26–29 June 1986. Stockholm, 223–28.

Barletta, B. A. 2001. *The Origins of the Greek Architectural Orders*. Cambridge.

Barringer, J. M. 2001. *The Hunt in Ancient Greece*. Baltimore.

______. 2008. *Art, Myth, and Ritual in Classical Greece*. Cambridge.

Barthes, R. 1982. *A Barthes Reader*, edited with an introduction by S. Sontag. New York.

Baxandall, M. 1972. *Painting and Experience in Fifteenth-Century Italy. A Primer in the Social History of Pictorial Style*. Oxford.

Beazley, J. D. 1922. "Citharoedus." *Journal of Hellenic Studies* 42, 70–98.

______. 1956. *Attic Black-figure Vase Painters*. Oxford.

______. 1963. *Attic Red-figure Vase Painters*, 2nd ed. Oxford.

______. 1971. *Paralipomena*. Oxford.

______. 1986. *The Development of Attic Black-Figure*, rev. ed. Oxford.

———. 1989. *Beazley Addenda. Additional References to ABV, ARV2 & Paralipomena,* 2nd ed. T. H. Carpenter with T. Mannack and M. Mendonça, eds. Oxford.

Bell, C. 1992. *Ritual Theory, Ritual Practice.* Oxford.

———. 1997. *Ritual. Perspectives and Dimensions.* Oxford.

Bérard, C. 2000. "The Image of the Other and the Foreign Hero." In Cohen 2000, 390–412.

Bérard, C., et al. 1989. *A City of Images; Iconography and Society in Ancient Greece,* D. Lyons, tr. Princeton, NJ.

Bernal, M. 1987. *Black Athena. The Afro-Asiatic Roots of Classical Civilization. Vol. 1: The Fabrication of Ancient Greece 1785–1985.* New Brunswick, NJ.

———. 1991. *Black Athena. The Afro-Asiatic Roots of Classical Civilization. Vol. 2: The Archaeological and Documentary Evidence.* New Brunswick, NJ.

———. 2001. *Black Athena Writes Back. Martin Bernal Responds to His Critics,* D. C. Moore, ed. Durham, NC.

———. 2006. *Black Athena. The Afro-Asiatic Roots of Classical Civilization. Vol. 3: The Linguistic Evidence.* New Brunswick, NJ.

Bhabha, H. K. 1996. *The Location of Culture.* London, New York.

Biers, W. R. 1992. *Art, Artefacts, and Chronology in Classical Archaeology.* London.

———. 1996. *The Archaeology of Greece,* 2nd ed. Ithaca, NY.

Blundell, S. 1995. *Women in Ancient Greece.* Cambridge, MA.

Boardman, J. 1972. "Herakles, Peisistratos and Sons." *Revue archéologique* 1972, 57–72.

———. 1974. *Athenian Black Figure Vases. A Handbook.* London.

———. 1975. *Athenian Red Figure Vases. The Archaic Period. A Handbook.* London.

———. 1978a. "Exekias." *American Journal of Archaeology* 82, 11–25.

———. 1978b. "Herakles, Delphi, and Kleisthenes of Sikyon." *Revue archéologique* 1978, 227–34.

———. 1985. *Greek Sculpture. The Classical Period. A Handbook.* London.

———. 1989. *Athenian Red Figure Vases. The Classical Period. A Handbook.* London.

———. 1991a. *Greek Sculpture. The Archaic Period. A Handbook.* London.

———. 1991b. "The Sixth-Century Potters and Painters of Athens and their Public." In Rasmussen and Spivey 1991, 79–102.

———. 1995. *Greek Sculpture. The Late Classical Period and Sculpture in Colonies and Overseas.* London.

———. 1996. *Greek Art,* 4th ed., revised and expanded. London.

———. 1998. *Early Greek Vase Painting. 11th–6th Centuries BC. A Handbook.* London.

———. 1999. *The Greeks Overseas. Their Early Colonies and Trade,* 4th ed. London.

———. 2001. *The History of Greek Vases. Potters, Painters and Pictures.* London.

———, ed. 1997. *The Oxford History of Classical Art.* Oxford.

Boedeker, D. and K. A. Raaflaub. 1998. *Democracy, Empire, and the Arts in Fifth-Century Athens.* Cambridge, MA.

Boegehold, A. L. 1999. *When a Gesture Was Expected. A Selection of Examples from Archaic and Classical Literature.* Princeton, NJ.

Borbein, A. H. 1996. "Polykleitos." In Palagia and Pollitt 1996, 66–90.

Bothmer, D. von, ed. 1985. *The Amasis Painter and his World. Vase-Painting in Sixth-Century B.C. Athens.* Malibu, CA and New York.

Brinkmann, V. 1985. "Die aufgemalten Namenbeischriften an Nord – und Ostfries des Siphnierschatzhauses." *Bulletin de correspondence héllenique* 109, 77–130.

______. 2008. "The Polychromy of Ancient Greek Sculpture." In Panzanelli 2008, 18–39.

Brinkmann, V. and R. Wünsche. 2007. *Gods in Color: Painted Sculpture of Classical Antiquity.* Exhibition at the Arthur M. Sackler Museum, Harvard University Art Museums, in cooperation with the Staatliche Antikensammlung and Glyptothek Munich, Stiftung Archäologie Munich, September 22, 2007–January 20, 2008. Cambridge, MA.

Buitron, D. and B. Cohen, eds. 1992. *The Odyssey and Ancient Art. An Epic in Word and Image.* Annandale on Hudson, NY.

Buitron-Oliver, D., ed. 1997. *The Interpretation of Architectural Sculpture in Greece and Rome.* Studies in the History of Art, 49. Hanover/London.

Bundrick, S. D. 2005. *Music and Image in Classical Athens.* Cambridge.

______. 2008. "The Fabric of the City: Imaging Textile Production in Classical Athens." *Hesperia* 77, 283–334.

Cahill, N. 2002. *House and City Organization at Olynthus.* New Haven, CT.

Camp, J. M. 1986. *The Athenian Agora. Excavations in the Heart of Athens.* London.

______. 2001. *The Archaeology of Athens.* New Haven.

Camp, J. M. and C. A. Mauzy, eds. 2009. *The Athenian Agora. New Perspectives on an Ancient Site.* Mainz, Germany.

Carpenter, T. H. 1991. *Art and Myth in Ancient Greece.* London.

______. 2009. "Prolegomenon to the Study of Apulian Red-Figure Pottery." *American Journal of Archaeology* 113, 27–38.

Castriota, D. 1992. *Myth, Ethos, and Actuality. Official Art in Fifth-Century B.C. Athens.* Madison, WI.

Champion, T. C. 1995. "Introduction." In T. C. Champion, ed., *Centre and Periphery. Comparative Studies in Archaeology.* London, 1–21.

Christiansen, J. and T. Melander, eds. 1988. *Proceedings of the 3rd Symposium on Ancient Greek and Related Pottery. Copenhagen, August 31–September 4, 1987.* Copenhagen.

Clark, A. J., M. Elston, and M. L. Hart. 2002. *Understanding Greek Vases. A Guide to Terms, Styles, and Techniques.* Los Angeles.

Cohen, B., ed. 2000. *Not the Classical Ideal. Athens and the Construction of the Other in Greek Art.* Leiden, the Netherlands.

______. 2006. *The Colors of Clay. Special Techniques in Athenian Vases.* Los Angeles.

Connelly, J. B. 1996. "Parthenon and Parthenoi: A Mythological Interpretation of the Parthenon Frieze." *American Journal of Archaeology* 100, 58–80.

______. 2007. *Portrait of a Priestess. Women and Ritual in Ancient Greece.* Princeton, NJ.

Cook, R. M. 1987. "Pots and Pisistratan Propaganda." *Journal of Hellenic Studies* 107, 167–9.

______. 1989. "The Francis-Vickers Chronology." *Journal of Hellenic Studies* 109, 164–70.

______. 1997. *Greek Painted Pottery*, 3rd ed. London.

Coulton, J. J. 1977. *Ancient Greek Architects at Work. Problems of Structure and Design.* Ithaca, NY.

Crielaard, J. P., V. Stissi, and G. J. van Wijngaarden, eds. 1999. *The Complex Past of Pottery. Production, Circulation and Consumption of Mycenaean and Greek Pottery (Sixteenth to Early Fifth Centuries BC). Proceedings of the ARCHON International Conference, Held in Amsterdam, 8–9 November 1996.* Amsterdam.

D'Alleva, A. 2005. *Methods and Theories of Art History*. London. [Previously published under the title *Look Again!: Art History and Critical Theory*.]

———. 2006. *Look! The Fundamentals of Art History*, 2nd ed. Upper Saddle River, NJ.

Day, J. W. 1994. "Interactive Offerings: Early Greek Dedicatory Epigrams and Ritual." *Harvard Studies in Classical Philology* 96, 37–74.

De Grummond, N. T. and B. S. Ridgway, eds. 2000. *From Pergamon to Sperlonga. Sculpture and Context*. Berkeley, CA.

Derderian, K. 2001. *Leaving Words to Remember. Greek Mourning and the Advent of Literacy*. Leiden, the Netherlands.

Dillon, S. 2006. *Ancient Greek Portrait Sculpture. Contexts, Subjects, and Styles*. Cambridge.

Dodd, D. B. and C. A. Faraone, eds. 2003. *Initiation in Ancient Greek Rituals and Narratives. New Critical Perspectives*. London/New York.

Donohue, A. A. 2005. *Greek Sculpture and the Problem of Description*. Cambridge.

Dougherty, C. and L. Kurke, eds. 1998. *Cultural Poetics in Archaic Greece. Cult, Performance, Politics*. Oxford.

———. 2003. *The Cultures within Greek Culture*. Cambridge.

Eagleton, T. 1996. *Literary Theory. An Introduction*, 2nd ed. Minneapolis.

Eco, U. 1979. *The Role of the Reader. Explorations in the Semiotics of Texts*. Bloomington, IN.

Elsner, J. 2007. *Roman Eyes. Visuality and Subjectivity in Art and Text*. Princeton.

Euphronios. 1991. *Euphronios. Peintre à Athènes au VIe siècle avant J.-C. Musée du Louvre, Paris, September 18–December 31, 1990*. Paris.

Fantham, E., H. P. Foley, N. B. Kampen, S. B. Pomeroy, and H. A. Shapiro. 1994. *Women in the Classical World. Image and Text*. Oxford.

Ferrari, G. 2002. *Figures of Speech. Men and Maidens in Ancient Greece*. Chicago.

———. 2003. "Myth and Genre on Athenian Vases." *Classical Antiquity* 22, 37–54.

Francis, E. D. and M. J. Vickers. 1983. "Signa Priscae Artis: Eretria and Siphnos." *Journal of Hellenic Studies* 103, 49–67.

Frontisi-Ducroux, F. 1996. "Eros, Desire, and the Gaze." In Kampen 1996, 81–100.

Fullerton, M. D. 2000. *Greek Art*. Cambridge.

Gadamer, H. G. 1989. *Truth and Method*, tr. J. Weinsheimer and D. Marshall. New York.

Garland, R. 1985. *The Greek Way of Death*. Ithaca, NY.

Geertz, C. 1973. *The Interpretation of Cultures*. New York.

Gell, A. 1998. *Art and Agency. An Anthropological Theory*. Oxford.

Gill, D. W. T. 1991. "Pots and Trade: Spacefillers or Objets d'Art?" *Journal of Hellenic Studies* 111, 29–47.

Goldhill, S. and R. Osborne, eds. 1994. *Art and Text in Ancient Greek Sculpture*. Cambridge.

Gombrich, E. 1968. "Style." In *International Encyclopedia of the Social Sciences*. New York, vol. 15, 352–61.

Gosden, C. and Y. Marshall, eds. 1999. *The Cultural Biography of Objects, World Archaeology* 31.2. London.

Greenblatt, S. 1980. *Renaissance Self-Fashioning. From More to Shakespeare*. Chicago.

Grossman, J. B. 2003. *Looking at Greek and Roman Sculpture in Stone*. Malibu, CA.

Gunter, A. G. 2009. *Greek Art and the Orient*. Cambridge.

Hales, S. and T. Hodos, eds. 2009. *Material Culture and Social Identities in the Ancient World*. Cambridge.

Hall, J. M. 1997. *Ethnic Identity in Greek Antiquity*. Cambridge.

———. 2003. "'Culture' or 'Cultures'? Hellenism in the Late Sixth Century." In Dougherty and Kurke 2003, 23–34.

———. 2007. "The Creation and Expression of Identity. The Greek World." In Alcock and Osborne 2007, 337–54.

Hannestad, L. 1988. "The Athenian Potter and the Home Market." In J. Christiansen and T. Melander, eds., *Proceedings of the 3rd Symposium on Ancient Greek and Related Pottery. Copenhagen, August 31–September 4, 1987*. Copenhagen, 222–30.

———. 1989. "Athenian Pottery in Etruria c. 550–470 BC." *Acta Archeologica* 59, 113–30.

———. 1999. "The Reception of Attic Pottery by the Indigenous Peoples of Italy: The Evidence from Funerary Contexts." In Crielaard, Stissi, and van Wijngaarden 1999, 303–18.

Hedreen, G. 1992. *Silens in Attic Black-figure Vase-painting. Myth and Performance*. Ann Arbor.

———. 2001. *Capturing Troy. The Narrative Functions of Landscape in Archaic and Early Classical Greek Art*. Ann Arbor.

Hemelrijk, J. M. 1984. *Caeretan Hydria*. Mainz.

Higgins, R. 1967. *Greek Terracottas*. London.

Hitchcock, L. A. 2008. *Theory for Classics. A Student's Guide*. London.

Holliday, P. J., ed. 1993. *Narrative and Event in Ancient Art*. Cambridge.

Hooper-Greenhill, E. 1992. *Museums and the Shaping of Knowledge*. London.

———. 2000. *Museums and the Interpretation of Visual Culture*. London.

Houby-Nielsen, S. 1995. "'Burial Language' in Archaic and Classical Kerameikos." *Proceedings of the Danish Institute at Athens* 1, 129–91.

———. 1996. "Women and the Formation of the Athenian State. The Evidence of Burial Customs." *Métis* 11, 233–60.

Hubbard, T. K. 2002. "Pindar, Theoxenus, and the Homoerotic Eye." *Arethusa* 35, 255–96.

Hurwit, J. M. 1985. *The Art and Culture of Early Greece, 1100–480 B.C.* Ithaca, NY.

———. 1999. *The Athenian Acropolis. History, Mythology, and Archaeology from the Neolithic Era to the Present*. Cambridge.

———. 2004. *The Acropolis in the Age of Pericles*. Cambridge.

Jay, M. 1993. *Downcast Eyes. The Denigration of Vision in Twentieth-Century French Thought*. Berkeley/Los Angeles.

Johnston, A. W. 1979. *Trademarks on Greek Vases*. Warminster, UK.

———. 1991. "Greek Vases in the Marketplace." In Rasmussen and Spivey 1991, 203–32.

———. 2006. *Trademarks on Greek Vases. Addenda*. Warminster, UK.

Junker, K. 2005. *Griechische Mythenbilder. Einführung in ihre Interpretation*. Stuttgart.

Kaltsas, N. and A. Shapiro, eds. 2008. *Worshipping Women. Ritual and Reality in Classical Athens*. New York.

Kampen, N. B., ed. 1996. *Sexuality in Ancient Art*. Cambridge.

Kannicht, R. 1982. "Poetry and Art. Homer and the Monuments Afresh." *Classical Antiquity* 1, 70–86.

Keesling, C. M. 2003. *The Votive Statues of the Athenian Acropolis*. Cambridge.

Keuls, E. C. 1985. *The Reign of the Phallus: Sexual Politics in Ancient Athens*. New York.

Koloski-Ostrow, A. O. and C. L. Lyons, eds. 1997. *Naked Truths. Women, Sexuality, and Gender in Classical Art and Archaeology*. London.

Kopytoff, I. 1986. "The cultural biography of things: commodization as process." In Appadurai 1986, 64–91.

Korres, M. 1995. *From Pentelicon to the Parthenon*. Athens.

———. 2000. *The Stones of the Parthenon*. Los Angeles.

Kousser, R. M. 2008. *Hellenistic and Roman Ideal Sculpture. The Allure of the Classical*. Cambridge.

Kurke. L. 1999. *Coins, Bodies, Games, and Gold: The Politics of Meaning in Archaic Greece*. Princeton, NJ.

Kurtz, D. and J. Boardman. 1971. *Greek Burial Customs*. Ithaca, NY.

Laks, A. 1999. "Soul, Sensation, and Thought." In A. A. Long, ed., *The Cambridge Companion to Early Greek Philosophy*. Cambridge, 250–70.

Langdon, S. 2001. "Beyond the Grave: Biographies from Early Greece." *American Journal of Archaeology* 105, 579–606.

———. 2006. "Maiden Voyage: From Abduction to Marriage in Late Geometric Art." In E. Rystedt and B. Wells, eds., *Pictorial Pursuits. Figurative Painting on Mycenaean and Geometric Pottery. Papers from Two Seminars at the Swedish Institute at Athens in 1999 and 2001*, Skrifter utgivna av Svenska Instituteti Athen, 4°, 53, Stockholm, 205–15.

———. 2008. *Art and Identity in Dark Age Greece, 1100–700 B.C.E.* Cambridge.

Langridge-Noti, E. forthcoming. "To Market, to Market: Pottery, the Individual, and Trade in Athens." In L. A. Riccardi and K. Daly, eds., *The Art and Archaeology of Ancient Athens*. Leiden.

Lawrence, A. W. 1996. *Greek Architecture*, 5th ed., revised by R. A. Tomlinson. New Haven, CT.

Lear, A. and E. Cantarella. 2008. *Images of Ancient Greek Pederasty. Boys Were Their Gods*. London.

Lefkowitz, M. R. 2002. "'Predatory' Goddesses." *Hesperia* 71, 325–44.

Lefkowitz, M. R. and M. B. Fant. 2005. *Women's Life in Greece and Rome. A Source Book in Translation*, 3rd ed. Baltimore.

Lefkowitz, M. R. and G. M. Rogers, eds. 1996. *Black Athena Revisited*. Chapel Hill, NC.

Lewis, S. 2002. *The Athenian Woman. An Iconographic Handbook*. London/New York.

Lexicon Iconographicum Mythologiae Classicae. Zurich, 1981–2009.

Lindberg, D. C. 1976. *Theories of Vision from al-Kindi to Kepler*. Chicago.

Lissarrague, F. 1990. *The Aesthetics of the Greek Banquet. Images of Wine and Ritual (Un Flot d'Images)*, tr. A. Szgedy-Maszak. Princeton, NJ.

———. 2001. *Greek Vases. The Athenians and their Images*. New York.

———. 2009. "Reading Images, Looking at Pictures, and After." In Schmidt and Oakley, 2009, 15–22.

Malkin, I., ed. 2001. *Ancient Perceptions of Greek Ethnicity*. Cambridge, MA.

Marconi, C. 2007. *Temple Decoration and Cultural Identity in the Archaic Greek World. The Metopes of Selinus*. Cambridge.

Marvin, M. 1989. "Copying in Roman Sculpture: The Replica Series." In *Retaining the Original. Multiple Originals, Copies, and Reproductions*, Studies in the History of Art, 20. Hanover, NH, 29–45.

———. 2008. *The Language of the Muses. The Dialogue between Roman and Greek Sculpture*. Los Angeles.

Mattusch, C. C. 1988. *Greek Bronze Statuary. From the Beginnings through the Fifth Century B.C.* Ithaca, NY.

———. 1996. *Classical Bronzes. The Art and Craft of Greek and Roman Statuary*. Ithaca, NY.

———. 2006. "Archaic and Classical Bronzes." In Palagia 2006, 208–42.

McNiven, T. 1982. *Gestures in Attic Vase Painting: Use and Meaning, 550–450 BC*. Ph.D. dissertation, University of Michigan, Ann Arbor.

———. 2000. "Behaving Like an Other: Telltale Gestures in Athenian Vase Painting." In Cohen 2000, 71–97.

Miller, M. C. 1997. *Athens and Persia in the Fifth Century BC. A Study in Cultural Receptivity*. Cambridge.

Mitchell, A. G. 2004. "Humour in Greek Vase-painting." *Revue Archéologique* 2004, 3–32.

———. 2009. *Greek Vase-Painting and the Origins of Visual Humour*. Cambridge.

Moignard, E. 2006. *Greek Vases. An Introduction*. London.

Moon, W. E. 1983. "The Priam Painter: Some Iconographic and Stylistic Considerations." In Moon, ed. 1983, 97–118.

Moon, W. E., ed. 1983. *Ancient Greek Art and Iconography*. Madison, WI.

———. 1995. *Polykleitos, The Doryphoros*. Madison, WI.

Moreno, P., ed. 1995. *Lisippo. L'art e la fortuna*. Milan.

Morgan, C. 1991. "Ethnicity and Early Greek States: Historical and Material Perspectives." *Proceedings of the Cambridge Philological Society* 37, 131–59.

———. 2001. "Ethne, Ethnicity, and Early Greek States, ca. 1200–480 B.C.: An Archaeological Perspective." In Malkin 2001, 75–112.

———. 2003. *Early Greek States beyond the Polis*. London.

Morris, I. 1987. *Burial and Ancient Society*. Cambridge.

———. 1992. *Death-Ritual and Social Structure in Classical Antiquity*. Cambridge.

———. 2000. *Archaeology as Cultural History*. Malden, MA and Oxford.

———, ed. 1994. *Classical Greece. Ancient History and Modern Archaeologies*. Cambridge.

Morris, S. 1992. *Daidalos and the Origins of Greek Art*. Princeton, NJ.

———. 2007. "Linking with a Wider World. Greeks and 'Barbarians.'" In Alcock and Osborne 2007, 383–400.

Neer, R. 2001. "Framing the Gift: The Politics of the Siphnian Treasury at Delphi." *Classical Antiquity* 20, 273–336.

———. 2002. *Style and Politics in Athenian Vase-Painting. The Craft of Democracy, ca. 530–460 B.C.E.* Cambridge.

Neils, J. 1996. *Worshipping Athena. Panathenaia and Parthenon*. Madison, WI.

———. 2001. *The Parthenon Frieze*. Cambridge.

———. 2005. *The Parthenon. From Antiquity to the Present*. Cambridge.

———, ed. 1992. *Goddess and Polis. The Panathenaic Festival in Ancient Athens*. Princeton, NJ.

Neils, J. and J. H. Oakley, eds. 2003. *Coming of Age in Ancient Greece. Images of Childhood from the Classical Past*. New Haven, CT.

Nevett, L. 1999. *House and Society in the Ancient Greek World. New Studies in Archaeology*. Cambridge.

Noble, J. V. 1988. *The Techniques of Painted Attic Pottery*. London.

Oakley, J. H. 2004. *Picturing Death in Classical Athens. The Evidence of the White Lekythoi*. Cambridge.

Oakley, J. H., W. D. E. Coulson, and O. Palagia, eds. 1997. *Athenian Potters and Painters*. Oxford.

Oakley, J. H. and O. Palagia, eds. 2009. *Athenian Potters and Paintesr, Volume II*. Oxford.

Oakley, J. H. and R. H. Sinos. 1993. *The Wedding in Ancient Athens*. Madison, WI.

Osborne, R. 1991. "Whose Image and Superscription Is This?" *Arion, ser.* 3, 1.2, 255–75.

______. 1994. "Framing the Centaur. Reading Fifth-Century Architectural Sculpture." In Goldhill and Osborne 1994, 52–84.

______. 1996a. "Desiring Women on Athenian Pottery." In Kampen 1996, 65–80.

______. 1996b. "Pots, Trade and the Archaic Greek Economy." *Antiquity* 70, 31–44.

______. 1998. *Archaic and Classical Greek Art*. Oxford.

______. 2007a. "Sex, Agency, and History: The Case of Athenian Painted Pottery." In Osborne and Tanner 2007, 179–198.

______. 2007b. "Projecting Identities in the Greek Symposion." In J. Sofaer, ed., *Material Identities*. Malden, MA and Oxford, 31–52.

______. 2007c. "Cult and Ritual. The Greek World." In Alcock and Osborne 2007, 246–62.

Osborne, R. and J. Tanner, eds. 2007. *Art's Agency and Art History*. Malden, MA and Oxford.

Palagia, O., ed. 2006. *Greek Sculpture. Function, Materials, and Techniques in the Archaic and Classical Periods*. Cambridge.

Palagia, O. and J. J. Pollitt, eds. 1996. *Personal Styles in Greek Sculpture*. Yale Classical Studies, 30. Cambridge.

Panofsky, E. 1955. "Iconography and Iconology: An Introduction to the Study of Renaissance Art." In *Meaning in the Visual Arts*, Garden City, NY, 26–54.

Panzanelli, R. with E. D. Schmidt and K. Lapatin, eds. 2008. *The Color of Life. Polychromy in Sculpture from Antiquity to the Present*. Malibu, CA.

Papadopoulos, J. K. and E. L. Smithson. 2002. "The Cultural Biography of a Cycladic Amphora: Islanders in Athens and the Prehistory of Metics." *Hesperia* 71, 149–199.

Parker, H. N. 2001. "The Myth of the Heterosexual: Anthropology and Sexuality for Classicists." *Arethusa* 34, 313–62.

Pasquier, A. and J.-L. Martinez, eds. 2007. *Praxitèle*. Paris.

Pedley, J. G. 2007. *Greek Art and Archaeology*, 4th ed. Upper Saddle River, NJ.

Polignac, F. de. 1995. *Cults, Territory, and the Origins of the Greek City-State*, tr. J. Lloyd. Chicago.

Pollitt, J. J. 1972. *Art and Experience in Classical Greece*. Cambridge.

______. 1974. *The Ancient View of Greek Art. Criticism, History, and Terminology*. New Haven.

______. 1985. "Early Classical Greek Art in a Platonic Universe." In C. G. Boulter, ed., *Greek Art. Archaic into Classical. A Symposium Held at the University of Cincinnati, April 2–3, 1982*. Leiden, 96–112.

______. 1986. *Art in the Hellenistic Age*. Cambridge.

______. 1990. *The Art of Ancient Greece. Sources and Documents*. Cambridge.

______. 1997. "The Meaning of the Parthenon Frieze." In Buitron-Oliver 1997, 51–65.

Pollitt, J. J., ed. forthcoming. *Painting in the Classical World*. Cambridge.

Pomeroy, S. 2002. *Spartan Women*. Oxford.

Preziosi, D. 1992. "The Question of Art History." *Critical Inquiry* 18, 363–386.

______. 1993. "Seeing through Art History." In E. Messer-Davidow, D. R. Shumway, and D. J. Sylvan, eds., *Knowledge: Historical and Critical Studies in Disciplinarity*. Charlottesville, VA, 215–31.

———. 1996. "Collecting/Museums." In R. S. Nelson and R. Shiff, eds., *Critical Terms for Art History*. Chicago, 281–91.

———. 2003. *Brain of the Earth's Body. Art, Museums, and the Phantasms of Modernity*. Minneapolis.

Rasmussen, T. 1991. "Corinth and the Orientalizing Phenomenon." In Rasmussen and Spivey 1991, 57–78.

Rasmussen, T. and N. Spivey, eds. 1991. *Looking at Greek Vases*. Cambridge.

Reeder, E., ed. 1995. *Pandora. Women in Classical Greece*. Baltimore/Princeton.

Ridgway, B. S. 1970. *The Severe Style in Greek Sculpture*. Princeton, NJ.

———. 1977. *The Archaic Style in Greek Sculpture*. Princeton, NJ.

———. 1981. *Fifth-Century Styles in Greek Sculpture*. Princeton, NJ.

———. 1989. "Defining the Issue: The Greek Period." In *Retaining the Original. Multiple Originals, Copies, and Reproductions*, Studies in the History of Art, 20. Hanover, NH, 13–26.

———. 1990. *Hellenistic Sculpture I. The Styles of ca. 331–220 B.C.* Madison, WI.

———. 1997. *Fourth-Century Styles in Greek Sculpture*. Madison, WI.

———. 2000. *Hellenistic Sculpture II. The Styles of ca. 200–100 B.C.* Madison, WI.

———. 2002. *Hellenistic Sculpture III. The Styles of ca. 100–31 B.C.* Madison, WI.

Robertson, M. 1975. *A History of Greek Art*. Cambridge.

———. 1981. *A Shorter History of Greek Art*. Cambridge.

———. 1992. *The Art of Vase-Painting in Classical Athens*. Cambridge.

Rowlands, M. 1987. "Centre and Periphery: A Review of a Concept." In M. Rowlands, M. Larsen, and K. Kristiansen, eds., *Centre and Periphery in the Ancient World*. Cambridge, 1–11.

Salomon, N. 1997. "Making a World of Difference: Gender, Asymmetry, and the Greek Nude." In Koloski-Ostrow and Lyons 2001, 197–219.

Schapiro, M. 1953. "Style." In A. L. Kroeber, ed. *Anthropology Today. An Encyclopedic Inventory*. Chicago, 287–312.

Scheffer, C. 1988. "Workshop and Trade Patterns in Athenian Black-Figure." In Christiansen and Melander 1988, 536–46.

Scheffer, C., ed. 2001. *Ceramics in Context. Proceedings of the Internordic Colloquium on Ancient Pottery held at Stockholm, 13–15 June 1997*, Acta Universitatis Stockholmiensis. Stockholm Studies in Classical Archaeology 12. Stockholm.

Schefold, K. 1992. *Gods and Heroes in Late Archaic Greek Art*, tr. A Griffiths. Cambridge.

Schmaltz, B. and M. Söldner. 2003. *Griechische Keramik im kulturellen Kontext. Akten des Internationalen Vasen-Symposions in Kiel vom 24.-28.9.2001 veranstaltet durch das Archäologische Institut der Christian-Albrechts-Universität zu Kiel*. Münster.

Schmidt, S. and J. H. Oakley, eds. 2009. *Concepts of Pictorial Representation in the Hermeneutics of Greek Vase Paintings*, Corpus Vasorum Antiquorum, Deutschland, Beihefte 4. Munich.

Schreiber, T. 1999. *Athenian Vase Construction. A Potter's Analysis*. Malibu, CA.

Scott, M. 2007. "Putting Architectural Sculpture into its Archaeological Context." *BABESCH. Annual Papers on Mediterranean Archaeology* 82, 321–31.

———. 2010. *Delphi and Olympia. The Spatial Politics of Panhellenism in the Archaic and Classical Periods*. Cambridge.

Shapiro, H. A. 1989. *Art and Cult under the Tyrants in Athens*. Mainz, Germany.

———. 1990. "Comings and Goings. The Iconography of Departure and Arrival on Attic Vases." *Metis* 5, 113–23.

———. 1991. "The Iconography of Mourning in Athenian Art." *American Journal of Archaeology* 95, 629–56.

———. 1992. "Eros in Love: Pederasty and Pornography in Greece." In A. Richlin, ed., *Pornography and Representation in Greece and Rome*, Oxford 1992, 53–72.

———. 1994. *Myth into Art. Poet and Painter in Classical Greece*. London.

Simon, E. 1983. *Festivals of Attica. An Archaeological Commentary*. Madison, WI.

Sinos, R. 1998. "Divine Selection: Epiphany and Politics in Archaic Greece." In Dougherty and Kurke 1998, 73–91.

Small, J. P. 1994. "Scholars, Etruscans, and Attic Painted Vases." *Journal of Roman Archaeology* 7, 34–58.

———. 2003. *The Parallel Worlds of Classical Art and Text*. Cambridge.

Smith, R. R. R. 1991. *Hellenistic Sculpture. A Handbook*. London.

Snodgrass, A. 1971 (repr. 2000). *The Dark Age of Greece. An Archaeological Survey of the Eleventh to the Eighth Centuries BC*. New York.

———. 1980a. *Archaic Greece. The Age of Experiment*. London.

———. 1980b. "Towards the Interpretation of the Geometric Figure-Scenes." *Mitteilungen des Deutschen Archäologischen Instituts, Athenische Abteilung* 95, 51–8.

———. 1982. *Narration and Allusion in Archaic Greek Art*, Eleventh J. L. Myres Memorial Lecture. Oxford.

———. 1987. *An Archaeology of Greece. The Present and Future Scope of a Discipline*, Sather Classical Lectures, 53. Berkeley, CA.

———. 1998. *Homer and the Artists. Text and Picture in Early Greek Art*. Cambridge.

Snowden, F. M. 1970. *Blacks in Antiquity. Ethiopians in the Greco-Roman Experience*. Cambridge, MA.

———. 1983. *Before Color Prejudice. The Ancient View of Blacks*. Cambridge, MA.

Sourvinou-Inwood, C. 1991. *"Reading" Greek Culture. Texts and Images, Rituals and Myths*. Oxford.

Sparkes, B. A. 1991. *Greek Art. Greece and Rome*. New Surveys in the Classics, no. 22. Oxford.

———. 1996. *The Red and the Black. Studies in Greek Pottery*. London.

Spivey, N. 1996. *Understanding Greek Sculpture. Ancient Meanings, Modern Readings*. London.

———. 1997. *Greek Art*. London.

Splitter, R. 2000. *Die "Kypseloslade" in Olympia: Form, Funktion und Bildschmuck. Eine archäologische Rekonstruktion*. Mainz, Germany.

Stansbury-O'Donnell, M. D. 1999. *Pictorial Narrative in Ancient Greek Art*. Cambridge.

———. 2006. *Vase Painting, Gender, and Social Identity in Archaic Athens*. Cambridge.

———. 2009. "Structural Analysis as an Approach to Defining the Comic." In Schmidt and Oakley 2009, 33–41.

Stieber, M. 2004. *The Poetics of Appearance in the Attic Korai*. Austin, TX.

Steiner, A. 2007. *Reading Greek Vases*. Cambridge.

Steiner, D. T. 2001. *Images in Mind. Statues in Archaic and Classical Greek Literature and Thought*. Princeton, NJ.

Stewart, A. F. 1977. *Skopas of Paros*. Park Ridge, NJ.

———. 1983. "Stesichoros and the François Vase." In Moon 1983, 53–74.

———. 1987. "Narrative, Genre, and Realism in the Work of the Amasis Painter." In *Papers on the Amasis Painter and his World*. Malibu, CA, 29–42.

———. 1990. *Greek Sculpture. An Exploration*. New Haven.

———. 1995. "Rape?" In Reeder 1995, 74–90.

———. 1997. *Art, Desire, and the Body in Ancient Greece*. Cambridge.

———. 2008a. "The Persian and Carthaginian Invasions of 480 B.C.E. and the Beginning of the Classical Style: Part 1, The Stratigraphy, Chronology, and Significance of the Acropolis Debris." *American Journal of Archaeology* 112, 377–412.

———. 2008b. "The Persian and Carthaginian Invasions of 480 B.C.E. and the Beginning of the Classical Style: Part 2, The Finds from Others Sites in Athens, Attica, Elsewhere in Greece, and on Sicily; Part 3, The Severe Style: Motivations and Meaning." *American Journal of Archaeology* 112, 581–616.

———. 2008c. *Classical Greece and the Birth of Western Art*. Cambridge.

Stillwell, A. N. 1948. *The Potters' Quarter*. Corinth 15, pt. 1. Princeton, NJ.

Stillwell, A. N., J. L. Benson, A. L. Boegehold, and C. G. Boulter. 1984. *The Potters' Quarter. The Pottery*. Corinth 15, pt. 3. Princeton, NJ.

Stissi, V. 1999. "Production, Circulation and Consumption of Archaic Greek Pottery (Sixth and Early Fifth Centuries BC)." In Crielaard, Stissi, and van Wijngaarden 1999, 83–113.

Svenbro, J. 1993. *Phrasikleia. An Anthropology of Reading in Ancient Greece*, tr. J. Lloyd. Ithaca, NY.

Tanner, J. 2006. *The Invention of Art History in Ancient Greece. Religion, Society and Artistic Rationalisation*. Cambridge.

———. 2007. "Portraits and Agency: A Comparative View." In Osborne and Tanner 2007, 70–74.

Thompson, D. B. 1975. *Ptolemaic Oinochoai and Portraits in Faience*. Oxford.

Trendall, A. D. 1989. *Red Figure Vases of South Italy and Sicily. A Handbook*. London.

Tsingarida, A., ed. 2009. *Shapes and Uses of Greek Vases (7th–4th Centuries B.C.). Proceedings of the Symposium held at the Université libre de Bruxelles 27–29 April 2006*. Brussels.

Vermeule, E. D. 1979. *Aspects of Death in Early Greek Art and Poetry*. Berkeley, CA.

Vickers, M. 1985a. "Artful Crafts: The Influence of Metal Work on Athenian Painted Pottery." *Journal of Hellenic Studies* 105, 108–28.

———. 1985b. "Persepolis, Vitruvius and the Erechtheum Caryatids: The Iconography of Medism and Servitude." *Revue archéologique* 1985, 3–28.

Vickers, M. and D. Gill. 1994. *Artful Crafts. Ancient Greek Silverware and Pottery*. Oxford.

Vidal-Naquet, P. 1986. *The Black Hunter. Forms of Thought and Forms of Society in the Greek World*, tr. A. Szegedy-Maszak. Baltimore.

Von Gennep, A. 1960. *The Rites of Passage*. Chicago.

Walsh, D. 2009. *Distorted Ideals in Greek Vase-Painting: The World of Mythological Burlesque*. Cambridge.

Watrous, L. 1982. "The Sculptural Program of the Siphnian Treasury at Delphi." *American Journal of Archaeology* 86, 159–72.

Weitzmann, K. 1947. *Illustrations in Roll and Codex. A Study of the Origin and Method of Text Illustration*. Princeton, NJ.

Whitehouse, R. D. and J. B. Wilkins. 1995. "Greeks and Natives in South-east Italy: Approaches to the Archaeological Evidence." In T. C. Champion, ed., *Centre and Periphery. Comparative Studies in Archaeology*. London, 102–26.

Whitley, J. 1991. *Style and Society in Dark Age Greece. The Changing Face of a Pre-Literate Society, 1100–700 BC*. Cambridge.

———. 2001. *The Archaeology of Ancient Greece*. Cambridge.

Williams, D. 1991. "Vase-painting in Fifth-century Athens. I: The Invention of the Red-Figure Technique and the Race between Vase-painting and Free Painting." In Rasmussen and Spivey 1991, 103–30.

———. 1992. "The Brygos Tomb Reassembled and 19th-Century Commerce in Capuan Antiquities." *American Journal of Archaeology* 96, 617–36.

Williams. D. and J. Ogden. 1994. *Greek Gold. Jewelry of the Classical World*. New York.

Woodford, S. 1982. "Ajax and Achilles Playing a Game on an Olpe at Oxford." *Journal of Hellenic Studies* 102, 173–85.

———. 2003. *Images of Myths in Classical Antiquity*. Cambridge.

Yatromanolakis, D., ed. 2010. *An Archaeology of Representations. Ancient Greek Vase-Painting and Contemporary Methodologies*. Athens.

Yatromanolakis, D. and P. Roilos, eds. 2004. *Greek Ritual Poetics*. Cambridge, MA.

Younger, J. G. and P. Rehak. 2009. "Technical Observations on the Sculptures from the Temple of Zeus at Olympia." *Hesperia* 78, 41–105.

Index